CAN COOK, WILL COOK!

Frank Stalley

Pen Press Publishers
London

First published in 2003 by
Pen Press Publishers Ltd
39-41, North Road
London N7 9DP

ISBN 1-904018-24-6

A catalogue record of this book is available from the British
Library

Cover design by Jacqueline Abromeit

Dedication

I would like to dedicate this book to Mons. S. Habert
and all the chefs at Kettners Restaurant,
for their great help and guidance.

Also to my wife and children for putting up
with my unsociable hours of work.

Introduction

This book is about my working life – over thirty years at present – as a chef in well known hotels, restaurants and clubs in London. It is also about the characters who inhabit this 'out the back' world of ours, and who I have had the privilege to work with. Some were well-known chefs, the innovators and motivators of their day.

I have tried to help the reader (if s/he is not a chef) to mentally picture the problems, the jokes, the stress, the quick-fire remarks of people existing under intense pressure every working day. Also, I hope to dispel the prevailing image of the head chef as a spoilt prima donna in white (in some cases, not so white), and to convince the reader that most chefs are not fat and slow but slim(ish), fast and witty.

By the end of this book, I will hopefully have offered the reader an insight into our world: what goes on in the kitchen when the cutomer's order arrives, what might be said when they order a chateaubriand or fillet steak well done ('Kinell, here's another gourmet!'), how we cope with difficult customers and complaints. On the way, I hope to tickle the sense of humour.

Readers will learn that the vast majority of chefs do not include a tin opener among the vital items they would take to a desert island. Being a chef takes skill and commitment, plus a real love of the job. Ever wondered how we keep sane whilst cooking maybe five different à la carte dishes at the same time? Then read on ...

By the way, there is no fictional element to this book: all the incidents recounted really did happen! If a rash of joke-playing breaks out after this book is published, then it is sheer coincidence.

CHEFS

Chefs are lively, fun and full of banter
Just like our proverbial Santa
We work hard, play just the same
Sometimes we manage to make our name
Well known throughout the land
Some are like a one-man band
They shout loud, move around quite fast
Just in case their star don't last.
Others are the mainstay of this world,
As the map of life starts to unfurl,
You'll find them all beavering away
For hotels and restaurants, they are the loyal who stay.
We speak kitchen French, but don't get the lingo,
And yet we love the French, by jingo!
Their food, their ways, their culture too.
Their cooking we love to do!
We are proud of the profession we have,
Nothing like office work, so boring and naff,
We don't know from day to day
What the customer wants or what they'll say,
We try our best, there's no doubt,
Our love for the job shines brightly out!

Haverstock Comprehensive, Chalk Farm, London. Catering student, 1955-57. City & Guilds 150

My love for the kitchen and all it entails began early in 1954, when one of the teachers at my school, in his/her infinite wisdom, decided that the boys doing woodwork and metalwork lessons, both of which I hated, would do a swap for a term with the girls. Thus, the boys would take basic cookery lessons (called 'home economics') and the girls would try either woodwork or metalwork. So, having spent all of '53 and the first part of '54 wondering what sort of job I could do when I left school, I was saved by one decision from this teacher at Haverstock, who solved the problem for me. I will always be indebted to him or her.

I so enjoyed the cookery lessons that when I found out that the school had started a course in catering, I asked my mother if I could stay on and do the two-year course. My mum was a real love; although things were hard financially, she didn't hesitate and agreed to let me stay on.

When I started, there was already a group in front of us, the forerunners of my own 'class of '54'. How many of them are still in the profession I don't know, but if any of you read this, then please get in touch, as I would love to see you all again.

Our teacher, Miss Watson, was a woman who had passed all the appropriate exams (though nowadays she would be Cordon Bleu trained). Miss Watson had a very good system of separating the men from the boys: if you played about and were not serious enough (bear in mind that this course was intended to set you up for life in a worthwhile profession), she suggested to the head and your parents that she didn't think you were really interested enough to take this up as a lifetime's work. You would then be advised to leave her class and take up something different. This was good, as the larkabouts were soon sorted out and only the dedicated ones were left. She was a very good teacher, quite fair, but she really put you through it; in short, she prepared you for life in the big kitchens.

Each day we used to do basic cookery lessons that also involved some French, English and Maths, as they would be used in the catering world. The French lessons mainly taught us to recognise and pronounce names of dishes, fruit and vegetables, how to say 'soup of the day', different

1

ways of cooking meat (roti, braise, etc). If anyone reading this is doing a catering course then I strongly advise them to get stuck in to French. Unfortunately I did not appreciate the importance of French in the kitchens until I had actually started work, and I found myself at quite a disadvantage. So give yourself a head start and pay attention to your French teacher.

The first year was spent learning how to cut vegetables for various dishes, and how to make basic sauces such as bechamel, espagnole, velouté etc. When we reached the second year, we were the kings, the number ones, the cocks of the walk, the bees knees. (As you might have noticed, we had a good opinion of ourselves.) We could cook and we were going to prove it. We were allowed to make lunches for the teachers in our own dining room two or three times a week, I remember.

There was no shortage of guinea pigs as the meals were subsidised and it only cost the teachers a few pence (Lsd, old money) to have a three-course meal, waited on in comfort. They lapped it up! Miss Watson would split us into two teams. One team prepared and cooked the menu, usually a choice of starter, two or three main courses, a couple of sweets and occasionally a cheese board. The other would be waiters, laying the tables, polishing the cutlery, making sure that the right glasses were on the table (they were allowed wine), making sure that the plates were in the hotplate. We even had proper tablecloths and napkins. Miss Watson showed us different ways of folding them, so for each meal we did them a different way. When the teachers started to arrive, the waiters had to greet them, check their 'bookings', seat them, give them the menus, take the orders and silver serve the meal. Wow!

I well remember the accidents that happened the first few times: spilt soup, burnt laps, over-flowing wine glasses, dropped dishes because the 'chefs' had a vicious streak and made the plates red hot. The poor waiter didn't realise until it was too late; then there was a quick dive to the service table to put the dish down and frantically blow your fingers as you thought dark thoughts about what you would do to the other team when it was your turn to be chef.

The chef team would slave away in the kitchen, a couple of people doing the starters, a couple preparing the main and vegetables, another pair doing the sweets. Every time we cooked we were on a different 'section', so we learnt to do all the points in the kitchen.

Come lunchtimes, the ones who were on the starters went and checked the hotplate and the servery, and lit the grill if it was needed. During service a 'runner' used to go into the servery and do the kitchen clerk's job, organising the orders, making sure all the garnishes were on and that the dishes were *very* hot (oh, wicked days!)

The first time I had to wait on the teachers, I decided that this side of catering was not for me. I much preferred the hustle and bustle of the kitchen with its deadlines and prioritising, working out what to start first, what to do next while you are doing the first part. This they call thinking on your feet, and it gave me such a buzz. I was completely at home in the kitchen, and these two years were the happiest times of my school life.

We were so contented in our work that, as we cleared up, we all used to have a singalong to the new rock 'n' roll songs that had just come out on record (the old 78s, remember them?) Imagine scrubbing out the pots and pans to the sounds of Elvis, Tennessee Ernie et al – it was great When I think of the racket we must have made, I realise Miss Watson was a real trooper – or maybe she just used ear plugs.

The only lads I can remember from the first year, the one above us, were called Tait and Flynn. Tait was long and lanky, Flynn shorter and more compact. After school Flynn got a job at the Rembrandt in South Kensington, and Tait got a job in the Hunting Lodge in Lower Regent Street. I never saw Tait again, but I met Flynn a year or so after I had started work. I met him at the St Martins in the Fields Club for commis and apprentice chefs, and he was still at the Rembrandt. I remember feeling quite good when he told me that the Rembrandt used tinned pureed spinach whereas Kettners, where I was working, did theirs fresh. The slight taste of one-upmanship was delicious!

The ones that were in my year were: Wyatt, who lived up Haverstock Hill; Wilde, whose dad ran an off-licence opposite Hampstead Tube Station; Peter Lockley, who lived in the flats at the back of the school. (I remember his older brother was in the Parachute Regiment, funny how you remember little things like that); George Kluger who lived in a turning off Adelaide Road; Mickey Knight, who lived in Peabodys in Victoria; Sidney Zagger, whose dad ran a vegetable shop (so he told us) in Mile End Rd; Rodney Smith, who lived at the back of the school. We also had two girls in our class. One was a rather large girl (gland problem) who had a bad limp. She was actually a very good cook, but unfortunately her weight plus her limp let her down: a chef must walk about ten miles in the course of a shift (though someone will no doubt come up with the statistics to prove me wrong). The other girl came from near Liverpool, I think. She was a bit of a flighty one and wore an ankle bracelet. Though she was quite good at cooking, she seemed more interested in 'getting known'.

As far as I know none of the tribe are still in catering, if they ever started. If I am wrong and they are still with us, then I hope they get in touch.

I still have the exam papers that we had to take to pass the City & Guilds 150. The menu we had to cook (for six people) was as follows:

3

Bread Rolls, grilled lamb cutlets, macedoine of vegetables, chipped potatoes, fruit flan.

After our exams, which I believe we all passed, we had to go to the labour exchange (now called the job centre). The man in charge of the catering vacancies went through the list for apprentices in the West End, and I was offered either the Rembrandt Hotel or Kettners Restaurant. I chose Kettners because it paid ten shillings a week more than the Rembrandt: a massive three pounds and ten shillings per week (now equivalent to the princely sum of £3.50).

After the exam and the visit to the labour exchange, it was a long wait till the end of term, when I would be starting out in a real live restaurant kitchen. In the meantime my mother was gradually buying my uniform and the three knives and palette knife that Mons. Habert, the sous chef at Kettners, had suggested I acquire before starting work. (Would you believe that I still have the palette and two of these knives? They made equipment to last in those days.)

Kettners Restaurant,
Romilly Street, London W1
Apprentice, 1957-62,
Chefs de cuisine: Mons. Moreau, Mons. Habert.

I started work at Kettners Restaurant in Romilly Street, Soho, on 10 August 1957, and was registered as number 954 by the apprenticeship council. (I still have my little blue book and my indentures.)

But my first impression of Kettners was before I even started work, and it was of going down into the bowels of the earth. After I had politely enquired of the doorman where I could find the chef, as I had an appointment with him, and after he had looked me over, probably deciding if I was worth the effort of an answer, he pointed to a small flight of stairs near the entrance and muttered, 'Down there!'

I reached the bottom, turned right through a door and found myself in this dungeon-like room. While I was standing there waiting for a ghost or some such apparition to appear, as if from nowhere a small, well-built man approached and asked in a heavy accent what I wanted. 'To see the chef,' I replied, at which he sniffed and promptly disappeared. This person turned out to be a kitchen porter called 'Pinnochio'. (I never found out why in the five years I was there; he just seemed to have arrived with that name.) Pinnochio was only 5'2", had a slightly hunched back and, with his craggy features, he could have been the model for the Hunchback of Notre Dame. He was the only person I have ever come across who could touch his ear and pick his nose with his tongue – especially effective during conversations with strangers!

After a few minutes, another short man appeared in a brilliant white uniform with a tall hat. I introduced myself and he explained that he was not the head chef (who did not condescend to see the likes of me, a mere apprentice-in-waiting), but the sous chef, Mons. Habert. He then quickly explained that I would have to have my own uniform and at least three knives (to start with), told me the best place to buy them and arranged my starting date – 10 August.

I turned up on my first day, full of nerves and wondering what I had let myself in for. I was taken to a changing room at the top of the building, overlooking the corner of Romilly and Greek Street, given a locker and left to get changed. The porter who had taken me upstairs was a chap called Gasco; he was a Spaniard who looked like Errol Flynn, and I later learned he had fought in the Spanish Civil War against Franco. He could not go back or he would be shot. I thought of Gasco when Franco died and Spain became 'normal' again, whether he was still alive and whether he had gone back to his family that he had not seen for all those years.

When I had changed I made my way down a winding staircase to the kitchen. Mons. Habert, the sous chef, met me and led me along past the plate room, with its group of Indian porters buzzing away washing last night's dishes and getting ready for the lunch service.

In the kitchen proper, a sudden rush of hot air hit me. I found myself standing by the hotplate on my right, looking down into a long narrow corridor. At the bottom was the hors d'oeuvres section, then the larder section. As I looked across the hotplate I noticed a sea of faces under tall white hats, all peering at me as if to say, 'Here's another one for the hell hole'. Mons. Habert then took me to the veg section where he introduced me to the entremétier, Joe Murtagh, a lovely man, a typical jovial Irish-man, about 5'10" with ginger hair, solidly built with hands like shovels. Joe was quite strict and you soon learned to do things how he wanted them done: how to pick (not trim with a knife) the french beans (haricots verts) or the mange tout, how to prepare and make soup, how to serve veg orders and how to keep the mise en place up. If you managed all this to Joe's satisfaction, then you were OK. If not, then look out, your ears were soon 'warmed up', and you learned very quickly what was right and what was wrong.

After Joe had introduced me to the others on his section, he asked me if I could make bechamel. Although I had spent two years learning the basic sauces at school, I had already decided that if I was asked what I could make or do, I would answer, 'Nothing, can you show me?' I figured that this way I would not make too many balls ups in my first few weeks, while I tried to get used to the pressures and the system of a busy kitchen.

The two main first commis on the veg section were Sotiris and Kola, both Greek Cypriots. Sotiris was stocky, with a lovely handlebar mous-tache; Kola was what you would call 'cuddly'. They both had a good sense of humour and lots of patience, especially with me. Everything was

6

freshly made: the game chips for the bar and the sauce service, the duchesse and armandines, the purée, the croquettes. The pommes frites and the pommes allumettes were cut by hand. The only veg that was not fresh was the petits pois fins, which came in a can (they were used to make petits pois à la francaise). All the soups were made fresh, a different one each day (soup du jour) and others for the à la carte menu, such as bisque d'homard, consommé, crème de tomate etc. Any pastries –for example, cheese straws and little profiteroles – were made by the pastry section. Sometimes the amount of work that we got through, just to keep en place, was remarkable, especially when we had a lot of functions on. I am always amazed, when I think back, how that amount of veg was served (with very few complaints) from such a smallish section of the kitchen.

On quieter days Joe used to go around the kitchen handing out boxes of beans to the other sections for them to pick. One thing about the chefs at Kettners: all the commis, chef de parties and even the sous chef and the aboyer all pulled together; nobody said, 'It's not my job', because they knew that when they needed a hand there would always be one at the ready. If, for example, the poor old sauce section was getting a right hammering, then both Joe and Ali (the poisonnier or fish chef) would help by sending a commis over to help, and vice versa. These chefs really taught me the value of inter-section co-operation.

Apart from the restaurant, Kettners had a number of private dining rooms. Rumour had it that the top of the building, now used as the offices and changing rooms, was once used as extra private dining rooms by the Prince of Wales, later Edward VII. There was supposed to have been a secret passageway under the road leading from the theatre opposite to the basement of Kettners, where the Prince would bring his 'special' guests to dinner after a show.

The early shift was from 9 am to 2.30 pm, then back at 5.30 pm till 9 pm. The guard shift was from 11 am until 3 pm, then back at 7 pm until 11.30 pm. This was worked on a five-day rota with alternate weekends or Sundays off. For the first couple of months (I was on a six-month trial) I was really all at sea. Nothing seemed to go right for me. Joe geed me along and roasted my ears on a daily basis, then all of a sudden things began to click into place. I could, for example, remember more than one order at a time. This memory tester, I was told later, comes with practice: the more pressure there is, the more orders you can remember.

Soon I began to enjoy myself. I felt that I was earning my wages of three pounds and ten shillings per week, and also that I was pulling my weight. As my confidence on the veg grew, Joe would give me another new thing to learn. After I had mastered the soups and the veg prep and service, he showed me how to carve elephants, monkey heads and faces out of potatoes. These were used for cocktail parties.

Joe had a wicked sense of humour (as have most chefs I've met – must be something to do with the heat!) One of his favourite tricks was to hide a raw egg in your mashed potato when you had a meal break. You can imagine what happened to the egg when you used your knife and fork on the mash. Also, if you were unwise enough to leave your plate unattended when you went to get a sweet, he used to swipe your meal and leave a raw cauli or a couple of potatoes under the cover. As the dining room was at the top of the building next to the changing room (three flights up), it was a bit frustrating to have to come back down to the kitchen in search of your meal, with Joe, a huge grin on his face, calling out, 'You're getting warm' or 'You're cold'. And if it wasn't busy, the rest of the kitchen would join in with completely useless bits of information as to where your food was hidden.

Some of the tricks we used to play on one another were priceless. We would send a young commis or apprentice with a request to the chef de partie for a long stand. After keeping the person waiting in the corner, while everyone at the section made out that they were busy and rushed around, the chef de partie would casually say, 'Go back and ask Joe, how long does he want it?' So the poor sod would be back and forth until the light shone bright.

Another great trick was the bucket of water gag. When chefs are doing a laborious job, such as cleaning beans, they have a habit of resting one leg over the corner of the table (this eases the pressure), then changing leg from time to time. The trick is to keep the chef talking while someone creeps up on his blind side with a bucket of water, places it next to his supporting leg, then sneaks away. Someone else would then call out the chef's name. The immediate reaction is to lower your leg to the floor and turn round. Many a person has had to do a shift with wet feet due to this despicable but hilarious trick.

Then there was the egg prank. You would blow out an egg, fill the empty shell with water, then throw it at someone. If the person (normally a waiter) is wearing black, the chef then rubs flour lightly on his apron and brushes past him. He might also dip the palm of his hand in flour and pat someone heartily on the back, leaving a lovely palm print that any detective would be proud to find.

An unsuspecting target might be given a handful of peppercorns and a huge knife, and told to cut them all in half; then there was the trick of asking a young apprentice for some filleted whitebait on toast (whitebait, as you probably know, are eaten whole); drying pomegranate seeds and swopping them for peppercorns; changing salt into sugar bowls and sugar into salt pots.

These were just a few of the things that we used to get up to; they all caused a smile or laugh and inspired a sense of camaraderie among the kitchen brigade.

After my first couple of hours at Kettners I was taken to see the head chef, Mons. Moreau – known to everyone as 'the old man'. He was about 6'1" and must have weighed 25 stone! Walking along in front of you, he looked like a ship in a storm; he seemed to roll from side to side and how he was never sea sick, I'll never know! Mons. Moreau said hello to me, told me to work hard and do as I was told, and I would keep out of trouble. These were about the last nice words he ever spoke to me in all the time he was my head chef. Thereafter, he either scowled at me or gave me a rollicking. Sometimes he'd tell my chef de partie off instead, which made me feel awful; but on reflection, this was probably to hammer home the point that it was not only me who was responsible for my mistakes – in other words, keep an eye on those working under you!

Mons. Moreau's favourite insult was to call someone 'a bloody shoe-maker', which didn't seem much of an insult to me; even at that young age I could think of worse. Victor Madere, the pastry chef, told me later that Mons. Moreau's father was a shoemaker. Victor assumed that for some reason Mons. Moreau did not like his dad, and so had turned his profession into an insult. Funny thing, life, isn't it?

There was an aboyer at Kettners, affectionately known as 'old Bill'. He was about 60 years old when I first knew him, and looked like a slimmer version of WC Fields, with a 'wide parting', as they used to say. He wore tortoiseshell glasses and walked with a bad limp; apparently he had been wounded as a junior officer in the First World War, and had also suffered from 'trench foot'. Bill could not speak French, yet he could call out the orders in fluent French! He was a great dog racing fan, as was the head chef, and at least twice during the day they would both disappear down to the chef's office to place bets and discuss the value of certain dogs. When Mons. Moreau was getting on everyone's nerves, old Bill would suggest that they go down and sort out some good tips that he'd been given. I think that was one of Bill's greatest assets, diffusing a tense situation before it got out of hand.

Mons. Moreau could keep a moan going for a few days, until the victim was in a right old state. The old hands just used to say, 'Yes, chef', 'No, chef', and 'Of course, chef', not really taking a blind bit of notice of what he was grumbling about. When he arrived back in the kitchen after a couple of good bets and a few glasses of wine, he was normally in a good mood again. But when he went home, the atmosphere changed: everyone seemed more cheerful, and a sigh of relief went up as he disappeared downstairs. 'Free till tomorrow!' was the silent cry.

On a Saturday, about midday, when the chef decided to go home, we commis and apprentices tried to get up to the changing rooms so that we could watch him climb the narrow stairs from the basement and get into his car. It used to take him five minutes or more to climb the stairs, both sides of his body touching the walls, almost getting himself jammed. (If you ever go to Kettners, look down these stairs and you can visualise how large he was.) His car was a black Citroen, just like the ones the French police use, and as he used to squeeze behind the steering wheel, the poor old car used to rock from side to side like it was in agony. I was told that one day when he was driving home, he caused a traffic jam around Cambridge Circus because, being so fat, he could only turn the wheel an inch or two at a time.

The beer quota for the kitchen staff was originally an ex-five gallon oil drum, fitted with a wire carrying handle and filled with mild beer. This was supposed to last a full day, but more often than not it didn't. The chefs then had to use their noddles to get extra beer, sometimes slipping waiters a decent lunch or dinner in return for a bottle of beer; or one of the chefs de partie would go down and sweet-talk the cellar man, who normally came evening time and was always a bit under the weather (having to sample various brews and wines to make sure they were all still good, you understand). If the chef returned triumphantly with, say, half a drum of beer, he was everyone's best friend for the rest of the evening. Towards the end of my apprenticeship the beer ration was changed to a couple of bottles of beer a day each, so obviously the 'black market' trade picked up.

After about four months I was transferred to the sauce section, where I met George Rascannière, the saucier. He was a great person who knew his sauces backwards (SECUAS, get it?), and he was lovely to work under. Although he was strict like Joe, he had a different sense of humour; his was more subtle. When the chef was seated on his bench on the other side of the hotplate, George would say, not very loudly, 'Come on, you're moving like a pregnant duck' or 'Don't burn that!' The chef, who I think could hear a feather land at fifty paces, would look across the hotplate and stare at the person who was on the receiving end of the comment. His scowl could shrivel a prune, and you learned very quickly that when the chef was about, you were really on the ball, en place and in front with the orders. I think this was George's way of making you realise that this was no game.

Our George looked as if he was of Mediterranean extraction, but he was a cockney Frenchman through and through. He was well built and about 50 when I knew him; he always wore his tall chef's hat at a jaunty angle and his eyes seemed to glint mischievously from behind his thick-rimmed spectacles. George had a slight limp (I think he was born with one leg shorter than the other) but it didn't stop him chasing you along the kitchen to give you a rollicking. He had a perpetual smile on his face, as if everything in life was a joke to him. (Judging from the tricks that he used to play, this was probably true).

George knew that the best way to make sure his 'partie' went well was to make sure he could trust the commis under him. Once you had achieved that trust he was a bit easier on you. If you were late for work on his section, George would say rather loudly, 'Got a touch of the shits, have we?' or 'I told you he was going to come in, didn't I?' to no-one in particular. This started everyone else off, and the friendly insults started flying around.

On a Sunday we used to have a sweepstake, trying to guess how many covers we would do for dinner that night. Each guess cost you half a crown (12½ p) and the winner at the end of service would collect the lot. If it was a tie then it was shared. George would sometimes keep the money inside the hotplate, and towards the end of service the coins would be nearly melting. He would quickly put them onto a cold plate, call over the lucky winner and pour the coins into his open hands. Well, the normal reaction was to drop the coins as you frantically tried to cool your hands down, and then you had to try and find the coins in amongst the sawdust on the kitchen floor. If you were not quick enough, the kitchen porter tried to sweep them up and put them in the pig swill bins. This used to cause quite a lot of merriment, especially if a newcomer won; and if the chefs, always so quick-off-the-mark (to go home), won, did they scramble for their winnings or did they run for the bus? What a decision!

Sometimes George would 'accidentally' drop the winnings into the bain-marie, so you had to try and fish the coins out of the boiling water. If he felt good, George might just drop them into a pint of beer, so you had to drink the beer to get the money. (Have you tried drinking luke-warm beer quickly?) The waiters also used to take part, which created a little bit of friendly rivalry, until the day one of the waiters got greedy. The only ones left in the sweepstake this particular evening were one of the chefs and one of the commis; if we did another three customers, then the waiter would win. Well, his mate came rushing in near the end of the evening with a check for four customers. George duly called out the order and we got on with the prep, but George must have had a feeling, so he went to check with the head waiter and found out he had actually shut the door a few minutes earlier.

From that day forth no waiters were allowed to take part. Shame really because until then, the waiters had been very good. Also, it lowered the prize money.

George was a very good sauce chef. Everything was done properly. The demi glace was made using roasted veal and beef bones with plenty of herbs, vegetables and stock. The sauce section used to have a large copper stockpot on the go all week. Flour and tomatoes were mixed well, then the sauce was boiled, put into the oven and left to simmer for about two days, being regularly skimmed and topped up.

We had a plat du jour menu that changed daily. This consisted of a cream soup or consommé, two different fish dishes, seven different meat dishes, and a daily specialities section.

To give you just a brief outline of the number of dishes on the à la carte menu at Kettners, here is a quick list:

Hors d'oeuvres:	29 different dishes.
Potages:	Five different soups, not including the daily ones.
Oeufs:	Four different sorts, including seven ways of serving an omelette.
Poissons:	Four different lobster dishes, ten different sole, two turbot dishes, and the Coquille St. Jacques.
Entrees:	15 different dishes.
Rotis:	Five varieties.
Grillades:	Ten different dishes.
Buffet froid:	Seven different cold meat dishes, not counting the assiette anglaise. Two game. This increased when wild duck, pheasant etc became available.
Legumes :	Nine different potato dishes, 14 vegetable dishes.
Desserts:	13 different sweets, not counting the various seasonal fruits.
Glaces:	12 ice cream dishes (all made on the premises).
Hot soufflés:	Four choices.
Savouries:	Three different, not including Scotch Woodcock.

This list is taken from a 1958 December menu. As you can see, there was always a lot of mise en place to do, especially considering we probably did about 100 dinners most days, not counting parties. George always liked to get the mise en place sorted out before service, as this gave you more time to concentrate on the orders that were coming in. The amount of duck, capon, chicken and poussin sold as plain roast kept one oven fully occupied all day. They were all served with the proper garnishes – fresh bread sauce, apple sauce, stuffing (sage and onion or herb), game chips, watercress and gravy. These were normally taken in whole and carved in front of the customer by one of the head waiters. You always knew when a special customer was in, because the manager, Mons. Bonvin (yes, 'good wine' really was his name!) would be flitting about 'like a horse on heat', as George used to say.

The restaurant had its own carver, one of the senior head waiters who was a smallish cockney Italian. During lunchtime he wore a starched white chef's hat and a chef's jacket, in the evening the traditional 'penguin suit'. Some of the joints he had to put into the carving trolley looked bigger than he was. We used to wait and see if he'd ever get a hernia lifting them, but he must have been quite strong as it never happened. His carving knives were very sharp, he could shave your arm with them, which he used to make a great show of doing. Sometimes he would grab an unsuspecting new commis waiter, pull his sleeve up and gently slide the edge of his carving knife up the person's arm, removing all the hair in the process. The guy normally looked on in terror, not wanting to move in case the knife slipped. We all used to watch, waiting for the day when the blade would slip, but in all the time that I was there it never happened.

Mons. Bonvin, the manager, was very tall, about 6' 3", well built and very smartly dressed both at work and outside. He walked with a sort of long-strided chicken gait. He and the chef used to have some lovely stand up rows, especially when a commis waiter had not told Mons. Bonvin or the head waiters that such and such a dish had sold out. Mons. Bonvin would come into the kitchen and try to get the chef to do a dish 'on the quick' so that he didn't have to go back into the restaurant and tell the customer that the dish he'd ordered was 'off'. The chef would delight in telling him, 'Not possible, your staff should have told you!' (I think that this used to make the chef's day, as he'd have a gleam in his eye and a smile on his lips). They would shout at each other for a couple of minutes, then a little later they would adjourn downstairs to the chef's office with a good bottle of wine, and reappear in good humour later.

The head waiter was a tall dapper man, always impeccably turned out. He was an Englishman – Arthur, I think was his name – a true gentleman, never got flustered, always on the ball, ('when all around are losing theirs' etc.) Most of the commis waiters were Cypriots, though the odd one was French or Italian. The head waiters were mainly Italian, with a couple of French and a couple of Cypriots. The banqueting permanent waiters were a Belgian and a Scot; they were helped by casual waiters as and when required. Sometimes, if a party wasn't very large, Mons. Bonvin would lend them a couple of commis, just to help carry the hot food up the narrow flight of stairs to the service room. On the whole everyone got on well together, and the majority of services were completed with good humoured banter between the chefs and waiters.

I remember once, one of the commis chefs lost a shirt. He'd put it over the back of a chair in the changing room and had forgotten to put it in his locker. Anyway, it disappeared without trace. We helpfully suggested that maybe the ghosts had pinched it – you can see that we were really concerned for the bloke. A few days later, as this commis was delivering an order to the hotplate, he happened to look up and noticed that the commis waiter had the same type of shirt on under his waiter's jacket. The next thing we knew, the commis chef had jumped across the hotplate, grabbed the waiter by the throat and was trying to rip his jacket off,

13

insisting that the waiter was wearing his shirt. And sure enough, his initials were found on the label. How daft can someone be, nick something and then wear it in front of the owner a couple of days later? Needless to say, the commis waiter left forthwith!

For a few months we had this Italian head waiter. He was about 6'1" and built like a wrestler, with shoulder-length, jet black hair swept back in the fashionable 'Tony Curtis' style. We used to watch him pick up the orders, waiting for his jacket to split open under his huge muscles. If ever any customers were getting bolshie or drunk, or disputing the bill, our friend was sent to deal with them. He was supposed to be very good at his job. And even if he wasn't, no-one would have told him otherwise!

In the cocktail bar there were two barmen. One was very nice and friendly, and always had a laugh with the chefs when he came for his meal. The other one was a miserable old sod. He had a sergeant-major moustache and it took him all his time to smile at you, let alone be pleasant. I'll always remember him the day my mother died. I had been trying in vain to get through to the chef's office (he was probably putting on his bets), so I phoned the bar and this barman answered. I asked if he could get Mons. Habert to the phone for me. 'No,' he said and put the phone down. I phoned back and told him that I thought he was a right bastard, and that if he didn't get Mons. Habert I would sort him out. I finally got through to Mons. Habert and told him my problem. 'Don't worry,' he said, 'just tell us when you're coming back.' When I returned it appeared that I had caused a minor upheaval. The barman had complained to the chef and Mons. Habert about me. 'What do you expect, after your behaviour to him,' said Mons. Habert, and I think that was when he told the barman his fortune, though I never found out for sure.

I was told that Mons. Habert had had a long conversation with this guy, and after that, when he came for his meals, he always tried to be friendly, but none of the chefs wanted to know!

During the summer, when there was a lull in business, we used to catch a fly, drop it into a bowl of water, wait for it to stop 'swimming', then lift it out and put it onto the table, lightly cover it with salt and, lo and behold, after a couple of minutes the fly would struggle out of the salt, shake itself and fly off. (I know that any animal rights campaigners reading this will say we were cruel and inhumane in the treatment of these flies, but please note that we never killed them, just cleaned them up a bit!)

We also used to have friendly competitions to see who could knock off the most flies in a shift. The rules were that they had to be knocked out of the air using only your oven cloth; you only got half a score if you hit them while they were 'resting'. This naturally ended with a few people getting a bit of a whack with the 'rubbers' (the kitchen name for oven cloths, not what you were thinking of!) To make your cloth go with a crack, the knack was to soak it in water, then it really disintegrated the fly, or left a nice red mark on someone!

Each year the residents of Soho organised the Soho Festival and Carnival. The carnival took place on a Sunday, I think in June, and everyone used to come out and line the streets. There were various floats and bands, complete with local celebrities and buskers, and it was a really good atmosphere. When we finished lunch service, we used to mooch around the streets, looking at the various displays and stalls, watching the buskers, hoping that maybe for once that guy would not get out of the sack. People used to come from all over London, as this was the forerunner of the now famous Notting Hill Carnival.

Soho in those days was very colourful. During the summer evenings, we would have our dinner break sitting looking out of the changing room windows at the top of the building, watching the world go by. At that time there were a lot of street buskers who made a living out of entertaining the passers-by; some were very good. I will always remember the 'Wilson, Betty and Kepple' crowd. They used to arrive dressed up as Egyptians, in fezzes and robes. One of the group would start playing a whistle and the other three, two blokes and one woman, would start by sprinkling sand on a long board they had laid down in the middle of the road, then they would 'do' the famous sand dance routine – highly hilarious.

Another night we would have the 'Samson duo'. One guy would do all the spiel and the other, who was only about 5'5", but with solid bulging muscles, would wrap himself in a long length of chain, get one of the crowd to lock the padlocks and make sure he was well bound up, then help him into a large sack and tie it up with string. Within about two minutes, after a lot of rolling about, huffing and puffing and strangled cries, he would emerge from the chains, and a hat would be passed around before they went merrily on their way with applause ringing in their ears. I thought the bloke who tied him up was a friend, but every time I saw them it was a different person they got from the crowd. Either they had hundreds of friends or these people were genuinely strangers. (I will soon be told, no doubt!)

Although Soho is still very cosmopolitan, nowadays you see too many business executives rushing about without a minute to spare. And whereas before, everyone seemed so happy, laughing and joking, especially the old cockneys in the Brewer Street market, today everyone seems so sad. Time marches on, eh!

After the late shift a few of us would sometimes go to one of the alleyway coffee bars, out-of-the-way cafes that local residents, workers and night owls used. They were always open till the early hours. We used to sit there with a coffee or tea and a fag, unwinding from the evening's toil and watching the 'working girls' and their minders (now called pimps) come in for their tea break and a gossip.

On the sauce for a while we had a Turkish Cypriot called Memet, who was so slim that if he turned sideways, you thought he'd gone away. He was the hairiest man I have ever seen: the only parts not covered in hair were his cheeks (on his face, that is!) Memet was nicknamed 'the Incinerator' because every time he put something in the oven, nine times out of ten he would forget all about it and it would burn. It is an unwritten law of restaurant kitchens that if you put something in the oven, unless you tell someone else about it, it's your responsibility. Dear old Memet would often, in the middle of service, give a strangled cry and rush to one of the ovens. After the smoke had cleared, we all used to gather round the 'corpse' and have guesses as to what it had originally been, much to the chagrin of Memet, who wanted to get rid of the burnt offering before George or the chef found out. He got quite a few rollickings.

Sometimes, on a quiet night when we were looking for mischief, we would wait until Memet put something in to roast, then one of us would engage him in conversation while the others removed his roast to another oven, filled 'his' oven with lightly greased, crumpled paper, shut the door and waited. After a few minutes the paper would catch fire and the oil would send out big smoke signals. We would then call Memet in panic-stricken voices, and he would come rushing back, dying a thousand deaths on the way, and frantically open the oven door. When it dawned on him what we'd done, he would curse everyone within earshot in a mixture of Turkish, Greek, English, French and Italian swearwords. (He was not really fluent in any of these languages, but boy, when he swore, he was just like a native!)

Also on the sauce was Hassan, another Cypriot. He was a huge fellow with enormous strength – he was about 5'10" and must have weighed 18 stone. Though he looked fat, it was all solid muscle. Hassan could fill a large, solid copper stockpot with bones, vegetables and water, then lift it unaided onto the stove top – a rupture case if ever there was one, but Hassan managed it without batting an eye. If you can imagine lifting four large sacks of potatoes at the same time, then you can see what I mean. Hassan knew his job, and he used to take over the sauce when George was off or was covering for Mons. Habert. Hassan had a large black moustache and deep brown, almost black eyes; they either twinkled with laughter or burnt through you when you made a mistake. 'What the fuck are you doing?' was one of his favourite expressions. Like George, he was a patient and good teacher and he took pride in the fact that he could pass his knowledge on, like all the chefs at Kettners.

Keeping it in the family, sometimes Hassan's brother Omar would work on the sauce. Everything was a laugh with Omar, he was a terrific guy. Then, for a time, Hassan's brother-in-law Joseph also worked there. This guy thought he knew it all, and believed he could give Errol Flynn a run for his money as far as women were concerned, despite being about fifty, paunchy and balding, with a nose that would have given W. C. Fields a run for his money. Joseph was like a fly round a honey-pot whenever one of the office girls came into the kitchen, always chancing his luck but getting nowhere. He was not a bad bloke on the whole, just bored you to tears with his exploits.

Later I was moved into the larder, where Sid reigned supreme. (I never found out his surname, it was always Sid.) If you listened to Sid speak, you would swear that he was a true cockney but in truth he was a native of Alsace in France. I think he was what they call Franglais, and he was one of the best. He had a bristly grey moustache that seemed fluffy when he was in a good mood, and spiky when he was about to let rip with a tongue lashing. You could hear Sid coming a mile off, he had a sort of sliding walk, very casual and slow, his knives were all ancient but sharp as razors.

Sid started me off by putting me under the wing of Ali, a Pakistani. Ali was young, with a boyish face, but he knew the hors d'oeuvres section like the back of his hand, and was always en place. Only now and again did he slightly crack under pressure, but when you have to do 20 plus starters in minutes, anyone would be running. Ali showed me how to thinly carve sides of smoked salmon and fresh parma ham; how to make mayonnaise in all its variations (marie rose, curried, chilli and various herb ones); how to make fresh horseradish sauce; how to clean and peel smoked trout, mackerel, eel; how to serve fresh foie gras and the best caviar, and the proper garnishes to go with each dish. There were, you may remember, 29 dishes on the menu, not counting those on the banqueting menus, so we were kept busy.

We also had to make up the salads as they were ordered: verte, panache, tomate, cocombre etc. The hors d'oeuvres section had a small walk-in fridge, just wide enough for a slim chef to enter. (Mons. Moreau used to stand at the door and just look in when he was doing his rounds. I don't think he had fitted inside since he went over 12 stone.) In here we used to build up our mise en place: about 30 portions of smoked salmon, ten or 12 of smoked trout and so on. When an order was called we took the plate out, garnished it up and put it out onto a multi-shelved, stainless steel cabinet so that the waiters could collect their order and take it into the restaurant to serve. We had to be on the ball as some of the waiters, instead of waiting their turn, would try and take part of someone else's order so they could give a quick service. Sometimes they tried to take a dish for themselves. The brighter ones often slipped you a beer, so that you had a touch of blindness when they absconded with an order to eat themselves. You also had to keep a wary eye on the head chef and sous, as they knew all the tricks (having probably done them themselves when they were younger) and you didn't want to get hauled over the coals for a miserly bottle of beer.

Near the hors d'oeuvres was the butcher's block, which was about five or six feet long and 2½ feet thick, really solid. (It would probably have taken about a week to burn.) The butcher was a chap called little Louis (this was because he was only about 5'3"), a Tunisian or Algerian. He was a very good butcher and taught me a lot. Sometimes the amount of meat on the bone that came in completely hid Louis, and all you could hear from behind this mound of meat was the sound of him cursing and the swishing of his knives as he ploughed through the meat, cutting the joints into sections and then trimming and cutting them into steaks etc. Louis used to spend about half an hour every day honing his knives on oil stone, then finished off lightly on a fine steel.

All the meat used to come in on the bone: whole sirloins, rumps, legs of veal, legs of lamb with the saddle attached, sometimes whole lambs and, now and again, a quarter of beef. The beef came from Scotland on the overnight trains, and Arthur used to collect it in his van in the early morning. Most of the poultry came in whole, feathers, giblets, the lot. Poor old Pinnochio and Gasco had the lovely job of cleaning and preparing them for roasting.

The turkeys were the worst to do, especially at Christmas. The only 'fun' part of cleaning a turkey was when you put meat hooks in its leg by the foot, and then hung it up on a rail suspended from the ceiling; then you literally had to hang onto the rest of the bird and pull like hell to get rid of the sinews from the leg. Sometimes, if the turkey's legs were strong, you ended up doing a Tarzan act, swinging along and pulling with all your might. Then, all of a sudden, the sinews would give and you would be left crumpled on the floor. The grouse, pheasant and partridge season were also 'mucky' and very smelly. My job also entailed sorting out the lungs, hearts, intestines and the livers (the latter were cleaned and used to make the pâté maison – lovely!)

During my time in the larder I had to learn how to pluck (I said *pluck*!) and tie up the fowls for service, and lard the game birds. When you had done a turn on the cleaning, you could guarantee a seat on the bus or train when you went home; the aroma lingered with you for quite a few hours and nothing seemed to really get rid of it. Sometimes, when you'd had some particularly ripe birds to do, you might even get the whole carriage to yourself!

During this time I was also taught how to 'blow' eggs, then fill them with water, seal them off and, when no one was watching, add them to

18

the trays of fresh eggs that the kitchen used during service. Imagine a busy night: you are just about to do a fried egg as a garnish for a veal escalope holstein. As you crack the egg into a pan with hot butter, a gush of water comes out, and if you aren't quick enough you might get splashed with the fatty water! The normal reaction was to call on the gods to strike down the illegitimate person who had played this rotten joke on you (bear in mind the embarrassment of knowing that everyone else knew you'd been had). You would make a dark note to get even, which you usually did at a later date, when the prankster had forgotten about it and was working on his next joke, and therefore wide open to attack from the rear.

In those days nothing was wasted. Chicken fat was saved and rendered down to make the chicken soup and velouté; all the fat from the roasting trays was saved in dustbins kept under the tables on the sauce section, and used to roast off the joints and make the demi glace. When it was 'tired' (beyond help), then it was given to the 'fat man', who would sell it to pig farms, or to soap-makers. Bones were scraped clean, roasted and used either for the consommé or the stockpot on the sauce section. The chicken livers were cleaned and used to make pâté, the beef trimmings were sorted out, and as the joints were boned the trimmings were put into three piles: one for rubbish (stockpot), the second for the mince, either for clarification or for bolognaise, and the third lot was the 'better' pieces that were added to or built up for the various sautées (goulash, bourgignon, and the steak and kidney pie mix). The steak and kidney pie was made mainly with topside and ox kidneys.

Louis used to cut about 40 assorted steaks ready for each service, and you could almost bet on it that they would run out during the service, so he had to set to topping up the mise en place again. Sometimes, when we had a lot of parties, especially at Christmas time, it took Louis and the others all their time to keep 'en place'. When you think that we used to do an average of 100 plus lunches and quite often over 200 dinners most days, you can see why Louis kept his knives like razors.

The knife grinders, two Italian brothers called Beltrami, used to call about once a fortnight. They'd come round to the kitchen, gather up all the knives that needed a 'tickle' and take them out to their van to 'do the business'. When the knives were returned to the kitchen the fun started, with an outbreak of nicks and gentle blood-letting as the chefs got used to their razor-sharp knives. The Beltrami brothers are still going strong, and they have 'done' the knives for the various kitchens where I have been chef over the years. They have always been cheerful, sharing jokes and making rude comments about the various chefs. (You must remember that a kitchen is a hive of crude jokes, language and actions, nearly always given and taken in good spirits – in the old days, probably literally!)

Also in the larder was the wet fish section, which was tucked away round the back of the main larder. All the fish used to come in on the bone: the soles needed skinning and either trimming or filleting; whole turbots had to be split in half after the head and fins were removed. The fish chef used to have the bones for his velouté and glace de poisson; the head was cooked by the larder and the meat was used by the hors d'oeuvres for the fish cocktail or salad. Lobsters came in live and were cooked on the premises. The 'cripples' (ones with a claw missing or some part deformed) could not be served whole, so they were cut up and used to make the bisque d'homard and the sauce americaine. For these, the shells were removed and pounded in a large marble mortar (you felt like one of those African women on the travel programmes pounding the corn). The resulting mess was returned to the soup/sauce and then the brains were mixed with butter and flour, added to the liquid and then cooked through. The eggs of the cooked lobster were dried and crushed and the powder was used for decorating the prawn cocktails and the like, as was the coral.

Under Sid worked a small man called Ernesto, an Italian we used to call Nesto. He was about 60, built like a feather and chewed tobacco all day, squirting a stream of juice into the rubbish bins as he passed along. Like the vast majority of 'old chefs', Nesto had worked around the world: America, Canada, the Middle East, you name it, he'd been there! He was a fantastic man, never got ruffled, no matter how the others tried to get him going.

The funniest thing I remember about Nesto was the day he was cooking a pot of live lobsters for the mise en place in the larder. He had a habit of turning the lobsters over, making sure they were alive and checking for any faults. This was quite safe, as they always came in with their claws tied shut with thick rubber bands. This time, though, there was one that had not been done and, obviously not too happy at being mucked about with, it decided to let Nesto know that it was alive all right. It pinched his forefinger and gripped hard for dear life. I can still see Nesto standing there trying to shake it off. Eventually, when we had all stopped laughing, Sid came over, managed to prise open the claw and released his finger. During all this Nesto had not said a word, just stood looking as if to say, 'I don't believe this is happening'. He was left with a nasty bruise on his finger which took a few days to clear up. From then on, he always checked the batch of lobsters carefully!

Several chefs (tournant and commis) came and went during my time in the larder. One was dismissed because he was caught one night going home with a whole side of smoked salmon wrapped around his waist! Another, Louis the Italian, was a right old whinger; nothing in this world was right for him. He used to try and get others to do his work while he just lazed about, so he was not very popular, as you can imagine. One night he was winding up this commis, a young Cypriot. Well, the guy lost his cool and whacked Louis on the head with a huge metal spatula. Louis sort of sighed and collapsed in a heap on the floor with a little blood flowing, while the Cypriot did a flying runner, out and away. Joe called the sous chef to tell him what had happened (very inconvenient as it was in the middle of the evening service). Mons. Habert popped down to tell the chef, who told Mons. Bonvin to call the police. So the lad had plenty of time to disappear. By the time the police arrived, Louis was back on his feet with a bit of a headache and the skin only just broken – no big deal, but he insisted on a bandage and going to hospital to have a check-up. The police tried to interview those who had been near at the time, but everyone was too busy doing the orders to have seen anything. As you can see, there was not much sympathy for Louis.

One guy used to pack up at 11 pm, regardless of how busy we were, change and go home. He only lasted a week – I wonder why. Another was called Robertson, a large, well built man who walked like John Wayne (or John Wayne walked like Robertson, as I think 'Robbo' was the elder). He spoke fluent French, as could most of the old British chefs. In the days before I began (about the 20s), you had to speak French to get on in the trade, but when I started it had begun to die out a little because of all the other nationalities coming into the kitchens.

Robertson liked to sup a little, and most afternoons he went to the ACF club in Old Compton Street just around the corner from Kettners. Most of the chefs in town used to go there during their break, have a few cheap drinks and chat or play cards, as the club was licensed all afternoon. When he was sober, Robertson was a lovely, fun man and a good teacher, well up on the garnishes and dishes. But when he'd had a few he got stroppy and was hard to work with. A couple of times he was even sent home early.

For sauces and fish dishes, wine, brandy and other spirits would be needed. These were collected from the chef's office, and before he gave you a newly opened bottle, he would pour in a few salt crystals and give it a good shake. One day I asked George why the chef did this, and he gave me a drop to taste. It tasted foul. The reason was to stop the chefs from drinking during service, or finding the bottles in their pockets on the way home. ('How did that get there?') Sometimes in the middle of evening service, Robertson would be dying for a fix. He would sidle up to the sauce or fish section, pour a shot of whatever was nearest into a cup, wink at you and whisper 'Shhhh!' Then he would nip back from whence he came and knock back his noggin. Robbo must have had a cast iron constitution as he never seemed to notice the salt content. For all that, when he was on form he was a very good chef; shame that he let himself down like that.

Another chef tournant was Charlie Roper, an Englishman with piercing light blue eyes and some fingers missing from one of his hands, which never seemed to hinder him in his work: he could carve, bone out and chop without any trouble. Charlie had a good sense of humour (most times) and was on the sauce quite regularly, when Hassan or George were off. He was very good at his job, but on quiet Saturday lunchtimes, when we were en place, he used to show me how to do various sauces 'à la minute'. In other words, if you ever had a problem, dropped a sauce or dish just before it was due to be served, then *this* was how you got out of the shit. Old Charlie impressed upon me that this method was for emergencies only – and have there been some emergencies!

One example is the time when a party was due to arrive. The host had come in to check the room and the layout, but when he looked at the menu he had a blue fit. It was not the menu he had chosen! The typist must have been in love the day she typed it up – she had not only got the main course wrong, but had printed the wrong starter too! The chef got over the starter OK – avocado and prawns instead of the smoked salmon he had expected. The main course was more problematic. It should have been entrecote marchand de vin, but was now supreme chasseur. Well, with a bit of sweat and fast cooking we made the chasseur in minutes flat, and as supremes don't take very long to cook it turned out well in the end. To pacify the client we gave him a lemon sorbet as a middle course for free. At times like these Charlie's teachings came in very handy!

One day poor old Sid died, literally on the job – just how he would have wished, I'm sure. Sid had had a very bad cold for about two weeks, but he insisted on coming in and pulling his weight. 'It'll be gone soon,' he said, 'I'm not letting a poxy cold get the better of me!' (Can you see the younger ones of today being so conscientious?). Our larder like all larders, was not the warmest of places, especially in the winter, and poor Sid just got worse. My last memory of him was him standing next to the mincing machine passing some scraps off for a clarification. He looked completely buggered! The chef was called and he told Sid what a silly bugger he was and that he would have to go for a check up. They sent him to the French hospital, which used to be in the top part of Shaftesbury Avenue. Gasco went with him and a couple of hours later he was back, saying that the doctors thought Sid had pneumonia, and they were going to keep him in.

Two days later, as we arrived for work in the morning, Gasco was waiting at the top of the stairs in the kitchen with the sad news that 'our Sid' had died peacefully the previous night. Everyone was in a state of shock, nobody had anything to say, no wise cracks during service, just the acknowledgement of the orders. Even Bill didn't seem to be calling out the orders as loudly as usual. It was just a bad, sad day that I shall always remember. Sid was a man of steel, nothing got the better of him, but now he was gone.

After a few weeks a replacement for Sid arrived, a German called Walter Blesse who was about 27. (That was very young in those days, normally you had to be 30 plus to get a gardemangre's position.) He spoke very good English, excellent French and a fair bit of Italian, and he was an excellent chef. I was privileged to watch him prepare a cold buffet that had been ordered late the night before for a 1 pm lunch. He had supreme jeanettes, lamb cutlets and cold roast sirloin to get ready, chaud, froid and glazed. He made it with time to spare, including setting them up on glazed dishes with garnishes. He had great organisational skills and the knack of getting the others in the larder into the swing of it all. His only trouble was that he liked to stir, winding up the French chefs about the war, how good Germany was and so on. He also used to tell us stories about his time in the Hitler youth, and of his being trained on the anti aircraft guns. I wasn't always sure whether the story he was telling was true or just a wind-up. He used to go home on a scooter (German, of course!), and as he was about 6'1", he looked like something out of space with his waterproofs, his hob-nailed biker boots and his helmet. Walter stayed about six months, then he left to emigrate to New Zealand. I presume he's still there, still winding people up!

After Blesse came a typical old stager. He must have been over 60 and was an Alsatian by the name of Zislin. He wore glasses perched on the end of his nose, and was always looking over them at you when he talked (or rather spluttered) like a headmaster. On his first day in the larder, I asked him what I should call him, expecting to call him by his christian name, as I did all the other chefs. He looked at me as if to fathom out who or what I was. Then: 'Call me Monsieur Zislin, or chef!' he spluttered. From that day I only spoke to him if I really had to; I never addressed him as Mons. Zislin or chef, I just used to stand next to him and say, 'Excuse me'. He was really bombastic and in his short time with us (about four months) he managed to upset and argue with practically everyone in the kitchen. The only ones who used to get to him were the Cypriots and Algerians – they would mutter away in their own tongue, smiling sweetly but really cursing him.

Another chef tournant was called Mason. I thought he was English, but I was told later that he was Belgian, so take your choice. (If he's still around, Mason himself can settle it.) He spoke French fluently, had 'pop' eyes, a swarthy complexion and a ready smile which was even bigger if he'd been up the club. Mason was quite a good chef who knew his 'onions'. I met him again a few years later when I went for a sous chef's position at a hotel where he was head chef.

About this time, little Louis decided to leave. His replacement was a German called Fritz who was built like a brick bog-house, with muscles

23

all over. Fritz was a really good butcher and he showed me his selection of master butcher credentials from Berlin, Hamburg etc. The certificates looked really impressive and he told me he'd had to go through a lot of hard work, practical and theory, plus a competition, to get them.

Then we had a Chinese chef tournant – yes, we certainly had an international kitchen. He was not too bad apart from the fact that he could not speak much English, let alone any French. (The old man must have been having a really bad day when he employed this fellow.) In the end he was used as the 'runner' for the larder (passing the orders to either the grill, fish or sauce). The one thing I remember about him was his love for grilled smoked salmon.

Then there was Jack Trigg, who was with us a couple of times as chef tournant and larder chef. Jack was in his late 50s and well-built, with a flattish face and large thick-lense spectacles. He was a true blue Englishman, not averse to having a go at the 'Frogs', as he called them, but he was good. He'd learnt his trade at a lot of different hotels and restaurants (like most of the chefs then). The highlight of his day was if he wound up the head chef before he went home. Jack had a sharp mind and a very quick tongue but he was never malicious. I met him again a few years later at L'Ecu de France. I walked in and blow me, there was Jack cooking up a storm on the roast/grill section. (More of this later.)

I remember a commis tournant called Simon. He was young and very confident in everything he did. Sometimes he used to get a bit uppity, but the chefs de partie soon shot him down. Apart from that he was quite well liked. George, Ali and Joe, plus the larder chef, knew that if he was on their corner things would go smoothly.

One day Simon and Mons. Moreau had a row. I never knew what it was about, but I can still recall the old man going scarlet and spluttering as if he was going to have a seizure, and Simon walking away calling the chef names in French. There was a stunned silence: no-one spoke to the chef like that and lived. It was only a few days later that Simon left; I still can't think why!

Swiss Charlie (to distinguish him from the other two Charlies, and yes, he was Swiss!) was another commis tournant. He was really crafty; when he was told to do such and such a job, he would take all day to do it, though after a while the chefs de partie caught on and chased him along. I think that the main reason everyone put up with Swiss Charlie, even the chef, was that he had a good-looking wife who used to come and meet him when he was on earlies (finishing at 9 pm). She was blonde, about 5'3" and very well put together. The temperature (amongst other things) used to rise when she turned up, usually wearing low-cut blouses or tight jumpers with a short skirt, stockings and high heels. Even the head chef smiled and was friendly to her, obviously wishing he was 20

24

years younger. If it was not too busy, she would be guided into the pastry and given coffee and biscuits or a sweet, then all the chefs de partie would take it in turns to pop in and chat with her. The ones who could speak French had an advantage, as she did not speak much English. (A few of us offered to give her private lessons, but that's another story.) Swiss Charlie was as tight as a midge's arse going backwards (one of my mother-in-law's sayings, lovely expression, eh!) Every night he used to wrap up two portions of meat or fish and two portions of veg, right down to a pinch of salt for their meal when he got home. He didn't spend a penny more than he had to.

For a short time we had a black tournant, the first black person I had seen with 'straight' hair. He told me once that he used special heated tongs every night to keep his hair straight. He was quite a nice bloke, but I think the speed that the kitchen worked and the pressure was a bit too much for him, and he 'sailed' over to other waters.

During this time we also had Young Charlie, who was English through and through. He'd start a row in the middle of Paris if he thought England was being put down. Charlie was a true nut case; everything he did was at top speed. He used to time himself when boning a joint of something and then next time try to do it faster. The trouble was that all this speed left a lot of meat still on the bone and in the end they gave him the trimming jobs to do because it didn't matter too much. When he was on the fish he used to give Ali palpitations, making a 30-egg sabayon in about four minutes flat, on a full fire. He'd just laugh when Ali shouted at him to do it slower and 'with love'. Young Charlie used to ride a motor bike, and looked like one of those ancient flyers with his goggles, helmet and loose-fitting waterproofs. I made the mistake one night of accepting a lift home on the back of his bike. If ever anyone had a death wish, or was very lucky, it was Young Charlie. After the first near-miss I tried to keep my eyes tightly shut and hung on tight, only squinting when I heard brakes being put on or curses filling the air. Charlie was good at making a near miss and then asking the other fellow what the hell he was doing on the road. Most of the guys liked him, he had a ready wit and did not take offence easily; he was just one of those 'rushers' in life. Charlie, are you still out there with your trusty bike?

When I first started at Kettners there was already an apprentice who'd been there about a year, Lionel Blanche. He was about two years older than me and was then called the senior apprentice. He was very good, and everyone believed he had good prospects. His only drawback was that he could not stand the sight of blood; he used to pass out cold. Sometimes, when one of the chefs had cut themselves, they would innocently call Lionel over, and while they asked him some silly question, they would accidentally let a drop or two of blood drop. If he hadn't noticed, they would say, 'Is that your blood or mine?' Well, Lionel would look, turn white and pass out. (There would always be someone next to him or behind him, so he was caught before hitting the floor – they were thoughtful like that!)

One year Lionel and his family went to one of these holiday camps, and Lionel was hauled up on stage to act as the stooge for the resident hypnotist. He was such a good subject that it took a while for him to come round, and from that day on he seemed to go doolally, doing the strangest things during service, or ignoring the orders. Everyone put up with his funny ways until he started to answer back, not jokey but really serious. The crunch came when he began to tell the chefs de partie how to do their jobs and then (sacrilege) told the head chef what he should be doing. It got so bad that Lionel left, and the last we heard, his family was suing the holiday camp, who had offered Lionel a job for life!

During this period I was told I had been accepted and was being enrolled with the apprentice council as an apprentice at Kettners restaurant. I was well pleased, I can tell you. Then I enrolled at Westminster College. All apprentices in those days had to attend a college for one day a week as part of their training. This was a real culture shock, because like the vast majority of apprentice chefs, I was used to using first-class foodstuffs: lobsters, Scotch beef, veal, turbot etc. Because the ingredients at the college were 'staff meal' quality (cod fillet, chuck steak, and so on), even the instructors apologised sometimes; but as they were on a tight budget for the day release lads, there was not much they could do about it. The sad part was that the guys who were full time (future managers etc) had all the good food and screwed it up, because they weren't interested in cooking; they just had to go through the motions as part of the management training. We often said, 'Why don't you give the crap to them and let us use the good stuff?' The college used to operate a restaurant offering lunch to outsiders, to give the full-timers a taste of à la carte service. No wonder some of the instructors lost their cool! (Who out there remembers Mons. Le Prince?)

Most of us were used to working with silver dishes and presenting food with garnishes, but at the college we had to use thick aluminium dishes – absolute crap! (I often wondered who had shares in the aluminium factory). Our first tutor was a man called Liegmes (I hope I've spelt it right). He was a really good chef who had been through the mill and knew it all. He used to get so frustrated at times with the quality of ingredients we were given to work with, but though he had a few discussions about the problem with the senior tutor, nothing changed.

We used to have the practical lessons in the morning and then after lunch (a quick sandwich in the nearby market, the college food was so poor) we'd have a theory lesson with Mons. Liegmes, during which he commented on the dishes we had made that morning. We were split into teams of two or three, depending on how many turned up (it was surprising how many chefs made the apprentices miss their college day because they were either busy or short-staffed. I must say that my chefs were very good and never tried to stop me going to college), then we would do either the starter, the main or the sweet. Mons. Liegmes was very constructive in his comments and was never vindictive.

After about three years Mons. Liegmes told us he was leaving to take up a more senior post at Portsmouth. We were sad at the news, but wished him all the best, and on the week he was due to leave all the lads had a whip-round for him, and bought him a bottle of Kirsch (his favourite) and a card, which we presented to him during the afternoon lesson. Over the years, I heard from various chefs who came into contact with him that he was doing very well. Sadly, I heard that he died a little while ago – another bit of history gone.

We soon met our new tutor, Mons. Bulot. Now Mons. Bulot was as different from Mons. Liegmes as chalk from cheese. He was a typical Frenchman: slim, with slicked-black hair and a pencil-thin moustache, so thin that I wondered if it had been drawn on with eyeliner. While Mons. Liegmes was softly spoken, calm and never gave us any bullshit, Mons. Bulot was very excitable and some of his stories had question marks over them. In other words, he was quite a pompous person and not many of us liked him much. My most vivid memory of him is when he was making a fondant gateau, but kept getting the fondant too hot so it slowly rolled off the sponge and formed a pool around the sponge. We looked on, wondering what he was trying to prove.

There were a few other tutors I remember. Mons. Vincent was one, and he was also the principal. His eyes seemed to zap right through you, but he could laugh too, and all the other tutors seemed to respect him. Since they had all done their time in the kitchens of the world before coming to the college, he must have been good.

Then there was Mons. D'Arsonval in the larder, a nice bloke with a lived-in face who never had to raise his voice (at least not that I ever heard). I remember one day we were sent down to the larder because Mons. D'Arsonval was going to do a butchery demonstration. Well, I'd thought that our little Louis was good, but this guy was something else. He had a side of pork and as he worked on it, his boning knife doing magic things, he gave a running commentary. I was told later that when the Queen had state banquets, most of the Westminster tutors were asked to go to the palace and help with the food, and apparently Mons. D'Arsonval was a regular.

An English chap, whose name escapes me but who was known as 'the farmer', was on the hors d'oeuvres and buffet section. As his nickname implies, he had the rugged high colour of a farmer. He too was good, all his timbales etc turned out perfect (at least every time I saw).

Mons. Lefevre was in the pastry section, another cool, calm and collected chef. We never actually had any of these tutors for lessons, but we heard that Mons. Lefevre was a very good teacher, and now that he has retired, I believe he is (correct me if I'm wrong) the consultant chef for the Lynx French House of Cointreau. Also in the pastry was a man called Burrows, a tall English chef who was apparently 'shit hot'. I was told later that before coming to the college, he had been pastry chef at the Grosvenor House in Park Lane, and that he'd done a pastillage model of the Queen Mary to celebrate her maiden voyage, which was presented at a banquet in the ship's honour. The model was, I'm told, a masterpiece.

Then there was Mons. Durand, a good all-rounder (he seemed to be on different sections every time we saw him). His memory is as good now as it was all those years ago and he is a fascinating bloke to talk to; he always has a story about some chef or other from the 'old' days. Some of his tales (all true, of course) would make a full time comedian weep with frustration, so you see, we do have a sense of humour, even if it is a bit on the wicked side.

And of course, there was Mons. Le Prince (who did not know Le Prince?), a phenomenon in his own lifetime whose short temper was legendary – you felt that if you touched him he'd go bang! I can remember passing through the sauce section on the way to the larder for a demonstration, and hearing a lot of shouting and cursing and the clang of a copper sauters as it landed somewhere after being thrown at some poor old full-timer, who had probably burnt something or asked Mons. Le Prince to repeat what he'd just said.

Back to Kettners now. The porters there were quite a permanent lot (not like today, when they change by the week, sometimes by the day!) One I could not forget (although I can't remember his name) was a little Algerian, who would only speak in Arabic with just a smattering of French. He was short and very thin, nearly a skeleton, but as strong as two horses. He was very dark-skinned, and covered from head to toe in tattoos, having spent a vast amount of his life working on boats in Algeria, Tunisia and around the world. I never found out how he came to end up as a kitchen porter in England, but some of the stories he told us (with Louis as interpreter) were mind-boggling and would fill a book by themselves.

We had two porters in the potwash, Maltese, I think, and their workload was pretty huge. We had so many types and sizes of pots, all in copper. The stockpots were so large that the average person could have a bath in one (and, judging from the state of some I saw, they probably had). At the end of the shift the porters' hands were pure white and crinkly, like tripe, and they used to rub their hands in salt to decrinkle them.

In the plate room, where all the plates, cutlery and silver dishes were washed, was a 'tribe' of Pakistanis. They hardly spoke to anyone, just got on with the job of directing the steady flow of clean plates and cutlery back into the restaurant and kitchen. Their 'foreman' was an old guy, Ali, who could speak fairly good English, so if the chefs wanted anything in particular, they would see Ali and he would sort out the problem. In all my five years I do not remember one argument occurring between them.

Then there was little Louis's brother – little, little Louis. He was a lovely fellow, only about 4'4", and the chefs used to play some rotten tricks on him. Sometimes they would lift him on top of the work tables and stand around idly while he tried to get down. They'd splash him with water ('Sorry, didn't see you down there') or say 'Get off your knees!' He took it all in good part, though he did get his own back. His favourite trick was to creep up behind you; then someone would call to you, and as you turned around he would headbutt you in the testicles. Once, for a joke, Ali grabbed him and stuck him in the milk fridge. After a few minutes of banging and the odd swear word, it all went quiet; when they looked in, there sat Louis, supping beer from the milk ladle. 'You can do that any time!' he said with a big smile.

Another of the chefs tournant was a smallish Polish guy. He looked a bit like Popeye's mate Mr Wimpey, was well rounded and always eating. We wondered how he could pack so much grub into his body each day until we found out he was a survivor of one of the German concentration camps. After he'd been with us a couple of months, he opened up a little, showed us the number tattooed on his forearm and told stories about the camps. Every now and again he would withdraw from life and for a day or two you would not get a word out of him; then he'd be right as rain. His eating habits stemmed from the camp days, so everyone understood when he'd reach over after you had finished eating and ask if he could finish off your meal.

Then I was put onto the fish section, where a Turkish Cypriot chap called Ali Hussein reigned supreme. I was told that he had started at Kettners as a commis and showed such promise that he was eventually promoted to poissonière. I think Ali was one of the best fish chefs I have ever worked with. He was so organised that even on the busiest nights you never saw him rushing around; he just seemed to move at a constant medium fast pace all the time. The day I started on his section, Ali put a list of the fish dishes on the wall (about 17, not counting the omelettes or the banqueting fish dishes). 'When you make three mistakes on each dish, then I'll give you a clip,' was his warning to me. I worked hard and did 'the business' from memory. I only slipped up once, and that was enough!

On that occasion, Ali grabbed my hand and explained to me how and why I had screwed up, then he gently squeezed my flesh between his thumb and forefinger. The pain shot up my arm and no matter how I tried I could not break free – Ali had me trapped with the use of only two fingers! Later on he showed me various holds and grips that he'd been taught by his various wrestling buddies while doing a stint at the YMCA. When I explain that Ali was built like a barn (all four sides), with upper arms so big you couldn't put your hands round them, you'll understand why I did not want to make too many mistakes.

Not that he didn't have a good sense of humour. It was Ali who taught me the 'hot spoon' trick. Every morning, just after the early shift had started, one of the porters made about three gallons of tea, milked, and left it on the hot plate in a large soup tureen with a ladle, so that everyone could help themselves. You know the pint and two pint heavy glass pourers, well these were our 'cups'. I graduated from a small half-pint job up to the full two-pinters. The idea is to casually engage someone in idle chit-chat, innocently stirring your tea, then quick as a flash you pop the hot spoon on the person's wrist. As they jump in pain, you say 'Oh, sorry I thought it was going on to the table', smile sweetly and walk away. But beware of *them* stirring *their* tea!

Another of Ali's party tricks was to creep up on someone who was deep in thought or concentrating on work, and squash an eggshell on the side of both ears at the same time. It made them jump because the echoes go right through the brain (assuming they had one, of course). Also on a hot night, when you are sweating like a good 'un, maybe doing an omelette on full fire, he'd come up behind you, say 'O.K.?' then swiftly pop an ice cube or crushed ice down the back of your jacket. The coldness against your sweat literally took your breath away.

But when it came down to work, with Ali everything had its place, both in the fridge and on the mise en place trays. He was quite right, of course, because as time went on and I picked up steam doing the orders and building up various garnishes and sauces, I could rush to the fridge, put my hand in and reach for whatever I needed without having to think. It was the same with the mise en place trays. These were done up fresh each morning and topped up during the course of the day. I could take the pan to the table and easily get the garnishes I needed without really looking, as all the bowls of garnish were laid out on the trays in exactly the same way every time. This saved precious seconds when we were under pressure (another name for being nearly in the proverbial). Ali had only two solid top stoves with ovens underneath to work on (the same as George and Joe), and he only had one commis to help him with the à la carte, table d'hôte and banqueting menus. Sometimes he had three or four different parties' dishes to sort out as well as a busy restaurant service and all the omelettes to do (except the cofiture ones, which were done in the pastry). Once you have worked under pressure you soon realise the benefits of a good mise en place.

I can honestly say that I cannot remember a time when Ali was in the shit or screwed up a dish, he was that smooth an operator. For a time Ali had Young Charlie (remember him?) as his commis. I think that if Ali had been a weaker guy, he'd have had a heart attack or a stroke with the antics that Charlie got up to. When you had to do the sabayon and the hollandaise for Ali, each one was at least a 15-minute job, because you had to 'tickle' the egg yolks along and whisk them well, normally in a figure-of-eight style. So that took you at least 30 minutes straight away. But not Charlie! He used to turn each one out in about five minutes flat! He'd take the rings off of the top and put the plat sauté on full fire and whisk like a banshee, smiling and sweating. Quite often he'd end up scrambling them, and if no one saw then he'd 'shoot' them quick and start again. With Charlie, everything had to be done for the Guinness Book of Records.

While I was on the veg with Joe, Ali had an Indian chap called Johnnie as his commis, who was always laughing and trying to please. When he was with Ali he was only slightly panicky. (Ali had a great calming effect; if he didn't run around, you thought, what the hell am I doing it for?) But after 9 pm, when Ali went home, Johnnie used to go completely to pieces, running from the stove to the fridge and back in utter panic. He would forget the orders just after they were called out and give the wrong orders when Bill called them away. But as he was such a likeable bloke all the others felt sorry for him and would help him out (who said chefs are hard-hearted and uncaring?) Ali had great patience with him and finally got him to slow down and use his brain, and not be so nervous about being on his own. Unfortunately, one day he made a real balls up of an order and the old man saw it. Not being in one of his best moods, he really roasted Johnnie, and from then on it was only a matter of time before he'd had his chips.

One section I really enjoyed working on was the fish, partly because once I had got the hang of the various dishes, preparation and serving, I was allowed to run the section on Sundays by myself, plus the late service during the week after the chefs de partie had gone home. It was a matter of pride being able to cope with the late orders and the Sunday service.

After about six months on the fish, I was sent into the pastry to continue my stint as an apprentice. The patissière was a Swiss bloke called Victor Madere who had been over here for 20-odd years, and he was shit hot! Victor told me that he had started his pastry career in Switzerland at a large pastry and bakery in his home town. The owner used to weigh out the various ingredients early in the morning before anyone was up and when the apprentices came down they learned how to make the special pastries and breads, but never the amounts of ingredients involved, as these were secret. As the custom in those days was to pay the creator if you wanted a certain recipe, the only way Victor could learn the recipes was to creep out of his room in the early hours of the morning, sit on the stairs and watch the owner weigh out all the ingredients, then make notes of the amounts.

Victor had arrived in London in the 1920s and started work for the Monnickendams, who were famous for their pastries and had quite a few shops in town. (It was strange that he should end his working life working for the son of his first employer at Kettners.) He'd also worked at the Carlton Hotel with Escoffier as a commis patissière, and was in the pastry team at the famous night club Café Anglaise during the war. One particular night, when Victor was off, during an air raid a bomb fell through the large glass dome above the dance floor, killing a lot of the customers and most of the staff. Victor always said that his lucky star was shining on him that night.

Victor was one of the best patissières I have ever met. He was Mr Cool, never lost his self control. Even when I screwed up a dish, he would quietly explain what had gone wrong, what I should do to correct it and then 'Start again and take your time!' he would say. He used to go through the ingredients, measures and methods of all the dishes on the menu, and then some! I will always remember returning to do my second shift one evening to find Victor decorating a gateau for a party the next lunchtime. He was 'painting' a scene of a brightly coloured bird sitting on a leaf-laden branch with a country vista in the background. It was as if someone had taken a photo and laid it on top of the gateau, but Victor was doing this freehand! Absolutely bloody marvellous, I tell you!

At Kettners they made virtually all their own ice-cream; the only ones brought in were vanilla, strawberry and chocolate. All the sorbets, bombes, parfaits and cassatas were made fresh in the pastry, and in the grill room we had two ice-cream making machines which were kept busy all week. The chef used to buy in things like charentals, melons, satsumas etc and Victor would turn them into sorbets, ice creams or mousses. Soufflés were made to order, from one to 50 plus. We used to have four soufflés on the menu – grand marnier, rothschild, chocolate and cheese – but we made any sort that might be requested (within reason).

When Victor did the fresh fruit salad, all his apples and pears were cut differently, so that if a customer ordered a fruit salad without pears, they were easier to see and take out. The (then) obligatory peach melba was also on the menu and Victor once told me how it had been invented. Apparently Dame Nellie Melba, the Australian soprano, was eating late and asked the chef, Mons. Escoffier, to do something special to surprise her. As he was just about to go home, he rushed into the pastry, looked in the fridge and found some fresh peaches that had just been peeled, some left-over raspberry sauce and a few toasted almonds. He placed the whole peach on top of some fresh vanilla ice cream, masked it with the sauce, sprinkled it with the almonds and, hey presto, a classic dish was born.

One evening, when service was slow, Victor started to talk about his younger days in the pastry. One of his stories has stuck in my mind like it has been superglued there. When he was pastry chef at a well-known hotel, the head chef was very demanding and, like Mons. Moreau, careful about giving wine etc for the dishes. Each Christmas Victor had to make a few hundred Christmas puddings for service and takeaways, and the chef stood over him while he poured brandy, port and sherry into the pudding mixture, to make sure the staff did not drink it. So he couldn't understand how, on Christmas Day, all the chefs got merry without him issuing any drink to them. The answer was simple: our Victor had a large hair sieve buried under all the mixed fruit, and as the chef poured the hooch over the fruit, the liquid slowly filtered through into the bottom of the bowl. When the chef had gone, Victor sieved the juice through a fine muslin, bottled it and stored it in a cool hiding place till Christmas lunch, then issued it to the troops, who thoroughly enjoyed it and proceeded to get tight.

Another time when it was quiet and Victor was in his reminiscing mood, he told me the following story (I have often repeated it because I think it is an absolute classic, so if you are one of the many who have already heard it, tough, 'cos here it is again!) One day, when Victor had only been in the business a few years, he and his brother were invited to a fancy dress party, so they decided to go as babies. They dressed up in 'nappies' (sheets tucked around their private parts), little bonnets and bibs and had sugar dummies. Just before they arrived at the party they emptied about two pints of light ale into a large potty and covered it over. A little later they told the host that they would do a little cabaret act. They got the potty, floated about four chocolate 'turds' in the beer, then put the potty in the middle of the room. Victor and his brother then sat on it to 'do their business'. They then took it in turns to drink the 'pee' and eat the 'turds'. Victor told me with some relish that some of the ladies present left the room to compose themselves!

Victor used to say that in all his life, he'd never had a headache, cold, flu or any illness whatsoever. (He used to arrive at work and go home wearing just a casual shirt, open-necked, casual jacket and slacks, even in the middle of winter with the snow lying thick; he just did not feel the cold.) Then one day his wife rang to say that he was not feeling too good and would not be in for a day or two. Sadly, within about three days, our Victor had died. The doctor said that he had caught a chill and as his body had never had to fight any germs, it was not able to fight when one struck. We could not believe it: Victor gone. Again it was poor old Gasco who had the job of telling everyone. We were all in shock, and how we got through the lunch service no one knows. Everyone had a whip-round for Victor; I'm not sure if they bought flowers or gave his wife the money, as Victor always said he was an atheist. M. Habert, George and old Bill went to the funeral, and we all thought of Victor on that day too.

Victor's first commis, a Cypriot (another one! I hear you cry) was very good, and most of the chefs thought he would take over; but he was either shy or lacking in confidence and he sort of cracked under the strain of running the pastry. So about a month later, the new patissière turned up. His name was Peter Cottat, a Frenchman with an 'Errol Flynn' moustache who was about 30. (Sorry if you weren't that old, Peter, but you had worry lines!) He was very easy-going and confident and seemed to fit in easily. Obviously Peter had a different style and system, but he was very good, very thorough like Victor. He liked the office girls and was always there to chat to them. In fact all the chefs de partie and sous used to pull rank when a pretty girl came into the kitchen – typical of chefs (must be the heat).

After about two months it was obvious that Peter and the commis did not hit it off (I think the commis could not adjust to Peter's system). Anyway, he upped and left – shame really cause he was a nice bloke, just needed that 'oomph' or maybe a quick boot.

When my time was up in the pastry, I was moved back into the kitchen with a bit more responsibility. I was to do the commis tournant's job; though I was still classed as an apprentice, I was now expected to be able to cope without any problem. I quite enjoyed this position as it enabled me to keep my hand in on all the sections: one or two days on the sauce, a day on the fish, a few in the larder, a couple on the veg – smashing! During this time I used to take over when Paul was off.

Now old Paul was a real case. He looked like a cross between Fagin and Shylock (or maybe the two combined!), was about 60 when I knew him, and guess what – he was a Greek Cypriot! Paul used to arrive in the morning and walk wearily through the kitchen as if he was on his last legs. He'd go and change, toddle down to the kitchen, say good morning to everyone, get himself a coffee, then retire to his grill room, where he'd have a little sit down to recover his breath before starting work. But when the time came to go home (especially in the evening) 'old Paul' would be up those flights of stairs like a greyhound after the rabbit! One night the sous chef, Mons. Favier, timed him from the moment he left his grill to the moment he passed him on the way out – just on four minutes! That was up three flights of stairs, into the locker room, off with his uniform, on with his coat and scarf, down the stairs and out. Now is that moving!

Sometimes a 'guard' would gather at the end of the hotplate a few minutes before the 'off', casually chatting and generally being obstructive. The sous would call out, 'OK, lads, goodnight!' and Paul would curse, shove, pant and puff until he managed to get past, accompanied by a string of curses. (It was rumoured that he had a very pretty young wife, and that he was in a rush to get his 'oats', so to speak.)

It was during this period that I had my worst run-in with the 'old man'. For quite a while he had been taking an interest in what I was having for supper. One night little Louis gave me a couple of cutlets, which I duly grilled (permission of Paul), then went into the pastry to see what sweet I could have. As I came back into the grill room with my sweet balanced on top of my dinner, Mons. Moreau came through the flap and stood in my way. 'What have you got?' he shouted at me. I was a bit cheesed off by now, so I said, 'Mind your own business, this is my supper.' He then grabbed my plate, muttering away in French. After some to-ing and fro-ing, I let go just as he decided to put extra force into his fro-ing. Well, the fruit salad with cream, the lamb cutlets and assorted vegetables with plenty of gravy went all over him: down the front of his pure white jacket, down his pure white apron – what a mess! He went red, then blue, and finally he told me to go home. I was really peed off by this time, so I muttered something about how his nuts should be cut off, and rushed upstairs to get changed. While I was changing, Mons. Habert came up and told me to stay off for a few days so he could cool the old man down. But on my way out, as I passed the hotplate, the chef grabbed my arm and told me I was sacked.

The next morning I woke up and took stock of my situation. I phoned the offices of the apprenticeship council, briefly told them the story, and made an appointment later that morning to see someone. I told the chap exactly what had happened, what I'd said and what the chef had said. He listened quietly then, as I sat there, he phoned Kettners and spoke to the boss, Mr Monnickendam, putting my side to him. He said it seemed to be a case of harassment by the chef and recommended that I go back and finish my apprenticeship. Anyway (it was a bit more involved, but to keep the story shortish), the chef was adamant that I would return over his dead body. So Mons. Habert had a word with Mr Monnickendam: as the chef was due to retire in about six months, how about I go 'on loan' for that period? The chap from the council agreed it would be a good idea, as this way I wouldn't lose my apprenticeship. Mons. Habert had a good friend, Mr Williams, who worked as first sous at the Westbury Hotel. He spoke to the chef, got him to agree and everyone's honour was saved.

And that was how I came to be sent on loan to the Westbury Hotel.

KETTNER'S

Restaurant Telephone : GERRARD 3437
Banquets   ,,   ,,   6437

ROMILLY STREET
Soho · London · W1

Carte des Vins

GRAVES

		Bouteille	½ Bouteille
1	Chateau la Vieille France 1953	18/-	10/-
2	Dry Select	18/-	10/-
3	La Fontaine d'or 1952	20/-	11/-
5	Chateau Olivier 1952	21/-	11/-
4	„ Carbonnieux 1949	32/-	—

SAUTERNES

9	Sauternes	21/-	11/-
11	Chateau St. Croix du Mont '53	21/-	11/-
12	„ Beauville 1953	25/-	13/-
13	„ Suduiraut 1949	36/-	—
17	„ Rieussec 1947	38/-	—
15	„ d'Yquem 1949-48	55/-	30/-
14	„ „ 1943	60/-	—

BARSAC

25	Agneau Blanc 1952	21/-	11/-
27	Chateau Coutet 1955	30/-	16/-
28	„ Climens 1947	45/-	—

BORDEAUX ROUGES

31	Carruades Ch. Lafite 1954	20/-	11/-
34	Chateau Moulinet 1952	21/-	—
30	Mouton Cadet 1952	20/-	11/-
33	Chateau la Rose Pourret 1952	25/-	13/-
35	„ Cheval Blanc 1954	25/-	13/-
36	Tauzia	26/-	14/-
37	Chateau Lafon 1949	27/6	14/-
38	„ Trois Moulins 1929	33/-	—

MISE EN BOUTEILLE AU CHATEAU

41	Chateau Montrose 1946	25/-	—
40	Clos Rene, Pomerol 1952	28/-	—
39	Chateau la Lagune 1950	30/-	16/-
43	„ la Dominique 1952	30/-	—
42	„ Mouton Rothschild '54	35/-	17/-
65	„ Ausone 1938	35/-	—
53	„ Calon Segur 1937	37/-	—
48	„ Rausan Segla 1937	38/-	—
60	„ Brane Cantenac 1929	40/-	—
64	„ Pichon Longueville Comtesse 1929	40/-	—
47	„ Mouton d'Armailhacq '47	40/-	21/-
49	„ Haut Brion 1948	45/-	—
52	„ d'Issan 1929	45/-	—
55	„ Lafite 1953	45/-	23/-
56	„ Petrus 1943	56/-	—
54	„ Latour 1934	60/-	—

MAGNUMS

330	Cheval Blanc 1954	50/-	—
331	Clos Rene 1952	60/-	—
332	Chateau la Dominique 1952	60/-	—
342	„ Mouton Rothschild 1954	65/-	—
334	„ Gruaud Larose 1949	80/-	—

BOURGOGNES BLANCS

80	Petit Chablis 1955	20/-	10/6
81	Pouilly Fuisse 1955	22/-	12/-
82	Puligny Montrachet 1955	23/-	12/6
79	Chablis 1955	25/-	13/6
86	Chateau Pouilly 1955	27/-	—
89	Meursault Perrieres 1955	30/-	16/-
84	Chablis Moutonne 1955	34/-	17/6
85	Chablis Vaudesir 1955	26/-	—
87	Le Montrachet 1952	45/-	23/-
88	Meursault, Hospices de Beaune Cuvee Jehan Humblot 1953	50/-	—
83	Le Montrachet Baron Thenard 1953	60/-	—

VINS DE LIMOUX

280	Limoux Maree (Sec)	27/6	—
281	Blanquette de Limoux (Mousseux)	35/-	—

LOIRE

271	Vouvray	19/-	10/-
272	Muscadet	20/-	11/-
273	Sancerre 1955	37/-	—
274	Pouilly Fumé 1956	36/-	19/-

VINS ROSES

260	Pelure d'Oignon	19/-	10/-
261	Rosé d'Anjou	19/-	10/-
262	Rosé de Provence	19/-	—
263	Tavel Rosé	20/-	11/-
264	Mateus Rosé (Portugais)	25/-	13/-

W & F 11-58

BOURGOGNES ROUGES

		Bouteille	½ Bouteille
90	Beaujolais 1955	19/-	10/-
92	Volnay 1953	21/-	11/-
94	Pommard 1955	25/-	—
40	Moulin a Vent 1955	25/-	13/-
91	Beaune Premiere 1953	26/-	14/-
95	Chambolle Musigny 1952	27/-	14/-
98	Nuits St. Georges 1955	32/-	17/-
102	Corton 1953	32/-	17/-
97	Grands Echezaux 1952	33/-	—
111	Aloxe-Corton 1955	30/-	16/-
99	Bonnes Mares 1952	35/-	18/-
100	Beaune Marconnets 55	40/-	21/-
105	Clos de Tart 1952-49	40/-	21/-
108	Clos de Vougeot 1947	45/-	23/-
101	Vigne de l'Enfant Jesus 1952	45/-	—
109	Romanee Saint Vivant 1952	55/-	—
106	Richebourg 1952	65/-	—
107	La Tache 1952	70/-	—

MAGNUMS

310	Beaujolais 1955	40/-
311	Moulin a Vent 1955	50/-
314	Nuits St. Georges 1953	60/-
312	Vigne de l'Enfant Jesus 1952	90/-
313	Le Chambertin 1926	90/-

CHAMPAGNES

		Bouteille	½ Bouteille
151	Moet Chandon 1953 Rosé	60/-	—
141	Krug 1949-47	55/-	29/-
142	Bollinger 1952	55/-	29/-
143	G. H. Mumm 1949	55/-	29/-
145	Charles Heidseick 1949	55/-	29/-
146	Perrier Jouet 1949-47	55/-	29/-
149	Veuve Clicquot 1949	55/-	29/-
150	Moet et Chandon 1949-53	55/-	29/-
147	Heidseick Dry Monopole 1952	55/-	29/-
152	Pol Roger 1949-47	55/-	29/-
154	G. H. Mumm N.V.	50/-	26/-
144	G. H. Mumm N.V. Double Cordon	50/-	26/-
153	Bollinger N.V.	45/-	23/-
155	Lanson N.V.	45/-	—
156	Pommery & Greno 1952-47	45/-	23/-
161	Pommery & Greno N.V.	40/-	—
162	Perrier Jouet N.V.	40/-	22/-
163	Gauthier Rose	40/-	22/-
135	Kettners Special Cuvee	40/-	—

MAGNUMS

370	Krug 1949	110/-
371	Charles Heidseick 1947-9	100/-
374	Perrier Jouet N.V.	80/-
375	Bollinger N.V.	90/-

SPARKLING

131	Veuve Amiot	32/-	—
202	Deinhards Sparkling Hock	33/-	17/-
132	Golden Guinea	35/-	18/-
215	Asti Spumante	35/-	18/-
180	Sparkling Burgundy	37/6	20/-
281	Blanquette de Limoux	35/-	—

SUISSES

231	Fendant, Sion Petillant 1957	27/-	14/-
232	Neuchatel 1955	30/-	—
233	Johannesberg Riesling 1954	30/-	18/-
234	Dôle 1956	30/-	—

VINS D'ITALIES

		Fiasco	½
210	Chianti Rouge	30/-	15/-
211	„ Blanc	30/-	15/-
212	Orvieto	25/-	—
213	Lachrima Christi	25/-	13/-
214	Est! Est! Est!	25/-	—

MOSELLE

		Bouteille	½ Bouteille
185	Veldenzer Kirchberg 1949	19/-	10/-
199	Piesporter Riesling 1955	22/-	12/-
186	Brauneberger Lay 1955	26/-	13/6
188	Piesporter Goldtropfchen 1953	30/-	16/6
193	Bernkasteler Maximiner 1955	33/-	—
192	Bernkasteler Rosenberg Riesling Spatlese 1955	38/-	20/-
194	Dhronhofberger 1949	42/-	—

HOCKS

203	Niersteiner Domtal Spatlese '53	26/-	—
205	Deidesheimer Hofstuck 1953	27/6	14/6
209	Assmannshauser Spatburgunder 1955	27/6	—
208	Liebfraumilch Klosterkeller '53	28/-	15/-
207	Hochheimer Berg 1953	30/-	16/-
187	Niersteiner Kransberg Riesling Spatlese 1949	30/-	16/-
189	Liebfraumilch, Hans Christofwein 1955	30/-	16/-
190	Liebfraumilch Langenbach 1955	30/-	16/-
191	Forster Neuberg Riesling 1949	30/-	16/-
204	Liebfraumilch St. Catherine 1955	32/-	16/6
198	Liebfraumilch Crown of Crowns	32/-	17/-
200	Rudesheimer Berg Roseneck Riesling Spatlese 1955	37/-	19/-
197	Schloss Johannisberger Spatlese 1953	50/-	—
201	Niersteiner Auflangen Riesling Trockenbeeren Auslese 1953	80/-	—

MAGNUMS

398	Liebfraumilch, Hans Christofwein '53	60/-

STEINWEIN

184	Horsteiner Abtsberg Riesling Auslese 1953	40/-	—
183	Markt Einersheimer Speckfelder Schlossberg 1955	32/-	—

COTES DU RHONE

121	Chateauneuf du Pape 1953	25/-	13/-
125	Chateauneuf du Pape 1953 Tete de Cuvee	32/-	—
122	Hermitage, Rochefine, Rouge 1953-50	24/-	13/-
123	Hermitage, Blanc 1949-42	25/-	13/-

VINS D'ALSACE

128	Riquewihr	22/-	—
129	Muscat 1952	28/-	15/-
126	Domains Dopff Riesling 1953	30/-	16/-
127	Gewürtztraminer 1953	32/-	17/-
130	Clos de Maquisard 1952	36/-	19/-

VINS ESPAGNOLS

220	Allela Blanc Sec ou Deux	17/-	9/-
221	Rioja	17/-	9/-

VINS PORTUGAIS

225	Dao Rouge	17/-	9/-
226	Dao Blanc	17/-	9/-
227	Vinho Verde	23/-	—

AUSTRALIAN WINES

245	Chalambar Burgundy	15/-	—
246	Rhymney Chablis	15/-	—

SOUTH AFRICAN WINES

240	La Gratitude	15/-	—
241	Chateau Libertas	15/-	—

PORTO

			Le verre
253	Ferreira 1945	45/-	4/-
254	Crofts 1945	45/-	4/-
250	Smith Woodhouse 1935	45/-	4/-
251	Warres Old Port	35/-	3/6
252	Cockburns	30/-	3/-

FINES CHAMPAGNES

			Le verre
***			3/-
	Fine Maison		4/-
	Armagnac, très vieux		4/-

BIERE

	Whitbread Pale Ale (La Bouteille)	2/-
	Lager	2/6
	Truman's Bitter	2/6
	Ben Truman (La Bouteille)	2/6
	Guinness (La Bouteille)	2/6
	Bass (La Bouteille)	2/6

Open Sundays : 12.30 2.30 p.m.
7 – 10 p.m.

Open Weekdays : 12 – 3 p.m.
6 p.m. – 12.30 a.m.

PLATS DU JOUR

13/12/58

Consommé Julienne 2/6 Crème Solferino 3/-

Filets de Sole Marguery 9/6

Turbot Poché Waleska 9/6

Steak & Kidney Pie 8/6

Sauté D'Agneau Fermiere 8/6

Rump Steak Marchand de Vin 11/6

Demi Poussin Polonaise 9/6

Goulash de Veau Hongroise 8/6

Risotto de Poulet Valenciennes 8/-

Poulet Forestiere 10/6

DAILY SPECIALITIES

....

Monday
Mignons de Veau a la Crème 14/-

Tuesday
Creme de Champignons 4/6
Moules Mariniere 7/-

Wednesday
Bisque de Homard 5/6
Chicken Pie 14/-

Thursday
Minestrone 3/6
Truite au Bleu 6/6

Friday
Tourte de Fruits de Mer 11/-

Saturday
Soupe a l'Oignon Gratinee 4/-
Escalope de Veau Cordon Bleu 15/-

Private Rooms
for Lunches, Dinners and Cocktail Parties
for 6 to 75 persons

HORS D'ŒUVRES	Tartelette aux Champignons 5/6 — Smoked Scotch Salmon 8/6 — Crevettes Roses 10/6 Oeufs Cocotte a la Creme 4/6 — Melon 4/- — Jambon de Parme 8/6 — Melon Cocktail 4/6 Caviare de Sevruga 35/- — Egg Mayonnaise 4/- — Pate Maison 5/- — Grape Fruit 2/6 Fried Scampi 9/6 — Scampi Provencale 9/6 — Lobster Cocktail 10/6 — Shrimp Cocktail 5/6 — Potted Shrimps 4/6 — Smoked Trout 6/- — Salami de Milan 4/- Spaghetti Bolognaise, Milanaise 4/- — Curry de Crevettes 6/6 — Escargots de Bourgogne 5/- per ½ doz. — Coquilles St. Jacques 8/6 — Sardines et Salade 4/- Foie Gras de Perigord 10/- — Blanchailles 6/6 — Salade Nicoise 5/6 — Huitres Natives No. 1's 17/6 — No. 2's 15/-
POTAGES	Clear Turtle 4/6 — Kangaroo Tail 4/6 — Consomme en Gelee 2/6 — Consomme 2/6 — Creme 2/6
ŒUFS	Princesse 5/- — Bercy 5/- — Brouilles 5/- — Omelette aux Champignons, Tomates, Crevettes, Jambon, Fromage, Paysanne 5/- Omelette Nature 4/6
POISSONS	HOMARD : Thermidor — Newburg — Mornay 15/- — Froid 13/6 SOLE : Grillee, Colbert, Frite, Meuniere, Breval, Bonne Femme, Waleska, Joinville, Veronique, 12/6 TURBOT : Poche Sauce Hollandaise, 8/6 — Grille, Sauce Tartare 8/6 Coquille St. Jacque 8/6 — Goujons de Sole Murat 10/-
ENTREES	VEAU : Escalope Viennoise 12/6 — Cote de Veau Grandmere 12/6 — Rognons Sautes au Madere 10/6 AGNEAU : Cotelettes Nicoise 10/6 — Espagnol 10/6 BŒUF : Tournedos Rossini 17/6 — Steak Tartare 12/6 Filet Mignon, Sauce Madere 15/- — Bœuf Strogonoff 12/6 17/6 Entrecote aux Pointes d'Asperges 16/- VOLAILLE : Poulet au Champagne 15/- — Chicken a la King 12/6 Vol au Vent Toulouse 10/6 — Demi Caneton aux Cerises 12/6 Supreme de Volaille Sous Cloche 17/6
ROTIS	Chapon de Surrey (3, 4 or 5 persons) 40/-. 60/- — Canard d'Aylesbury (2, 3 or 4 persons) 30/-. 50/- — Saddle of Lamb (60 minutes, 4 or 5 persons). Carre of Lamb (25 minutes) 2 persons — Poussin 14/- — Half 7/6
GRILLADES	Mixed Grill 12/6 — Entrecote Minute 11/6 — Lamb Cutlets 9/6 — Rump Steak 13/6 Mutton Chop 9/6 — Entrecote 13/6 — Veal Chop 12/6 — Filet Steak 15/- — Entrecote Double Bearnaise 30/- (2 persons) — Chateaubriand 35/- (2 persons).
BUFFET FROID	Jambon 7/6 — Bœuf 8/6 — Poulet 10/6 — Poulet et Jambon 11/- Salades 2/6 — Aile de Poulet Froide 12/6 — Canard et Salade d'Orange 14/-
GAME	Faisan Roti — Civet de lievre aux Nouilles 10/6
LEGUMES	Pommes Natures 1/6 — Rissolees, Purees, Lyonnaise, Alumettes, Frites, Sautees 2/- „ Nouvelles 2/- — Croquette 2/6 — Petits Pois au Beurre 2/6 — a la Francaise 2/6 — Haricots Verts 2/6 — Carottes 1/6 — Artichauts au Beurre 3/- — Epinards au Jus, a la Creme, en Branche 2/6 — Chouxfleur 2/6 — Oignons Frits 2/- — Aubergines Frites 2/6 — Champignons a la Creme 7/6 — Celeris Braises 2/6 — Endives Braisees 2/6 — Choux de Bruxelles 2/6
DESSERTS	Macedoine de Fruits 3/6 — Ginger and Cream 3/6 — Marrons Glaces 6/- — Figues a la Creme 3/6 — Crepes Suzette 7/6 — Creme Caramel 3/- — Ananas Frais Creme 5/- Ginger Pancakes 3/6 — Meringues Glacees 3/6 — Profiteroles au Chocolat 4/- Ananas et Glace 3/6 — Sabayon 5/6
GLACES	Vanille 2/6 — Sorbet Citron 2/6 — Sorbet Framboise 2/6 — Coupe Nesselrode 4/- Bombe Tutti Frutti 4/6 — Moka 4/- — Praline 4/6 — Parfait Chocolat 4/6 — Peche Melba 4/6 — Poire Belle Helene 4/6 — Cassata 4/- — Omelette Surprise (2 persons, 20 minutes) 10/-
SOUFFLES (20 minutes)	Grand Marnier 7/- — Rothschild 5/- — Chocolat 5/- — au Fromage 5/- —
SAVOURIES	Canape Diane 4/- — Mushroom on Toast 3/6 — Welsh Rarebit 2/6
FROMAGES	au Choix 2/6 — Brie 4/-
CAFE	1/6 — Cafe Creme 2/6 — Cafe Turque 2/- — The 1/6

39

The Westbury Hotel,
New Bond Street, London W1
Commis tournant, June-October 1960
Chef de cuisine: Mons. Dutrey

The chef de cuisine at the Westbury was a man called Marius Dutrey, one of the famous old chefs. Although with all head chefs there was someone with a story about them, you normally took that with a pinch of salt and made your own judgement. Mons. Dutrey had a flattish slavic face and crafty eyes that seemed to look at you from round the corner. On the whole he was a quiet man. When he arrived in the morning he would go round, shake hands with everyone, wish them good day, then vanish into his office in the kitchen. During the morning he would venture out to inspect the mise en place or cadge a fag from either Mons. Marco or George on the grill. Then he would come out just before service and, with some spoons in a bowl of water, he would taste all the soups and sauces for the day's menu. Mons. Dutrey's pet saying was 'Needs a bit more salt and seasoning', so he'd bring out of his office his magic crystals (mono/glute), place one crystal in about two gallons of soup, stir lightly and taste again. 'Lovely,' he'd purr. When he decided to do the aboyer, everyone was on tenterhooks, as he had a quiet voice (I never heard him shout in all the time I was there). Since the orders had to be given to the larder downstairs by tannoy, with Mons. Dutrey's quiet voice and French accent you can imagine the chaos that reigned. Mr. Williams, the sous, used to discreetly send the orders down written on a piece of paper so as not to offend the chef.

The Westbury was a fairly new hotel that had only been open a couple of years when I arrived. The story goes that when Mons. Dutrey was engaged as the chef de cuisine shortly before it was due to open, he was taken on a guided tour of the hotel. When, after the tour, he was asked if he had any comments or questions, Mons. Dutrey was supposed to have replied, 'Well, the hotel is really lovely, but there's one small matter I'd like to raise: where's the kitchen?' Believe it or not, they had forgotten to build a kitchen! Here was this large hotel with all the mod cons, and they had forgotten its very life blood! After much consternation and looking at the plans, they eventually squeezed the main kitchen into a corridor behind the restaurant. The still room was nearly bigger than the kitchen, and what was going to be the underground car park was transformed into the grill room and banqueting suites. What a cock-up, eh!

The staff in the main kitchen were all long-timers who had been there since the opening. There was Mr Williams, the first sous, a lifelong friend of Mons. Habert, my sous at Kettners. He had eyes that laughed at you behind his spectacles and a really wicked sense of humour. But though he was good for a laugh, you knew who was boss! Mr Williams ran the kitchen in all but name; he used to do all the ordering, staff organising etc. His knives were razor sharp and he could split a honeydew melon with just a tap of his knife, yet I never saw him cut himself in all the years I knew him. He was fluent in French, with a good shot of Italian for luck. Mr Williams was good at his job, and he was a fair man, liked and respected by everyone.

One day Mr Williams was threatened by this big, drunken kitchen porter. Mr Williams had asked him to do something and he had taken the knock, threatened to punch Mr Williams. Within seconds the KP was surrounded by the other chefs and was in danger himself. Even Mons. Mario, the sous chef in the grill room, had come running to help sort out this bloke who'd had the audacity to threaten Mr Williams. The porter was literally manhandled out of the back door, one of the porters got his clothes from his locker and sent him on his way. That evening, when Mr Williams had finished, he was accompanied by a couple of the chefs to the main road, just in case the KP was waiting. That was the sort of loyalty Mr Williams commanded.

It was a sad day for the trade when he was taken ill (I think it was a brain tumour) and had to semi-retire. He was never quite the same person again. It was even sadder when he passed away; the kitchens, I was told, went into mourning for a week.

On the grill was George, a Greek. His fastest speed was about four miles an hour (that was on a good day), but in the Westbury kitchen you didn't have far to move anyway. He was a nice guy who had done his bit for the hotel, and this was his 'winding-down' job. George was very good on the grill and his presentation of the dishes was lovely.

Next to George was Mons. Marco (who didn't know Mons. Marco?) This man was a legend. He had travelled the world then settled in London, and could speak French and English, as well as his native Italian. He must have been over 60, but his mind was as sharp as Mr Williams's knives. He knew all the classic dishes backwards, sideways and diagonally. Sometimes we younger commis would try to catch him out. We'd dig out an old book, find some obscure dish, then casually ask Mons. Marco, 'Do you know what this dish is?'

He would look at you with his laughing, brilliant blue eyes and, with an expression that said 'You're at it again', he would proceed to rattle off the ingredients, method, and sometimes he would even throw in the story behind the dish for good measure. (I presume everyone knows that many classic dishes are named after someone or somewhere).

Mons. Marco's speciality was wind-ups, as he had a wicked sense of humour. He was also very interesting and got on famously with Mr Williams. On a quiet night if you could get the two of them reminiscing, it was fascinating!

Although he was getting on in years, Mons. Marco was a very hard worker and it was a pleasure to work under him. The sauce section he ran was very busy. Not only did we have to make sauces for all the meat dishes, but we had to do the fish as well – enough to puff out a young guy, let alone an older one. But he seemed to thrive in a hectic atmosphere. I was told one day that he was alone in the world, having lost his wife and daughter in a car crash a few years earlier. The only thing that kept him sane, it was said, was his work. He was supposed to drink a bottle of scotch every night when he got home, but if he did it never affected his work. I didn't have the nerve to ask him if it was true, so I never knew for sure.

Next to him was the veg section. The veg chef at that time was an Irishman called Jerry Tiernan, who was just 'holding the fort' until a certain sous chef's position became vacant. Jerry had a strawberry birthmark on his face, and he was a great bloke: cool, calm and collected. He was always willing to teach you how to do things with plenty of patience. We became good friends and my girlfriend (now my wife) used to baby-sit for Jerry and his wife. Jerry at that time was teetotal, (yes, I know, unusual for an Irishman, but true) and the only time I ever saw him lose his rag was when Mr Williams was threatened.

Up the winding staircase was the pastry, where Mons. Meuniere reigned supreme. This room was nearly as big as the kitchen (well, everything was as big as the kitchen; the main changing room was *bigger*!) Mons. Meuniere wore a constantly sour expression, as if he had the worries of the world stashed away at home. He was blind in one eye, I think, and as it sort of stared at you, it was difficult to know if he was looking at you or not. But the sweets they turned out from that small room were amazing. Mons. Meuniere's main helper was a short Italian chap called Aldo, who seemed to turn out most of the work. Considering the shortage of space, I think they did brilliantly. Aldo's passion was to make pastillage models, which were the centrepieces for the petits fours dishes (all made on site) served with coffees and liqueurs. One model I always remember (do you, Aldo?) was the one of a bull-fighter all done up in his finery with his cloak and sword. Really great! Apart from doing the sweet trolley for the restaurant, the pastry had to do one for the grill room and for the parties, so they really had to move at times.

Downstairs in the basement was the larder, the staff dining room and laundry. In the larder there were two Joes: one was the larder chef, Maltese Joe, and the other was Polish Joe. M.J. was about 5'5" and round with it. He used to peer at you through his little round glasses with an astonished expression every time you spoke to him. Although I never worked in the larder I was told he was a bit of an 'old woman', always moaning about something or other (sounds like the wife; no, only kidding). P.J. was a bit taller and wore the thickest pair of glasses I have ever seen (and I mean thick!) He was the butcher (don't laugh) and when he was boning out, his face was about three inches from the carcass he was working on. We used to think that he butchered by touch rather than by sight and the joke going round was 'Don't stand near P.J. when he's boning or you could end up with your arm butchered out'. How he managed to do all that butchery I'll never know, and I never saw him cut himself either.

Also in the larder, but acting as a sort of tournant, was our Ted. Now Ted was not for the faint-hearted. He was also Polish, about 6'3" and built like a brick shit-house. Really, I have yet to meet a person who covers so much space! But Ted was a typical gentle giant, all fun and laughter. (Let's face it, if Ted told a joke, you laughed!) Seriously though, he was a very nice guy, and often used to tell us stories of his younger days in Poland, about his time in the Polish army during the last war and the rough time he had trying to get into England afterwards. I believe his first wife and child were killed by a German air-raid while he was fighting at the front, hence his utter hatred for anything German. One story that has stuck in my mind is of the time his unit had held up a German advance because he and a few other 'big guys' (if Ted said they were big, they must have been enormous!) could throw grenades over 100 yards, so the Germans had to wait until they could bring up some large guns to shell them with before they could dislodge Ted's unit. They were so good with their throwing that as soon as they saw a German movement they could lob a grenade right into their laps!

Once or twice a week Ted did the staff meals, and about once a week he did the breakfast service. On these days the waiters were on their best behaviour, never moaned about the service, never tried to hurry him up (when it was ready it was ready) or wind him up. Nobody took a chance with Ted; he could break your arm just by shaking your hand. I don't think he ever appreciated his own strength. One day my girlfriend and I were walking along Kilburn High Road when all of a sudden a dark cloud seemed to cover us. I looked up and there was Ted in his trilby and long overcoat (imagine a Russian KGB agent) standing there covering the pavement and laughing like a drain, a huge smile on his battered face. Ted thought it was a great joke to frighten the crap out of you, but for all that he was a hard worker and a good laugh.

The staff cook was a bloke called Bernard. He was about 60, not very tall and around 20 stone. ('Don't stand anywhere close when I'm cremated,' he used to say.) Apparently he had been a very good chef in his younger days and had travelled widely, but when I met him he was on the verge of retiring (unlike today, when you've had it if you're over 40!) and had lost some of his enthusiasm. He was like Mr Williams and Mons. Marco, very knowledgeable and interesting to listen to when he started to reminisce about the 'old' days.

The breakfast chef (or chefess) was a woman called Lily. She was Jewish, I think, about five foot nothing, stocky and a fast worker. When you think that she used to do a couple of hundred brekkies on her own, that was running. All the time she'd be cursing and having a go at someone, but as you got to know her you realised she was an expert winder-upper with a terrific sense of humour. She used to have to put up with the tricks that the others played on her, though she wasn't slow in getting them back. My favourite trick was to carefully save egg shells and place them on a tray so that it looked full. Then, when Lily went to the loo, I'd change it over for one of her full trays and wait. 'Six fried eggs!' the waitress would cry; Lily would grab the eggs, discover they were just shells, check the rest of the tray to find they were all lulus, then chuck it at whoever she saw first. 'Not me, not me Lil!' they would yell. 'You'll do,' she'd say, 'until I find out who.'

Every now and again Mr Williams would get Fred, the floor's head waiter, to call out just as she was clearing up, 'Hold on, Lil, we've a big order coming through!' Then he'd give her a really vicious docket with practically everything on it. With a lot of grumbling and cursing, Lily would start to get things ready. Mons. Marco would make sure that he took over all the stove and gave her hassle when she tried to get on it. By now she would be very unladylike, and the air would be turning dark blue. After a few minutes Fred would call out that the order was cancelled, as the customers could not wait so long for breakfast and were going elsewhere. Then Mr Williams would wind Lil up, saying she was getting slow, and Mons. Marco could have done the order while he was doing up his mise en place. Well, that finished poor old Lily, who prided herself on getting orders out quickly. After she had cursed the hind leg off a donkey, both Mr Williams and Mons. Marco would burst out laughing and offer her a cup of tea as a pacifier. Sometimes Lily threw it at them in temper, sometimes she drank it. But it was all taken in good spirits. Unfortunately, nowadays chefs seem to be too serious for their own good; a little joke helps to lighten the pressure they work under.

The dispense bar was the domain of Mary. She must have been about 60 and, with her long dresses and jumpers, her hair always in a bun, she looked like a throwback to the 1920s. But she was as sharp as a pin, really on the ball, and never forgot who asked for what or, most importantly, who had not given her a docket for their order. I saw her refuse to serve a waiter again until he had given her a docket for his previous order.

In the still room was Tony, a Maltese with a balding head that was constantly sweating. He was always smiling and cheerful, and nothing was too much trouble for him. When Mr Williams or Mons. Marco arrived he would have a pot of tea or coffee served to them just as they were entering the kitchen; he seemed to have a sixth sense about this sort of thing. He used to make all the teas, coffees etc for the whole hotel, and really worked hard. It was a sad day when a few years later, I was told that he had collapsed at work and been taken to hospital, but no luck, he passed over.

The grill room was supervised by a cockney Italian called Mario. He had a lump about the size of a small egg on his forehead, caused by an accident with a rifle butt while he was fighting in Korea against the north Koreans. Mario was another brilliant wind-up merchant. He was born here and all the male members of his family, I was told, worked at Smithfield Market. They were quite disappointed when he didn't follow suit. Mario used to make his own wines and his speciality was morello cherries in brandy – wicked! Get drunk eating the cherries and then a return visit to bacchus by drinking the juice.

Mario had two assistants in the grill room. One chef, who did the grills and helped out on the sauce, was a large, solid black man called David, who was about 5'8" and built like Tyson. He was youngish, always laughing, joking and full of fun. When he was with men David was a joker; with women, especially young ones, he oozed charm. He was also a 'getcha' merchant: if you wanted something then David could get it for you. He forever had things to sell cheap; they might have been a bit 'warm', but you could never get a straight answer from him. He used to tell us about his younger days back home in Jamaica. When the American sailors were getting ready to sail, the kids would crowd round them with special offers, trying to sell them the local rum at a good price. The trouble was that the 'good' quality dark rum and the 'special' light rum were not all they seemed: the dark rum was tea with a little blackjack in it, and the light rum was just weak tea, all in pukka bottles and sealed. They kids were lucky that the sailors only found out when it was too late to do anything about it!

The other one of Mario's team was a little fellow called Pannis – yes, he was Greek! He was tiny, very stocky and as strong as a horse (he used to eat like one, so that was probably why). Pannis drove an Austin Cambridge, a fairly large car, and you could just see him over the top of the steering wheel. He had a habit of driving fairly fast, but when he was talking to you he would be looking at you, not the road (time for a heart pill, I think). Pannis did the veg, but he, David and Mario worked as a team, all mucking in and helping each other on busy sessions. They also did all the parties and sometimes I had more laughs with them than I did upstairs.

As I was on loan to the Westbury, I still had to go to college once a week (Thursdays at this time), which counted as my day off. So, as the two brigades took it in turns to work weekends, I was seconded every other week to Mario's team.

During the first few months at the Westbury, Mons. Dutrey had a chef called Raymond Zarb as a sous chef 'floater'. Apparently Zarb had just returned from working in the Middle East and was waiting for a head chef's position to become available, so Mons. Dutrey employed him as the 'Arab specialist' to cook authentic dishes for some Arab princes who were staying there. Raymond Zarb was a large man, about 6'1", and must have weighed about 20 stone, but he was still quick on his feet. He used to cruise up and down the kitchen doing his bit, and I have never seen a man sweat so much. It was like watching a miniature Niagara Falls some nights, he must have lost at least a couple of pounds each service. Later he started his own restaurant in Westerham called, I think, The Marquis De Montcalm, but then I heard that he'd been in a bad car crash and had semi-retired. (Is this true, Raymond?)

After about six months, Mons. Habert sent a message that it was OK to come back to Kettners to finish off my apprenticeship. Then Mons. Dutrey called me into his office and offered me the veg chef's position if I stayed on at the Westbury (more money, of course). I called Mons. Habert, told him about the offer, and asked if it would be possible to get a small rise so I didn't lose out too much, Mons. Habert said to come back and he would sort something out – so I have Mons. Dutrey to thank for getting me an extra rise that year!

I was welcomed back to Kettners like I'd never been away, but while I had, things had been happening.

My nemesis Mons. Moreau had, of course, retired, and Mons. Habert was the new head chef, though he'd had to fight for the job. Apparently the boss, Mr. Monnickendam, was going to look outside for the replacement so Mons. Habert had asked for a chance to prove himself – he had, after all, been running the kitchen as sous chef for about four years. Mons. Habert apparently told Mr. Monnickendam that if he did not get the chance, then he could stick his job somewhere. I think this could well be true because Mons. Habert was a straight talker who didn't mince his words, which is why he was well respected. Apart from being a good chef, you knew where you were with him: if there was something wrong he'd tell you, if it was right he would be ready with the praise.

The new sous was a cockney Frenchman called Oberoffer. He was supposed to be a good fish chef, but unfortunately by the time I knew him he was going to pot. We were getting the beer ration in bottles now, and he is the only person I know who could drink a crateful during evening service and still talk sensibly. He lasted about six months, then got himself another position elsewhere.

One day Mons. Moreau came in to say goodbye, as he was leaving and going back to France to end his days. Everyone was amazed at the amount of weight he had lost; he was down to about 16 stone and his suit was loose on him. (I only heard this from the others because when Mons. Habert heard Mons. Moreau was coming in, he sent me down to the cellar until the 'old man' had gone, not wanting to upset him on his last visit.) When he left everyone commented on how ill he had looked, then the stories started to come out. At home he was apparently not allowed to smoke, drink or gamble. So now we knew why he loved it at Kettners! The poor bloke looked knackered, and I think the word for his condition was 'henpecked'! To no-one's real surprise, we heard from his wife about five months later that Mons. Moreau had gone to that great kitchen in the sky – from boredom and frustration, was the general opinion!

The next sous was a guy called Favier, a Frenchman (surprise, surprise!) with dark flashing eyes that could be full of fun or threaten to skin you alive. He was very good and confident, as well as being a good teacher, and soon settled in with the others as they could smell a bullshitter a mile off. It was during his time as sous that Mons. Habert entered me for the London Apprentices' Competition, which was open to all third year apprentices working in London. About a week before the competition Mons. Habert received the menu that was to be cooked and 'handed' me over to Mons. Favier so he could advise me on the best way of doing the dishes. With the help of George and Victor, we had a couple of dummy runs, all pure classics.

The big day arrived. I duly turned up at the college and, along with seven or eight others, did my 'stuff'. At the end of the day I came second – not bad out of the whole of London! I think the difference between us was only a point or two, so I was quite pleased. Of course Mons. Habert. Favier, George and Victor all reckoned I should have come first, but they might have been biased! Later I received a copy of Sauniers Repertoires de la Cuisine as my prize. I still have this book today, a little dog-eared but still in working order!

A while after, Mons. Favier was offered a position as executive chef for Birds Eye, the frozen food company, and moved to Norfolk to take up the position. The next guy to take over the sous position was a bloke called Joel Defaut. He was about 26 (young in those days) and wore shaded glasses all the time. At first I thought he was just being flash, but I soon found out that one of his eyes had been badly scarred in a fishing accident so he wore shades to avoid stares. He turned out to be very good and was well liked. My girlfriend at the time (now my wife) thought he was very sexy and mysterious because of his glasses and his habit of wearing leather jackets! Shortly after, I believe he became head chef at Kettners for a while, then later became the chef/patron of the Beaujolais wine bar/club near Cambridge Circus. He is still there to this day.

It was during this period that our Bill decided to retire, which he did gracefully. Then a new aboyer started, a Mauritian (not a martian, though from some of the orders he used to call out, he might well have been!) He was small, a bit like Peter Lorre (who? I hear you ask. Ask your dad or grandad!) Although he could speak French, I don't think he had much kitchen experience, as he seemed to have trouble calling out the dishes properly.

Towards the end of my apprenticeship at Kettners Mr Philip, the boss's son, asked if I would like to help him out by transferring for a short while to the L'Escargot Restaurant in Greek Street, just up the road from Kettners. Apparently his father had bought him L'Escargot to set him up in business on his own. It all made sense about 18 months later when Mr. Monnickendam sold Kettners to the De Vere Group of hotels. They had a few hotels in town and the rest of the country, but they were a bit down-market compared to what Kettners had been, and I believe this was the start of the decline of Kettners as one of the best restaurants in London. Mons. Habert left not long after the takeover – more of him later.

Anyway, I said yes because I had enjoyed my time at The Westbury and thought that a little more experience wouldn't do me any harm.

L'Escargot Restaurant
Greek St, London W1
Commis tournant, June-September 1962

The first morning I arrived at L' Escargot was a shock; I felt I was stepping back 20 years. The kitchen was fairly small (one room) and was in the basement with just a tiny glass 'window' looking out on to the street. The changing room was right next to the kitchen, so the smell of food got into your outdoor clothes. Two stoves were raised on a slab of concrete about a foot high, so you had to 'step up' to cook. The larder was in the corner under the 'window' and as for the fridge ... Well, if you were thin you could squeeze in; if you were over ten stone, forget it! (though if you turned sideways you had a chance.) I have never seen such a small fridge.

The head chef was Italian. He'd been there quite a few years (since the restaurant was built, I think) and he was like a walking skeleton who'd been dead for a while but no-one had told him. His English was very bad, but as all the others were Italian, he didn't need much anyway; even the suppliers were Italian. The sous was another Italian (see, I told you) who was also the sauce chef. Considering the space he had to work in, he turned out some good work; his soups and sauces were excellent. The veg/pastry chef was – you've guessed – an Italian. The porters were Pakistani and every few hours they would all toddle off to the changing room, lay out their prayer mats and off they'd go, praying to the wall (very strange, I thought, until they explained that they were facing Mecca). I'd always thought, until then, that Mecca was a bingo hall: you live and learn!

The standards at L'Escargot were not as high as at Kettners but they had their particular methods – some rather antiquated. The chef still pickled his own fish, mainly mackerel and herring, which were filleted and layered in salt crystals in a large wooden barrel. After a few days,

49

they were taken out and served. Next to the stoves there was an old 'pushme-pullme', a hand-operated lift used for service: one went up, one down. The restaurant was always quite busy for lunch and dinner so they must have been doing something right.

In all honesty, I didn't really enjoy this portion of my apprenticeship at L'Escargot, but it certainly was an eye-opener.

L'Escargot Menu

I returned to Kettners in September 1962 and finished my 'time' in August. Mr Philip, as everyone called him, presented me with a book, *Escoffier's Culinary Art*, with an inscription inside: just my name and the dates I'd worked at Kettners. I really treasured this book and kept it on display with my other books in my various offices so the younger lads could look through them and learn. That is, until I went on holiday during my time at the Royal Westminster Hotel, leaving the running of

51

the kitchen to my first sous, and the second sous, who had only been there a few weeks. On my return I found that my beloved *Escoffier* had vanished, along with my second sous; he'd just done a runner one day. If anyone should come across a dark blue Escoffier's culinary art book with my name inside, please return it and you will earn my everlasting love (or, if you're a bloke, my thanks!)

I was then put to work as a chef tournant. I must admit I grew comfortable here and could have stayed for good, unconcerned about finding another job. The truth was, I was getting in a rut and didn't know it. Then one day Mons. Habert called me into his office and gently explained the importance of getting experience outside Kettners: it was time, he said, that I started to 'swim in the big pool'. He arranged for me to see a friend of his, Mons. Metivier, the executive chef at Cadby Hall, in the experimental kitchen near Olympia.

Mons. Metivier always had a smile; everything seemed a laugh to him. He was another cockney Frenchman who had worked in some good places, had loads of experience and was a fine teacher, although after I got to know him a bit better, he turned out to be a real worrier who was a bit of an 'old woman' at times.

The general brief of the experimental kitchen was to produce classic dishes as cheaply as possible and to market them under the name of Frood Frozen Foods (remember the name?), the trade name for J Lyons & Co. The idea was a good one: to give 'ordinary folk' the chance to buy famous dishes from the supermarket at a reasonable price. Let's take as an example poulet chasseur. In a 'posh' establishment the chicken would be a young roaster; you'd use button mushrooms, fresh tarragon, freshly chopped tomatoes and onions, and a good demi glace. Put them together and voilà! But now the ingredients were weighed right down to the last gram, then sent off to be costed. The answer would come back: 'Too costly, make it cheaper!' So we'd put in cheap boiling fowl, mushroom stalks, dried tarragon, a 'quick' demi glace and eventually we'd turn out a version of poulet chasseur that the costing boys were happy with. Then it would go into production. A few meetings would decide the style of packaging, what should be put on the label etc. So in practice, the dishes were anything but classic.

At Cadby Hall I was employed as a commis tournant. With Mons. Metivier and me was another chef, Bruce, who had worked for the company for umpteen years. His pronunciation of French dishes could be quite funny and many a time I caught Mons. Metivier wincing. (In Kettners I was taught to pronounce dishes correctly in French and also managed to pick up a smattering of Greek, German and Italian. I couldn't hold a proper conversation but I could make myself understood.) Apart from that, Bruce was good: he knew how to make the dishes even if he couldn't say them! Years later, when I attended one of the Earls Court Hotel Olympia exhibitions (in those days you could get free tickets if your chef was a member of a chef's club), I saw Bruce working for a frozen food company on one of the stands. He still looked the same, and no doubt his pronunciation was too!

The kitchen consisted of one large room with a couple of fridges and two 'flat top' stoves along one wall. Along the other were two swing doors leading into the domain of Mr Hallet (as he liked to be called), the chef in charge of quality control in the then well-known Lyons Corner Houses. He was an Englishman with piercing eyes that 'shot' through his glasses. He was one of those super confident blokes we all meet as we go through life. Everything he ever did was spot on – you know the type.

The first day I was sent down to the canteen for lunch, I got the shock of my life: I had to pay! For a chef the food was always free as far I was concerned. The first and only time I visited the canteen, I rustled up something in the experimental kitchen instead at no charge!

Every now and again, Mons. Metivier would have to go on a tour to make sure the dishes were being turned out correctly, stored at the right temperature etc. Often he would take me along and explain what was happening on the various floors. All the dishes were made here; nothing except the raw ingredients were brought in.

Another room (I call them rooms but they were large factory-type floors) housed the baking ovens. On a conveyor belt the dough would go in one end and be baked by the time it came out the other. Another was the slicing room, where umpteen loaves would be loaded and sliced, packed and stacked as you watched. Another room had a long line of slow-cooking ovens for the famous baked beans (who needed Heinz?) and the slow cooking of joints for various meat dishes. When they were ready and cooled off, a long conveyor belt would feed the exact amount of sauce, gravy or whatever onto the silver foil portion dishes. They would go along, watched by bored women who were supposed to keep a beady eye on the portions to make sure the machine didn't go off course. Then they were loaded into 'cages' and taken down to the freezers in the bowels of the earth. The next day the cages would be brought back and put through another type of machine. This was the sealer for boil-in-the-bag dishes. The frozen dish was turned out into a plastic bag, passed through a meat bar to seal it, then packed all in one motion. Then the finished products would be packed off back to the freezers again, ready to be sold.

The buildings were supposed to have a few ghosts wandering around, though I never saw any. I presume they were new workers who had got lost and were destined to wander the passages forever. The freezer rooms were, I think, the most creepy of the lot. By the time the lift had slowly descended to the basement, you had a feeling you might soon reach Australia. Anyway, when you arrived you were met by silence and two large plastic doors. Along the wall leading to these doors were heavy anoraks and a pile of heavy gloves. When I asked Mons. Metivier what all the coats and gloves were for, he said, 'I'll show you', and took me through the plastic doors. Well, the coldness hit you like a whack on the head, I cannot describe it (though those who have been to the Arctic will know). All I could see was a vast cloud of 'smoke' and some shadowy figures going to and fro in absolute silence – a bit like the Village of the Walking Dead! After about a minute I could feel my jacket getting stiff and we both made a quick exit. 'Now you know,' said Mons. Metivier with a sinister smile. From then on I was one of the first into the 'gear'. I believe the men who worked down there could only stay inside for a few minutes at a time.

We had a black porter in the experimental kitchen and one day he took me down to the freezers to show me how and where he stored our dishes. We went up this passage and down that passage until finally he said, 'Here', pushed the cage into a recess and went out. If you can imagine walking round your house with your eyes shut, leaving something then knowing exactly where it is without looking – well, was what it was like in those rooms. You were lucky to be able to see more than a few feet. Our porter would toddle down to bring up the dishes we would be testing and even if they had been down there for a few weeks, he'd come back with the correct ones every time. Truly amazing!

The sort of head manager of the Frood section was a 'Billy Cotton' type – large, red-faced and jovial. The trouble was, he didn't know one dish from another. When we had sample tastings and he was showing prospective customers how good the products were, we would set up the range of dishes required on a table in the kitchen with a nice white tablecloth, china plates and silver cutlery. This chap would walk along the table with the list of dishes in his hand, bullshitting away, calling out, 'I think we'll taste the fish provençale first'. Mons. Metivier would casually walk along the table and rest his hand near the dish; the 'boss' would look along the table and say, 'Here we are, try this, it's really marvellous.' In truth, he didn't have a clue which dish was which and if it was left to him to sort out the dishes, the chicken would probably have ended up as beef! I think this was partly the reason Frood was taken over: the bosses were too busy bullshitting one another and not busy enough making decisions about selling the dishes.

Another thing that opened my eyes was that every time the bosses, the Glucksteins and the Salmons, had any private or business parties, they would ask the chef to send over some samples of say, canapes, to their offices. There, they would pick out the ones they wanted. Now, not being used to this sort of 'outside catering', I was always mystified as to why we had to keep precise details of the decoration of each canape or cold buffet dish. The reason, Mons. Metivier told me, was that the boss or his wife used to take a colour photo of each dish they'd chosen. Then, on the day of the party, whether it was the next day or four weeks later, as the food was being brought in, the dishes were compared with the appropriate photo. Woe betide you if the decoration was not the same as the sample!

On these days, usually Saturdays, we had to get in for about 6 am so that we could do everything fresh and have it ready to go by 11 or 12. Talk about bum-quivering! The managers of each section involved would have to make sure their best men were on the job.

On the top floor was a massive room that was sometimes filled with 'cages' of old bread. On the floor along one side were large manholes. The unused bread was stored up here until it was hard, then it was 'shot' down the manholes, which funnelled it down into large grinding machines a floor or two below. This was then mixed with other bits and pieces and sold as animal fodder. Neat, eh!

Another eye-opener was the manager's restaurant on the top floor of the next building. Talk about bedlam! Kettners on a busy day was quiet compared to this place. Everyone seemed to be shouting and arguing with each other, running around like headless chickens. No wonder they always had service problems!

We used to make some weird and wonderful dishes at Cadby Hall. At the time J Lyons were trying to break into the passenger and fishing boat market. With frozen dishes, there was no need for lots of chefs on board a boat or ship; you would only need a couple to defrost and serve the food. We had to do quite a few Norwegian and Danish dishes. The companies used to send over the recipes and we'd make up about 20 portions of each, store and freeze them in long trays. Then they were vac packed and stored in a freezer until required. The bosses or reps of the different companies would come over now and again and we would prepare a sample showing for them.

The other thing Lyons was trying to get into was airline meals. The idea was that before the flight, meals would be prepared and frozen, then defrosted and heated up inside the aircraft using convection ovens. A good idea, I hear you say, but the trouble was, the immediate bosses could never make a decision. They huffed and puffed, then decided to leave it until 'next time'.

Sample tastings of dishes were held in a glider (kept in a yard), so that the guests from the various airlines could be entertained as they would be on an actual aircraft. The only trouble was that all the dishes served while I was there were cooked fresh that morning, foiled and wrapped, then taken over to the glider. One of the chefs used to go and reheat the food, and they had a waitress who served the 'customers' and generally looked after them. A bit of a cheat really, but that's business!

The one thing that amazed me about some of these managers was that they had been doing the same job for years. Imagine, for example, that you are the manager of the braised beef section where all that happens every day is that large joints are put into slow ovens and cooked for four of five hours. The joints cool off, are placed in the slicers, cut to the required thickness, weighed to the correct weight and put into foil dishes. Then the right amount of gravy or sauce is added and the lot is sent down to the freezer. Next day or so, the are all packaged and passed out for sale. Such routine work would have driven me potty but these blokes seemed to love it.

One of the amazing things at Cadby Hall was the way soups and sauces were made. First the exact amount of ingredients would be gathered together with the method sheet. The ingredients would be put into a large 'bathesphere', water or stock added, and after the prescribed time of pressure cooking, the contents would be 'shot' along various pipes to whichever department needed them. It was amazing to think that 20 or 30 gallons of boiling liquid was whisked along these pipes through the building.

The pastry unit was also mind-boggling. They had these huge machines where the ingredients were put in at one end and the finished pastry came out the other, rolled to the required thickness. These rooms always had a fine mist floating about due to the flour; I used to hold my breath when going through them. It was here that I met one of the lads from school, Micky Knight. He was very good at pastry and I thought he'd gone to one of the West End hotels for pastry work, so I was surprised to see him there. I often wonder what happened to him.

I only stayed at Cadby Hall six months, as I knew this part of the industry was not for me. The only thing I really learned there was how to freeze and store goods correctly. I got in touch with Mons. Habert and told him that I felt restaurants and hotels were more me, so he put me in touch with Mons. Cippola, the chef de cuisine at the Carlton Towers Hotel. Mons. Habert really was a lovely man; not many head chefs would put themselves out to assist a young chef in his career, helping him to get into good establishments under good chefs and generally 'being there' if needed.

The Carlton Towers Hotel
Sloane Street, London SW1
Commis tournant, May-August 1963
Head chefs: Mons. Cippola, Mons. Antosch

I started as a commis tournant in the restaurant kitchen at the Carlton Towers, mainly on the sauce and veg section, though I was occasionally put in the larder. Although the hotel had not been open very long, it already had a good name, especially the restaurant, and the Rib Room was also mentioned in guidebooks. The kitchen brigade was about 80 per cent French and the rest were a mixed batch.

Mons. Cippola, the head chef, always had a different way of presenting a dish. One day he'd come along and show you one way; then, a few days later, just as you were getting used to doing it, he'd come along and do it differently. You could never be bored, but the chef de partie was driven mad trying to keep up with the latest method.

The amount of class work produced in that long, narrow kitchen was incredible. One of the popular dishes was the flaming sword shashlik. The waiters used to hate this dish as they had to carry a burning sword, held high, into the restaurant for all to see, and if they weren't careful, they would find their arm smouldering by the time they reached the customer. I am surprised that there were no serious accidents with this dish (now I have said that, some smart alec is going to tell of a serious accident that happened).

The hors d'oeuvre section was run by a Frenchman. He was very good and creative but, like most of the Frenchmen there, he didn't mix with the others very well. They all seemed to have little time for jokes or laughter. I know they were trying to make their names, but being stuck up with your commis didn't help foster the comradeship you usually find in kitchens.

The sauce chef was English, though he looked French and spoke French well, having spent a few years working in the South of France. He was very good and a bit more cheerful than the others. The poissonière was the smallest chef I have ever come across – about five foot nothing. He had to stand on a box to work as he could not reach inside a pot if he didn't, but he was a brilliant fish chef. The veg chef was English and the larder chef was Spanish. He was the surliest of the lot, a real miserable bugger who was not much good and used to delegate a lot, thus taking the credit when things were good and giving out the rollockings when they were not. It was a good job he had good commis under him.

The butcher was a large Irishman who had his own 'room' downstairs with fridges where he did all his butchery for both the Rib Room and the restaurant. The pastry chef was English, a really good pastry chef who unfortunately had a twitch; as he talked his head would keep moving, hence the nickname 'Noddy'. This was said with respect as he was very talented and, so I was told, treated his staff well. The three sous chefs, all French, were all very good and between them they kept the lads on their toes.

The chef in charge of the Rib Room was a bloke called Sparrowhawk. Apparently he was well-known in the trade, but I had never heard of him. Mr Sparrowhawk's main claim to fame was his Yorkshire puddings – they rose to bursting. (Every one a winner, baby!) I was once told a story about him. Apparently the Carlton Towers had once sent him off to America to promote the hotel to the American market, and he had mystified the Yanks by producing a whole roasted sirloin, half rare and the other half well-done! When asked how he had achieved this marvellous feat, he said that it was a special way of roasting; but later he confided to the chef that all he had done was to have a very hot oven, roast the joint rare and then leave half of it out of the oven while the rest was cooked well done – crafty, eh!

While I was at the Carlton Towers I met Fritz again. He started as second larder, but although his work was still good, by now he'd really gone round the bend. He kept talking to himself and the floor, the fridges, the ceiling. The others were a bit wary of him, understandably, I suppose. Anyway, he only lasted a couple of weeks and then he went 'trotting away', and I've never seen him since.

The chef's office was at the far end of the kitchen, and you had to walk past it to go out. Mons. Cippola always came out to shake your hand and wish you goodnight or good morning – a real gentleman.

One of my favourite stories about the Carlton Towers is when the Duke who owned the land took over the whole restaurant one night for (I think) his daughter's birthday party. (When the landowner says he wants the use of the restaurant for the night, you say 'yes', of course!) The poor customers had to either use the Rib Room or have room service that night. The band that played was Billy J Kramer and his group (they were one of the 'in' groups then). As I recall, the menu was five courses and it ended with a special display from our Noddy. He had carved, out of a large block of ice, a crinoline lady about six foot high. He had hollowed her out and fitted coloured lights inside, so that when it was wheeled into the restaurant, all the lights were dimmed and she shone bright and true.

Another story concerns Mons. Cippola himself. One evening when we returned for the evening shift, we saw the three sous huddled together in the chef's office, but no sign of the chef. We were told he'd had a huge row with the general manager (who had apparently wanted to interfere with the running of the kitchen). Anyway, the upshot of it was that Mons. Cippola had literally packed his belongings and left. The commotion grew worse as the chefs de partie joined the sous in the office to find out what was wrong. No-one was very interested in working until they knew what had happened. The sous then called for a meeting with the GM. When they were told the story, they asked for Mons. Cippola to be reinstated but the GM said no, so they all resigned, gave the GM their hats and aprons and went home. A few minutes later, when the chefs de partie were informed ,all the French ones resigned too. It just shows you what a popular guy Mons. Cippola was. Apparently the GM was left poe-mouthed by all of this.

The amazing thing about this story is that, apart from causing shock waves through the West End, within about three weeks Mons. Cippola had found every one of the guys who had supported him a job in various West End establishments. Now that's what I call looking after your staff!

For a few weeks after Mons. Cippola's departure, the kitchen was run mainly by the remaining chefs de partie, and the Maltese sous chef from the Rib Room was seconded to the restaurant kitchen to help with the running until the managers sorted themselves out. He wasn't a bad bloke really, just thought he was better than he really was and used to tell everyone who would listen. He could talk up a storm, shame he couldn't work the same.

During the time in limbo, quite a few chefs came and went. One of the guys was maybe 70, a short, round Italian. He was supposed to have been the head chef at a famous restaurant in Piccadilly for a number of years and had retired but was 'called up' for the duration. He might have been very good in his day but I'm afraid he was a bit past it by now. He was very forgetful and no-one really had much time for him – shame really 'cos he tried hard. He stayed as first sous for about two months together with a large (both in height and weight) Dutch chef who also came to fill in as sous. His name I never found out except that he was known in the trade as 'Dutch Peter'. This bloke was in his late 50s, 6'2" and about 19 stone (I think six stone was beer, but that's another story). Peter was a good chef, he had the right attitude, firm but fair with the staff. Most of the young chefs respected him and took notice when he told them something. He was always a happy type, cracking jokes and generally helping the kitchen to pull together again, believe in what we were doing and getting our confidence back.

Dutch Peter used to tell us some hilarious stories about various places he'd worked. One concerned a well-known head chef with a big 'hooter', who was having a row with a chef de partie. The head chef was trying to give this chef de partie a rollocking but the guy was not standing for it. Anyway, the outcome was that the chef said, 'No-one threatens me. See this nose, no-one has ever got near it!' At this, the irate chef de partie smacked him one and broke his nose. 'You won't say that again,' said the chef de partie as he left.

Another tale concerned the time when Peter was working at the Grand Hotel on the corner of Trafalgar Square. The kitchen was on the top floor, some five or six floors up. Peter was, I believe, the sous chef there and was having trouble getting one of the chefs de partie to do as he wanted (a right load of trouble, these chef de parties, eh!) The chef de partie was a very small bloke, so Peter grabbed him and half held him out of the kitchen window until he agreed to do as he was told. Talk about gentle persuasion!

One day we were told we had a new chef coming. His name was Antosch, and he was 'imported' from Austria, where he had, so they said, a good reputation. The day came and he duly arrived, spoke to the sous and chefs de partie but forgot all the commis. Rotten sod, we thought, he wants us to support him but can't be bothered to speak to us. He wasn't a bad chef, just a bit remote; whether it was because it was his first time in this country (I know, I'm about to be told different), or that he was shy, we never found out. Later I heard he had gone north and was the executive chef at the Gosforth Park Hotel in Newcastle.

By this time I was getting a bit fed up with the general attitude of the Maltese sous chef. His overbearing manner was becoming suffocating, so I decided to move on.

L'Ecu de France, here I come!

The Gourmet's Choice

Surrey Chicken à l'Estragon (2 cvts.) 35/-

AYLESBURY DUCK WITH ORANGE SAUCE, 19/6
and garden peas

Poussin and Bacon 21/-   Aylesbury Duckling (4 cvts) 60/-

(These dishes are made to order)

COLD SUGGESTIONS

Fresh Scotch Salmon	21/-	York Ham	10/6
Roast Norfolk Turkey	12/6	Chicken Salad	17/6
Cornish Lobster Mayonnaise	21/-	Lobster Salad	21/-
		Ox Tongue	10/6
Roast Sirloin of Beef	12/6	Best End of Lamb	15/6
Chicken Wing	15/6	Steak Tartare	17/6
Chicken Leg	10/6	Aylesbury Duckling	17/6

VEGETABLES

Baby Marrow	4/6	Egg Plant Fried or Sauté	4/6
Carrots Vichy	3/6	Leaf or Creamed Spinach	3/6
Garden Peas	4/6	Braised Celery or Endives	3/6
Bouquet of Broccoli	4/6	Corn on the Cob	5/6
French Beans	4/6	Cauliflower Hollandaise, au Gratin or Polonaise	4/6
Broad Beans	3/6		

POTATOES: French Fried 2/6   Creamed 2/6   Lyonnaise 3/6
Steamed 2/6   Hash Brown 3/-   Croquette 3/6

SALADS

Asparagus Tips	5/6	Potato	3/-
Heart of Lettuce or Endive	3/6	Japonaise	5/-
Russian	3/6	Fresh Cole Slaw	3/-
Tomato	3/6	Mixed Green	3/6
Waldorf	4/6	Beet	3/6

DESSERTS

Parfait Astoria	10/6	Crêpes Suzette	12/6
Coupe Maltese	7/6	Baked Alaska (2 cvts.)	15/-
Crêpe Soufflé Montreuil	7/5	Soufflé Glacé Patricia (2 cvts.)	15/6
Cherries Jubilee	10/6	Marrons Mont Blanc	8/6
Pear Suchard	6/6	Banana Singapore	8/-
Zabaglione au Marsala	10/6	Ice Cream Cake American	7/6
Omelette Soufflé Milady	15/6	Orange Elysée	7/6
		Ice Creams, Various	4/6
Brandied Banana or Peach Flambé	12/6	Sorbets, Various	4/-
		Fresh Fruit Salad au Kirsch	7/6
Soufflé Grand Marnier (2 cvts.)	15/6	Apple or Cherry Strudel	5/-

SAVOURIES

Canapé Diane	4/6	Canapé Baron	4/6
Welsh Rarebit	4/6	Soft Roes on Toast	4/6

Our Special Cheese Soufflé 10/6

Our Choice Cheese Board   Selection 5/-   Brie or Stilton 6/-

Fruits in Season

Coffee	2/6	Tea	2/6
Mint Tea	3/-	Café Hag	4/-
		Tilleul	3/-

HOMARD "IMPERIALE" (prepared in room) 22/6
Our latest gastronomic creation.

CHATEAUBRIAND SARAH BERNHARDT (2 Cvts.) 55/-
A double tenderloin of beef, cooked to your taste, garnished with tomatoes, mushrooms, braised endives, pont-neuf potatoes and served with Sauce Bearnaise.

SUPREME DE VOLAILLE A LA KIEV 21/-
Wing of chicken stuffed with spiced butter, fried and served on bed of Rice.

MEDAILLON DE VEAU "AUERSPERG" 31/-
Topped with mushroom sauce, garnished with nuts, tips of asparagus and butter noodles.

THE BALKAN SWORD (4 Cvts.) 75/-
Tenderloin, calves liver, lamb chop, bacon, pimentos, tomatoes aubergines, onions and mushrooms, grilled and served on a flaming sword. Garnished with rice and onion salad.

POUSSIN FARCI "NICOLE" 19/6
Stuffed spring chicken, braised and served with sauce Bressaise.

CHOPPED TENDERLOIN "CARLTON" 17/6
Finest Scotch beef mixed with onions and special seasonings cooked in butter, garnished with croquette potatoes, French beans and sweetcorn, Madeira sauce served separately.

ORIGINAL WIENER SCHNITZEL 19/6
Served with mixed salad.

CAUCASIAN SHASHLIK 21/-
Tenderloin of lamb, marinated in red wine and olive oil, with mushrooms, onions and tomato, broiled and then brought to your table on a flaming sword. Garnished with rice and pimentos, and a devil sauce.

APPETIZERS

Caviar Beluga (per oz.)	30/-	Strasbourg Foie Gras	21/6
Scotch Smoked Salmon	12/6	Cornet of Smoked Salmon and Shrimps	15/6
Fresh Fruit Cup Florida	6/6	Fresh Lobster Cocktail	15/6
Pâté Carlton Tower en Croûte, Sauce Cumberland	10/6	Crevette Cocktail de Luxe	10/6
		Chilled Melon, from	10/6
Potted Shrimps	6/6	Avocado Mexicaine	12/6
Snails Burgundy Style (½ doz)	9/6	Avocado Vinaigrette	10/6
Swedish Herring in Sour Cream	9/6	Hors d'Oeuvre Parisienne	10/6
		Smoked River Trout	9/6
Salade Niçoise	8/6	Prosciutto with Melon	15/-

Globe Artichoke: Hot—Sauce Hollandaise, Cold—Vinaigrette 8/6

SOUPS

Clear Turtle Amontillado	7/6	Lobster Bisque	7/6
Cream of Chicken	4/6	Cream of Tomato	4/-
Consommé Double en Tasse	4/-	Cream of Peas	4/6
		Cold: Vichyssoise	5/-
Bortch en Gelee	6/-	Madrilène	3/6
		Consommé en Gelée	3/6

FISH

FRESH SCOTCH SALMON: Grilled 21/-   Poached 21/-
SCAMPI: Fried 13/6   Provençale 15/-
DOVER SOLE: Colbert 15/-   Grilled 15/6   Belle Meunière 15/6
FILLET OF SOLE: Olga 18/6   Caprice 17/6   Bonne Femme 15/6
TORBAY TURBOT: Poached, served with Hollandaise sauce 15/- (20 min.)   Broiled, Mirabeau style, with anchovy, tomato and black olives 17/6

Whole Broiled Lobster	35/-	Lobster Newburg	22/6
Turban of Prawns Bombay	15/-	Lobster Thermidor	22/6
River Trout Meunière	15/6	aux Amandes	17/6

ENTREES

Tournedos Rossini	27/6	Supreme of Chicken Maryland	21/-
Escalope "Cordon Bleu"	21/-		
Pepper Steak	22/6	Chicken in Casserole Garnished	21/-
Calf's Liver and Bacon	15/6	Chicken à la King	19/6
Kidneys Sauté Turbigo	15/6	Steak Diane	22/6
Fillet of Beef Strogonoff	18/6		

FROM THE GRILL

Entrecôte à la Planche 21/-

Prime Fillet Steak	22/6	Rumpsteak	21/-
Lamb Cutlets	15/6	Veal Chop	18/6
Double Lamb Chop	19/6	Spring Chicken	21/-
Kebab à la Grecque	17/6	American (2 cvts)	35/-
Entrecôte Double (2 cvts), Sauce Bearnaise, Pommes Frites	35/-	Mixed Grill Carlton Tower	19/6
		T-Bone Steak de luxe	28/-

L'Ecu de France
Jermyn Street, London W1
Chef tournant, August 1963-February 1964
Head chef: Mons. Pannier

The quality and standards at L'Ecu de France were excellent, as business showed. It was one of the premier restaurants in London at that time, which was good as there was a lot of competition.

The kitchen at L'Ecu was situated in the basement, and to reach the entrance you had to go around the back of the building, up an alleyway and then down some steep stairs. As you arrived at the bottom of the stairs, you saw a bright light in front of you – this was the hot plate with the kitchen behind it. There was a passage between the kitchen and the larder which led to the changing rooms and the pastry. To the right of a short passage was the chef's office and further on, the entrance to some of the private rooms and the veg prep room.

The first sous was a guy called Bill Lacey (I was told that his wife was a well-known restaurant critic). He looked like a sergeant major, big and round, with a tight crew cut, a bristly moustache and the manners of a traffic warden on heat. He used to stand by the changing room at two minutes to eight in the morning and give you the third degree if you arrived a couple of minutes late. Bill was a very sarcastic person, but the trouble was, he wasn't funny with it. I don't think he had a sense of humour at all, he was too busy trying to browbeat everyone, so he was not the sort of sous you looked up to. I think he only kept his position because he was very strict with everyone. He left much later, having been head chef there, to start his own restaurant but after a while it faded into the mists of time.

The other sous was an Italian, a nice quiet person who got on with the job, no fuss, no panic. He created a sea of calm when he was on though he was a bit soft on the guys, he inspired more respect than Bill ever did. I often wonder if Mons. Pannier employed these two opposites on purpose.

At L'Ecu there were two brigades: one early, one late. These shifts were done a week about. The early was from eight till four and the late was from four till 11.

The kitchen was split up into sauce, fish roast/grill, larder and pastry. The pastry was in its own room behind the kitchen. The main pastry chef, Bernard, only worked earlies, and a guy called Heinz worked the nights. All the petits fours were made on the premises, as were all the sweets – none of this buying in, wot! Bernard was an easy-going bloke, anything for peace, not like Heinz (he was German by the way!) Heinz was an excellent pastry chef who already had a morning job (a bugger for punishment), and he used to wind Bill up something wicked. The pastry was connected to the hotplate by an intercom so that the orders could be called through, thus saving time running up and down. Bill was sneaky and used to listen in to the conversations that were going on in the larder and the pastry by flicking a switch. Now Heinz soon got wise to this. Every time Bill switched in there was a faint click, and as soon as he heard this Heinz started to call Bill all the names, saying what a prat he was and so on. When Bill came round and asked about it, Heinz would smile sweetly and deny all knowledge of it. Bill couldn't very well tell Heinz that he'd been listening in on him, so he just used to mutter dark threats and go back to the hotplate.

Heinz moved as though his bum was on fire, everything was done yesterday with him. I later heard that he was having trouble with his ankles and was not surprised; he must have worn out the joints.

In the passageway opposite the entrance to the pastry, there was the petits fours cupboard. This consisted of about 20 shelves where the petits fours were stored. I have never seen so many different types of petits fours, the selection was amazing.

There were two sauce chefs. One was an Italian called Scania (I hope this is spelt right). He didn't let Bill get away with any remarks, he always gave back an answer. The last I heard was that he was the chef at the Cafe Royal restaurant, which doesn't surprise me as he was a very quick and competent sauce chef. The other was an English chap called Roger, about my age. He was good, though a bit laid back and not quite as strong as Scania.

One of the poissonières was Swiss. He was supposed to be shit hot but when he served a fillet sole vin rouge with a near chocolate-coloured sauce, his ratings fell a bit. He was a nice enough chap but not really 'with it'. The other was an English guy with thickish glasses, he used to look at you with a surprised expression as if to say, 'You talking to me?' He was a bit on the lazy side and where all the others would stock up on the sauters for service and, if necessary wash their own to save time, he would only get a couple and when he ran short he would calmly take one of yours. One day I was on the sauce and the fish was getting hammered, and there he was nicking my pots. When he wasn't looking I slipped one into the oven, got it red hot, then put it on top of my pile of pots. Sure enough, the next order was for him. He calmly reached down and nicked my special pot – I could hear the sizzle from six feet away! It took a couple of seconds for his brain to realise it had been had and he let go of the pot and rushed to the cold water tap. I really enjoyed that evening service and so did the others! The only one who didn't was my friend the poissonière – I wonder why! I must say he never pinched one of my pots again, so it worked. (He just pinched from someone else.) But it just goes to show, you don't have to argue with people to make your point!

Next we come to the veg. One of the chefs was called Ram (I don't know if that was his name or nickname), he was about 45 and very well organised and precise. He worked to a system and although he didn't seem to move quickly he was always on time with the orders. He was either Anglo-Indian or Mauritian, I never found out which. The other was a Yugoslav with a worried face, not quite as organised as Ram and a bit prone to having mini-breakdowns in the middle of service (you know the sort).

Then on the roast section we had dear old Jack Trigg, one of the good old boys. It was nice to meet Jack again – he was still the same, winding up all and sundry as quick as he could. He used to wind Bill up every chance he got. The other roast was a young English guy who, I think, had come from the Trocadero. Bill used to have a go at him (I think it was because he couldn't get to Jack), but this guy had strong staying powers so he didn't take much notice of Bill.

The larder had three chefs and, if I remember, a couple of commis. One of them was Italian, another Spanish and the third, I think, French. The Italian was called Joe, he was very good at cold buffet work, just seemed to fiddle about with a dish and, hey presto, it looked great. I remember at Christmas Joe had made a pheasant pâté. He turned it out onto a salver, added a few feathers and tail feathers and it looked like a pheasant on a nest – really effective. Joe later went on to become head chef at the Ivy Restaurant. The Spaniard was called Romil, and I later found out he was Gasco's great friend and they had fought against Franco in the International Brigade together. Small world, isn't it! Actually Romil looked like Gasco – medium build, Errol Flynn moustache, wavy hair – they could have been brothers. Romil was good and he and the other larder chefs all seemed to get on well together. The third was called Maurice, but he never seemed to be in the same class as the other two.

In the veg prep room they employed a woman, an Italian, I believe, who only worked mornings. She was very good and quick, picking the spinach, doing the beans, peeling the potatoes. You name a veg and I bet she had cleaned it! She left all the veg neatly in containers and the chefs just took what they needed.

Mons. Pannier, the head chef, was a lovely man. He walked with one shoulder slightly lower than the other as if he was carrying a sack of potatoes around. He made up the menus daily and had them printed on site, though the first copy was handwritten. (He had lovely writing, a sort of scroll effect.) Mons. Pannier used to wander into the kitchen a couple times before service and go around and see everyone, making sure they were all right. He always looked slightly worried, but he had a good sense of humour. His lopsided walk made him seem laid back but he was sharp as a needle, really on the ball. Some of the dishes that appeared on the menus really made you hunt for the recipe. In the end you had to go to Mons. Pannier's office, knock on the door and say, 'Please, chef, what is X?' He would smile slowly, casually reach behind him to his bookcase, pick one out from the year dot and say, 'Page so and so'. Mons. Pannier's bookcase was the length of his office wall and some of the books must have been in the ark. He would never allow them out of the office, you had to read the recipe or copy it down in the office.

Let me give you an idea of the amount of work that was done at L'Ecu during the course of a day. The daily table d'hôte consisted of at least 12 starters, five plats du jour for lunch and another five for dinner. The à la carte section consisted of 24 hors d'oeuvres, nine soups, seven egg dishes and six different omelettes, 16 fish dishes and four different lobster dishes, 15 entrees, 11 cold buffet, 15 grills and 18 different sweets. Quite a lot to remember, let alone do to order.

They had a small Frenchman as carver for the restaurant (why are they all small fellows?) He was only about 5'2" but round (a bit like Tweedledee) and always wore a brilliant white chef's coat with a long white apron, topped off with a tall toque (a chef's hat, for the uninitiated). True to French tradition, he had a small thin moustache. Every day he had to carry the joints of meat up a flight of stairs into the restaurant so he must have been quite strong. Most days we had the usual ribs of beef with all the garnish, stuffed saddle of lamb, capons, turkey etc. Then every so often, chef would put a medium leg of veal on and the poor little bugger (sorry, carver) used to have a hell of a job getting this big chunk of meat on a large salver up the stairs. He often had to get help from a couple of waiters. I often wondered if this was the chef's perverse sense of humour, or just his way of making the guy earn his tips.

Most of the L'Ecu waiters were Italian – nothing new there, then! But unlike most other places, they never seemed to hang around the kitchen or service area. This was probably because Bill used to have a go at them for making the place untidy and sometimes he would report them to the manager for being lazy. Bill's way of being on top, I suppose.

L'Ecu was a very busy place. The ground-floor restaurant seated about 100. Some days we were on the go from the moment the doors opened (those were the days of the luxury expense account) until they closed, especially at Christmas time. The private rooms (I think there were about six of them) were situated in the basement at the back of the kitchen. This made it easier for service as the private room waiters only had to walk along the passage, whereas the others had to keep climbing up and down the stairs. Our favourite trick was to give a restaurant waiter only half of his order so that he'd have to come all the way back down. 'Oh sorry about that,' we'd say with a concerned look (lying buggers that we were!) We often had new waiters starting; they probably took the job to train for the Olympic Games, doing the uphill race or some such thing.

Although the kitchen at L'Ecu de France wasn't as friendly as Kettners or the Westbury, the guys weren't too bad (apart from Bill). But eventually Bill got to me. When I was on the veg, towards the end of lunch service we used to get bits en place for the evening shift. This particular time I had made some pommes duchesse, nice and firm, and put them in the larder to cool down at about 2 pm. At around a quarter to four, Bill came over and said that the duchesse was a bit runny. When I checked, sure enough it was wet so I stayed on and did some fresh. This happened a couple of times, so one day I checked the mixture at about 3.30. It was fine, nice and firm, so I started to clear up and get ready to go home. Then at quarter to four Bill came over. 'Duchesse runny!' he said. When I checked it, sure enough – crap! I said to Bill, 'That's funny, I only checked it a few minutes ago.' Although I could not prove it, I was sure that a certain someone was playing the saboteur (any guesses who was number one suspect?)

Anyway, that finished me and I started to look around for a new job. I was soon told about a chef tournant position going at Crockfords Gaming Club in Carlton House Terrace. (Thanks again, Mons. Habert!)

A L'ÉCU DE FRANCE

111 Jermyn Street, S.W.1

TELEPHONE : WHITEHALL 2837

(G. TOURNANT – AUG. '63 – FEB '64)

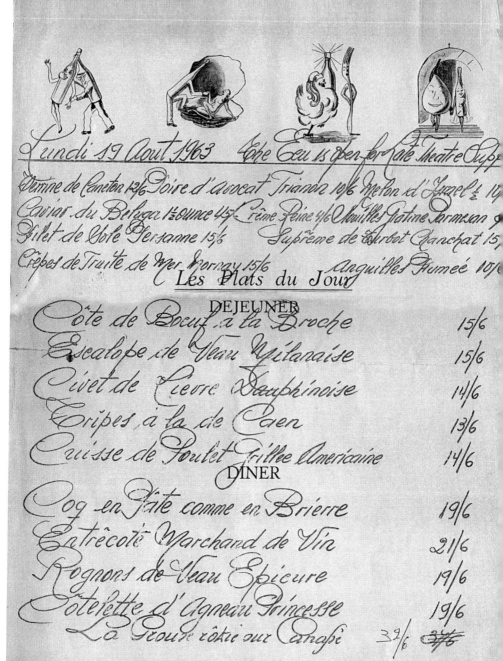

Lundi 19 Aout 1963   The Eu is open for late theatre suppers

Terrine de Caneton 12/6 Poire d'avocat Trianon 10/6 Melon d'Israel ½ 10/
Caviar du Beluga 1½ ounce 45/ Crème Reine 4/6 Nouilles Gratine Parmesan 9
Filet de Sole Persanne 15/6   Suprême de Turbot Archat 15/
Crêpes de Truite de Mer Mornay 15/6   Anguilles Fumeé 10/

Les Plats du Jour

DEJEUNER

Côte de Boeuf a la Broche	15/6
Escalope de Veau Milanaise	15/6
Civet de Lievre Dauphinoise	14/6
Tripes à la de Caen	13/6
Cuisse de Poulet Grillée Americaine	14/6

DINER

Coq en Pâte comme en Brière	19/6
Entrecôte Marchand de Vin	21/6
Rognons de Veau Epicure	19/6
Cotelette d'Agneau Princesse	19/6
La Geoure rôtie sur Canapé	32/6 ~~34/6~~

Nos Salons Privés

Le Salon Rose - de 6 à 12 personnes   La Cave - de 10 à 14 personnes   La Taverne - de 12 à 45 personnes

LES HORS D'OEUVRE

Melon Frappé	Hors d'Oeuvre Variés 10/6	Saumon Fumé 15/6
Thon à l'Huile 8/6	Truite Fumée 7/6	Artichauts Lucullus 10/6
Anguilles Fumée 10/6	Bouquet de Langoustine	Artichauts Vinaigrette 7/6
Truite Marinée Ecu 12/6	Cocktail de Homard	Florida Cocktail 5/6
Crabe Dressé	Potted Shrimps 5/6	Caviar (1½ oz.) 45/–
Jambon de Bayonne 12/6 avec Melon 15/6	Foie Gras au Porto 25/6	Pâté du Chef 8/6
Cocktail de Crevettes 10/6	Oeufs en Gelée 3/6 pp.	Avocado Pear 7/6
Terrine du Chef 8/6		Charcuterie 12/6

LES POTAGES

Minestrone 4/6	Velouté de Tomates 4/6	Vichyssoise 5/6
Bisque de Homard 8/6	St. Germain aux Croûtons 4/6	Gaspache 7/6
Tortue Claire au Xérès 7/6	Consommé de Volaille 4/6	Madrilène en Gelée 4/6

LES OEUFS et LES FARINAGES

Omelettes: Jambon, Fromage, Tomate, Champignon, Reine, Espagnole 10/6 — Œufs Pochés Argenteuil (2) 10/6

Œufs Brouilles aux Foies de Volaille 10/6	Œufs en Cocotte Rossini (2) 10/6	Œufs au Plat Bercy 8/6
Nouilles au Jambon 8/6	Gnocchis Romaine 8/6	Raviolis Biarrotte 8/6

LES POISSONS

Homard: Americaine, Thermidor, Biarrotte, Xavier		Truite Saumonée Doria
Scampi Newburg 17/6	Scampi Frits Tartare 15/6	Saumon d'Ecosse Poché ou Grillé
Filets de Sole Walewska 15/6	Filets de Sole Véronique 15/6	Filet de Sole Frit en Goujon 16/6
Tronçon de Turbot Poché Hollandaise 15/6	Suprême de Turbot Dugléré 15/6	Grenouilles Provençale 17/6
Truite de Rivière au Bleu 12/6	Truite de Rivière Amandine 14/6	Coquille de Fruits de Mer Mornay 14/6
Sole au Champagne, Belle Meunière ou Nantua 18/6		Brochette de Scampi Ecu 17/6

LES ENTREES

Escalope de Veau Cordon Bleu 17/6	Suprême de Volaille Remoise 21/6	Ris de Veau Princesse 22/6
Tête de Veau Sauce Gribiche 13/6	Suprême de Volaille Hawaiienne 21/6	Côte de Veau au Romarin 20/6
Noisettes d'Agneau Niçoise 17/6	Feuilleté de Poulet Financière 15/6 Caneton Poêle aux Cerises ou Orange (demie) 27/6	
Entrecôte Chasseur 21/6	Poussin Grand'Mere Tournedos Opera 22/6	Foie de Veau Fines Herbes 15/6
Jambon Braisé aux Pêches 21/6		Kehbab d'Agneau Orientale 18/6

LE BUFFET FROID

Homard Froid	Salade de Homard	Saumon d'Ecosse	Truite Saumonée Sauce Verte		Filet de Sole Dugléré
Jambon	Boeuf	Agneau	Langue	Poulet Suprême de Volaille Jeannette Salade de Poulet Œuf en Gelée	

LA BROCHE

Le Poulet de Grain	Le Poussin	Le Carré d'Agneau (25 mins.)
	Le Caneton (60 mins.)	

LES GRILLADES

Scotch Fillet 21/6	L'Entrecôte 20/6	Le Tournedos 21/6
Chateaubriand (2 pers.) 45/6	Chop d'Agneau 15/6	Mixed Grill 17/6
Entrecôte Minute 18/6	Rognons au Lard 15/6	Côte d'Agneau Double 15/6
Porterhouse Steak (2 pers.) 45/–	Paillard de Veau 15/6	Cotelette d'Agneau 15/6
Côte de Veau 20/6		Brochette de Foies de Volaille Vert Pre 15/6

LES SALADES

Laitues 4/6	Endives 5/6	Tomates 4/6	Romaine 4/6	Cresson 4/6	Orange 5/6 Japonaise 5/6

LES LEGUMES

Chouxfleurs Gratin 4/6	Petits Pois à la Française 4/6	Epinards à la Crème 4/6
Haricots Verts 4/6	Brocoli 4/6	Courgettes Provençale 5/6
Carottes Vichy 4/6	Choux Verts 4/6	Petits Pois à la Menthe 4/6
Artichauts Hollandaise 8/6	Maïs à la Crème 4/6	Epinards en Branches 4/6
Pointes d'Asperges 7/6	Fèves au Beurre 5/6	Les Asperges

LES POMMES

Lyonnaise 2/6	Sautée 2/6	Purée 2/6	Allumettes 2/6	Frite 2/6	Croquette 2/6

LES DESSERTS

Patisserie Parisienne 4/6	Biscuit Ecu 4/6	Mont Blanc 7/6
Mousse au Chocolat 4/6	Compôte de Fruits 5/6	Flan aux Fruits 4/6
Crème Caramel 4/6	Macédoine de Fruits Frais 5/6	Gâteau Maison 4/6
Pêche Dame Blanche 6/6	Bombe Pralinée 5/6	Soufflé aux Liqueurs 12/6
Soufflé Harlequin 10/6	Meringue Glacée 5/6	Sabayon Marsala 8/6
Poire Hélène 5/6	Crêpes Suzette 10/6	·Glaces Variées 4/6

LES CANAPES

Canapé Maison 6/6	Canapé Diane 6/6	Welsh Rarebit 4/6	Scotch Woodcock 5/6

FRUITS DE SAISON	Café 2/6	Hag 3/6	Sanka 3/6	Nescafé 3/6	FROMAGES ASSORTIS 4/6

Crockfords Club
Carlton House Terrace
Chef tournant, February 1964-January 1965
Head chef: Mons. Ritter

Crockfords Club (one of the best gaming clubs in London at that time) was situated at number 16 Carlton House Terrace, at the far end to the left as you came from Pall Mall into Waterloo Place. It was an imposing building (still is), built around the late 1700s. The inside was very plush: large rooms with high ceilings, it just reeked money.

The kitchen was in the basement and the restaurant was on the first floor. Behind the restaurant was a small servery where the finishing touches were added to the dishes. The starters and salads were also made here to order. There were two lifts that came straight up from the kitchen, a small hotplate just to hold the dishes prior to serving (they were sent up from the kitchen at the last moment). The checks were sent down by means of a metal pipe, via steel-tipped 'bullets'. The chef who normally did this job was called Ali Khan, a well-spoken middle-aged, upper-class Pakistani who'd obviously had a good education. He had been there a few years when I got to know him and one day we got chatting. He told me that he lived in a one-roomed flat, never went out, didn't eat out, and sent all his spare cash back to his brother in Pakistan. They were buying land to start a farm; Ali was supplying the dosh and his brother was overseeing the work. Ali reckoned that after another four years he would be able to go home and retire as a landed gentry farmer. I often wonder if he made it. I hope so, as he was a nice guy, always ready to help out, always smiling and never raised his voice or got angry.

Crockfords' kitchen was in the basement along with the changing rooms and the chef's office, the staff dining-room and, just off it, 'the gods' domain' – the croupiers' room. They were classed as the saviours of the club and were regarded as special people – and by Christ, did they know it! They were a snobbish, stuck-up lot. The rest of the staff were OK, they always spoke and had a joke with you. Serving the staff and the croupiers were two women – well, one woman and a young girl. It was a bit difficult to tell the girl's exact age as she had about a ton (no, that's unkind, half a ton) of make-up on. She was nice enough, a sort of prototype Essex girl. The other was a mother figure (well, maybe a grandmother).

Along the passage were the stairs leading up to the clubroom, a small restaurant for customers who wanted a snack rather than a big meal, or just wanted to be quiet and maybe reflect on their losses. There were four regular waitresses who served here, all Irish. One was a small, thin colleen, the other was about 40-ish and claimed to be able to read tea leaves. (Oh yeah, I hear you say. Well that's what I thought until she read my tea leaves and told me that a young blond boy I knew would have a fall and hurt his leg. A while later my wife's blond brother, who was about six at the time, fell off a wall outside the flats where they lived and cut his knee. Now I always give any predictions the benefit of the doubt, because seeing is believing!) The other two waitresses were sisters, and all four used to get on with the customers and kitchen lads, so it was a good atmosphere.

Now we come to the kitchen. The sous chef was an Italian in his 50s, a nice bloke who knew his stuff, but when the place got very busy he used to lose it and get agitated. Then the waiters started to hassle him, which made him worse, and he would curse them, telling them to go to distant lands and look for their parents etc.

The larder was presided over by Mario, a lanky six-foot Italian whose one redeeming physical feature was his gold front tooth. When he smiled it was like the sun had risen. Mario had an eternal smile; I think he was trying to get his money's worth from that tooth. He was good in the larder, never panicked, just got on with the job. No matter how busy he might be he always had time for a chat. The other chap, who worked mainly in the larder but was, I think, like a second sous, was ... wait for it ... Italian! He was called Batista and had a limp (leg, not wrist!), but he was a good class worker. His cold buffet dishes were good, especially when we had special parties. Batista had the place 'sewn up'; if you wanted to know anything, then ask *him*.

Just next to the larder, in a sort of large converted coal hole, was the pastry. This was run by a small Englishman who was very good, made everything fresh even the petits fours. He had the looks of a farmer, with his rosy cheeks and soft voice: a typical, unflappable Englishman. He had a good sense of humour, a bit dry for the Italians, but the rest of us appreciated it. His favourite pastime was making pastillage models for the petits fours to be served with; his crinoline ladies were always lovely to see. With him in the pastry was a young lad about my age, a French cockney called Raymond Thevenet. We got on very well as we had the same sort of outlook on life. Then, surprise surprise, I found out that Mons: Habert was his uncle. Well, knock me down with a rolling pin – what a small world! Raymond only stayed a couple of months, then he emigrated to a small island off New Zealand. I heard a few years later that he was still there and had settled in well. Raymond, if you ever get to read this, how about getting in touch?

In the next room were the sauce and veg sections. The sauce was run by a few men while I was there. One was called George Good – 'good by name, good by nature' was his favourite expression. He was a good (sorry about the pun!) sauce chef in the old tradition. You name a dish, he'd tell you what it was. When the chefs de partie finished about 10 pm, George used to get changed like his life depended on it, just so that he could get home to his local and have his pint of beer with a port chaser before the pub closed.

When he was on form George was very funny, he had the kitchen in stitches time after time. But sadly, like most gifted people, he had a down side which reduced him and nearly us to (real) tears. He'd apparently had a very sad life and, like most clowns, he hid his loneliness behind his jokes. George loved his beer and he could open his bottle and drink it straight down before you could open yours. He had an open gullet for drink but he never got drunk on duty; I shudder to think how much it would cost to get him drunk! George was always willing to show you how to do things and always telling you tales of what he used to get up to when he was younger. (How can you lock a head chef in a fridge for an hour and get away with it? Well, George did!)

While I was at Crockfords I met Mons. Mason again, a chef I'd known at Kettners. He came as the saucier and it was nice to see him again but he only stayed for a few months and then moved on. Then we had Andre, who thought he was the reincarnation of Casanova himself. He used to spend more time chatting up the female croupiers than working – 'like a fly round a bit of shit' was the sous' expression. I remember one day Andre, just before lunch service, was going to fry off some crisps for garnish. He happened to see a new female croupier pass by, so he just dunked the basket full of raw crisps (game chips) into the hot fat and nipped to the door to chat her up. Well, the fat boiled over, *whoosh!* on the hot stove, and lo and behold there were flames, bloody big ones! The only funny thing was the look of sheer horror on Andre's face as he looked back and saw what had happened because of his philandering ways. He went white and promptly ran out of the kitchen and into the yard – so much for the macho man image! After we had got together and put out the fire by smothering the inside of the stove with soda crystals and slinging a fire blanket over it, dear old Andre came back looking very sheepish. All of us in turn gave him a right old rollocking (richly deserved), and until the day he left (which was not that far off), Andre never worked on the sauce again. His actions in running away were both dangerous and stupid; he should have stayed and tried to fight the fire that he had started. If it wasn't for our quick thinking things could have been very serious; the trunking could have caught fire and then set both the restaurant and rooms alight.

Vitorio, the veg chef, was also a great Casanova in the kitchen, though outside I think his wife had him in a full nelson. Apparently, out of work he rarely said boo to a goose, but at work, well, he was another instigator of the touch-ups, kisses and other general molestations that occurred. (Mind you, most of the others weren't far behind in coming forward!)

Every day Vitorio spent more time organising his own lunch and dinner than he did on the customers, while his commis did most of the work. His meals were something to see: maybe a lovely double portion of turbot, lovingly cooked in butter or a sauce, freshly cooked vegetables. He used to just sit down and have his meal, completely oblivious to any orders. 'I'm eating,' he'd say and they let him get away with it.

One quiet night, Vitorio and I were larking about throwing pinches of cayenne pepper onto each other's stoves (burning cayenne stinks and makes you catch your breath) when all of a sudden the restaurant manager came steaming into the kitchen screaming blue murder. The extractor had taken the cayenne smell up the trunking, into the servery and into the restaurant! Vitorio put on his most surprised look and immediately blamed me (thanks a lot!) Well, I apologised profusely and said that the edge of the frying pan had caught fire. I don't think the manager believed me, but still.

Yet another Casanova was ... right again ... an Italian! He was a chef tournant and was actually quite ugly but in his own rose-coloured vision he saw himself as irresistible to women and the best love machine ever. Like Andre, he was always chatting up the women: *puttanas* (prostitutes), he used to call them when they weren't there. When they were, he was like a lake of oil, he was that smooth – a real life gigolo. From the number of women he claimed to have 'had', it was a wonder he ever found time to come in to work! We only took a portion of his 'conquests' as real. He had a skin that would shame a rhino and according to him he was the originator of the Kama Sutra. (Don't tell me, you've met someone like him too!)

Mons. Ritter was a good chef, although we didn't see much of him in the kitchen. He was either in his office or upstairs in the restaurant. He had the inevitable moustache and used to look at you through his glasses with his brown 'happy' eyes. Everyone respected Mons. Ritter and looked forward to his menus, a table d'hôte every day and an à la carte about every four months. The standards and quality were first class: if you needed truffles you had truffles. Mons. Ritter had made a name for himself in various establishments and was well-known in the West End. I was told once that he was a member of the Ritter Courivauld (dry stores) family, but I never did know for sure. (Is it true, Mons. Ritter?)

One of my best memories of Crockfords was the time we did the post-premier party for the James Bond film Goldfinger. (I still have the buffet menu.) The club had a large patio at the back and to get to it you had to cross one of the gaming rooms and go through big french windows. They had fixed up a large marquee covering the whole area, big enough to seat about 200 people, and had done it out like a beautiful restaurant with plenty of gold. We had all been working extra hours for a couple of days before, getting various dishes ready: cold hams, turkeys, sirloins of beef, lamb cutlets, all glazed and decorated. There were whole salmons, lobsters and crayfish, all decorated; freshly carved sides of Scottish smoked salmon, giant tins of caviar all laid out in the marquee in a traditional style buffet. Some of us served behind the buffet, others were the 'gofers', fetching and carrying replenishments for the buffet up two flights of stairs. Yet others were in the kitchen topping up the mise en place. I remember that the chef had enlisted the help of a few chef trainers from Westminster Tech, who caused a little bit of ill feeling as they only wanted to serve on the buffet and not get their hands dirty. But apart from that, the kitchen worked well as a team. Batista chatted to his friends the waiters, and for some extra portions of food we were supplied, on a regular basis, with champagne. Lovely jubbly! (We all managed to take home a bottle of bubbly each – spares, of course!)

I really enjoyed the evening, even though we did not finish until about three in the morning (The guests did not even start arriving until after 10.30 pm.) A couple of the chefs, Mario and Batista, stayed on with the head chef until the very end, about five I think. It was the first time I had helped on such an occasion, and though it was very tiring, it was also very satisfying, something to look back on in the future and reminisce on.

One day an older (60-plus) chef joined Crockfords as a saucier. He was French and a bit of a misery (if he had a sense of humour, he'd left it at home), though he was quite good on the sauce. He had a real knack, obviously practised over the years, for carving mushrooms into a fish or turtle, or doing a fancy design on the top – really effective. The only trouble was that he would not show anyone how he did it; he'd turn away so you couldn't see. He was not willing to show or help younger chefs – pretty naff, eh! Still, it makes sense when you think that in days gone by, the young chefs only learned how to do things by paying the experienced chefs to show them, and that some chefs made their name by being the only one able to do a dish in a certain way.

In the club room, some days the girls weren't too busy and spent most of the time chatting to the customers. Other days, they would be rushed off their feet. This is where Vitorio came in. The girls had to come into the kitchen to deliver the orders and then collect them. Vitorio would rub flour onto his hands, creep up behind them and grab either their breasts or waists, though his favourite was to grab their bottoms and leave white handprints for all to see. Then the lads would have fun brushing the flour off the girls' black uniforms – sometimes brushing where no flour existed, know what I mean! Sometimes Vitoria touched so gently that the poor waitress did not feel a thing and as no-one let on, she went up to the clubroom with two lovely white handprints on her bottom! While they were serving a customer it would be pointed out to them that they had been 'branded', which often caused quite a laugh for both the clients and the chefs.

Once one of the prettier waitresses engaged Vitorio in deep 'friendly' conversation. He was thoroughly enjoying it when one of the older waitresses crept up behind him and poured a bucketful of iced water all over him. We had quite a laugh over that one. Another time Vitorio was being chased by the girls over some trick he'd pulled on them. He shot into the gents' changing room and hid in the loo, but one waitress stood guard outside whilst the other two unrolled a hosepipe, went into the gents and literally 'flushed' him out. He looked like he'd had a 20-mile swim but he took it in good part and he always seemed to get a kiss from them at the end of the day. Amazing what some people can get away with, isn't it!

The kitchen used to pack up at around 11 pm, and about 10.30 a chef de nuit would come on and would serve any customers whatever they wanted until the place closed – generally 5 am. This guy was a small dapper Frenchman who never seemed to laugh – miserable old sod. He always had some moan or other about the night before: this wasn't left, there was not enough that – a right old whinger. He had enough time most nights to do everything from scratch, but he always expected us to leave him plenty of mise en place, so that he could have a 'break'.

The club used to have its share of regular customers, and most of the time they lost or had only modest wins. Occasionally there was the big winner who started with, say, a £10 000 stake and walked out with maybe £80 000 or more. One day we would hear of a punter losing £10 000 in one night and then a few nights later the same guy would win perhaps £40 000 in a night. But, like the bookies, the club always won more than they lost. We always knew the 'house' was winning when complimentary dinner slips started coming down to the kitchen; the manager had ordered all the most expensive dishes and wine – free of charge –

for the losers so that when they went home they did not feel too bad after a good nosh and sup, and would probably return, pushing their luck again.

My favourite Crockfords story was the time when a famous film director came to chance his arm at the roulette table. Crockfords had what they call 'car jockeys', guys who took your car as you arrived at the entrance and parked it for you. When you were ready to go home, they would collect it and deliver it to the entrance. Well, on this night the 'jockey' who took the director's American car away was new and, not being used to the main entrance gates, he knocked the front wing and dented it. The club always took full responsibility for any cars left in their care and prided themselves on quickly and efficiently sorting out any problems. So, the manager went to tell the 'great' man, in very apologetic terms, about the mishap. The guy listened to the apology, took out a pen and a writing pad, wrote a name and number on it and said to the manager, 'This is my chauffeur's number, tell him to bring Rolls here at about three o'clock, thank you'. He didn't turn a hair, just got back into the game – is that money or what! Needless to say, the car was fixed up in double quick time at no cost to the punter, but at a loss to the jockey. (I believe they had to have their own insurance to cover themselves against accidents, so it probably cost the poor bugger a few bob overall.)

One of my nicest memories of Crockfords was when my son Mark was born. I had phoned in to say that I would be a bit late as I was going to the hospital first to see him and my wife. When I arrived at Crockfords later, the catering manager Mr Edmonds, with the chef behind him, came up to me and gave me a bottle of champagne to celebrate the birth of my son. My wife and I were very touched by this gift, and it taught me another thing – treat others as you would like to be treated. Even though it was a simple gesture which didn't cost them much, we still remember it to this day. Mr. Edmonds later left the club and became the secretary of Boodles Club, a position he still holds, I believe.

Though I was happy at Crockfords, my time here was drawing to a close. One day Mons. Habert phoned me and offered me a position in his new kitchen appointment. The money was better and the challenge of producing authentic Greek food was appealing, so I accepted the position of chef tournant at the Bristol Restaurant.

CROCKFORDS

Les Hors d'Oeuvre

Melon Rafraîchi 5/6   Potted Shrimps 5/6   Terrine Maison 6/6
Coupe de Crevettes 7/6   Truite Fumé 6/6   Anguille Fumée 7/6
Salami 8/6   Mortadella 8/6   Hors d'Oeuvre Variés 8/6
Saumon Fumé 10/6   Jambon de Parme 10/6
Crevettes Rosé Méditerranées   *Cocktail de Homard
Foie Gras de Strasbourg   Caviar de Beluga   *Huîtres Natives

Les Potages

Crème de Tomates 3/6   Crème de Champignons 3/6
Crème St. Germain 3/6   Consommé Chaud ou Froid en Tasse 3/6
Vichyssoise 4/6   Minestrone Milanaise 4/6
Bisque de Homard 7/6   Tortue Claire au Sherry 7/6

Les Spécialités

(minimum 20 minutes)

Le Filet de Sole Otéro 18/6   Le Grenadins de Veau Suzanne 16/6
Le Suprême de Volaille Crockford 17/6   Le Tournedos à la Melba 16/6
Les Rognons de Mouton Liègeoise 12/6   Le Suprême de Volaille Ambassadrice 17/6
Le Homard à la Michèle   Le Caneton Lucullus (2 cts) 45/-
*Le Médaillon de Saumon à Chambord (2 cts)

Les Oeufs et Farinages

Oeufs Pochés:- Mornay ou Washington 4/6   Bénédictine 4/6
Oeufs sur le plat:- Bercy ou à la Turque 4/6   Ravioli Portugaise 6/6   Spaghetti Bolognese 8/6
Omelettes:- Fines Herbes 6/6   Fromage 6/6   Espagnole 8/6   Tomate 8/6   Jambon 8/6
Cannelloni Niçoise 7/6

Les Poissons

Scampis:- Frits 12/6   Meunière 12/6   Provençal 15/6
Sole de Douvres:- Frite 14/6   Grillé 14/6   Meunière 14/6
Délice de Sole:- Bonne Femme 10/6   Véronique 10/6   Palace 10/6   Walewska 14/6
*Saumon d'Ecosse:- Grillé—Meunière—Poché   *Homard:- Cardinal—Mornay—Newburg—Thermidor

Buffet Froid

Langue de Boeuf 10/6   Jambon d'York 10/6   Assiette Anglaise 12/6
Côte de Boeuf 10/6   Poulet du Surrey 12/6   Dindonneau de Norfolk 12/6
*Demi Homard   *Saumon Frais

Les Entrées

Rognons Sautés Turbigo 12/6   Côte de Porc Charcutière 12/6
Escalope de Veau:- Viennoise 12/6   Holstein 12/6   Napolitaine 14/6
Foie de Veau Lyonnaise 12/6   Jambon Cuba 12/6
Poulet en Cocotte aux Champignons 15/6   Suprême de Volaille Maryland 15/6
Caneton:- aux Petits Pois 17/6   à l'Orange 17/6   Paysanne 17/6
Tournedos Rossini 25/-

The Charcoal Grill

Kidneys and Bacon 12/6   Lamb Cutlets (2) 12/6   Gammon Steak 12/6
Lamb Chop 14/6   Pork Chop 14/6   Mixed Grill 15/6   Veal Chop 15/6
Steaks:- Rump 13/6   Sirloin 14/6   Fillet 16/6   T. Bone 25/-

Les Rôtis

Caneton d'Aylebury   Poussin au Cresson   Poulet du Surrey
*Perdreau   *Faisan   *Grouse

Les Légumes et Salades

Petits Pois à la Française ou à la Menthe 3/6   Haricots Verts au Beurre 3/6
Choux-fleur Nature 3/6   Choux de Bruxelles 3/6   Céleris au Parmesan 3/6   Epinards en Branches 3/6
Pommes:- Frites—Persillées—Lyonnaise—Sautées 2/6
Salades:- Coeur de Laitue—Française—Panachée 3/6

Les Entremets

Crème Caramel 3/6   Glaces au Choix 3/6   Salade de Fruits 5/6   Coupe Jacques 5/6
Meringue Chantilly ou Glacé 4/6   Crêpes à la Confiture ou au Citron 5/6   Pêche ou Poire Melba 5/6
Soufflés Variés   Ananas Flambé   Crêpe Suzette

Les Canapés

Sardines sur Toast 3/6   Welsh Rarebit 3/6   Laitances sur Toast 3/6   Canapé Diane 4/6
Buck Rarebit 4/6   Canapé Baron 4/6   Champignons sur Toast 4/6   Anges à Cheval 10/6
Le Plateau de Fromages   Les Fruits Frais

Le Café 1/6

Vins En Carafe

	CARAFE	DEMI CARAFE
Anjou Rosé	16/6	9/-
Bourgogne Blanc	16/6	9/-

Vintage Port by the glass 5/6

	CARAFE	DEMI CARAFE
Beaujolais	16/6	9/-
Hock	17/-	9/6

Château d'Yquem by the glass 5/6

10% Service   *Vin Saison

CROCKFORD'S HANDICAP
GALA DINNER
Menu

BUFFET FROID
Le Saumon fumé d'Ecosse
La Dinde de Norfolk, Cranberry Sauce
Le Jambon de York
La Langue écarlate
Le Poulet de Surrey
Le Homard froid, sauce mayonnaise
Le Saumon frais d'Ecosse
L'Entrecôte de Boeuf Angus, sauce raifort

SALADES ASSORTIES
Pommes de terre, salade des légumes
Endives, Laitue, Concombres, Tomates

ENTREMETS
La Salade des fruits, crème fraîche
La cassata Denise
Les mousses assorties
Les gateaux au fromage
Le panier des fruits de saison
Les petits fours

POMMERY & GRENO

Bristol Restaurant
Stag Place, London SW1
Chef tournant, January-May 1965
Head chef: Mons. Habert

Mons. Habert's restaurant was called the Chanticleer and was situated on the first floor of Stag House, a very swish apartment block where the likes of (so I was told) Max Bygraves lived. Lord Douglas Hume also had an apartment there, plus quite a few other well-known personalities.

The kitchen was in the basement, as was the Bristol Restaurant, which I would be cooking for. You could only get to the kitchen via the car park. It was quite a narrow kitchen but fairly well equipped, unlike some kitchens I could name.

The sous chef was an Austrian called Rudi, who had come from the London Hilton, where he had been offered a job while he was still in Austria. (At this time the kitchen of the Hilton in Park Lane was mainly staffed by Germans and Austrians. Oh no it wasn't, I hear the cry! Oh yes it was!) Rudi walked with a 'John Wayne' swing, and spoke very good English with a German lilt (or should that be an Austrian lilt? I think that's a bird!) His main job was to oversee the service in the Chanticleer Restaurant both for lunch and dinner, though at other times he worked in the larder section helping to prepare the various dishes, cold buffet and the butchery. When Rudi was upstairs he'd send the checks down with the orders and we would then cook, prepare and send them up in the lift so that he could finish them off – not a bad system really.

The sauce chef was a middle-aged Indian. I'm not sure whether Mons. Habert inherited him or had found him somewhere. He was not a bad sauce chef, but he thought he was better than he really was. Also, he did not really help any other section – a bit lazy really. The veg chef was also quite good, a young English chap whose name I cannot remember. As we were a small team, we all tended to work together, which was good as it stopped you getting bored. This variety of work was why I always preferred to take chef tournant positions.

During the lunch service the restaurant manager was Lord Vivian. This was, I thought, a nickname, but I soon discovered he was a living, breathing, pucker Lord. He was working for the money as he was not quite as wealthy as other lords. He was a very nice man who used to come down and have a coffee with the chef each morning and discuss the bookings or any problems. I was told that he used to 'sign on' at the House of Lords most days.

Having Lord Vivian as manager was a good business move as quite a few of our lunch regulars were from the House of Commons/Lords. As he knew most of them, it made for a good atmosphere, and they knew that they could entertain without having the press tipped off.

The lunchtime menus were French/English table d'hôte, with a small à la carte available. Sometimes poor old Rudi was rushed off his feet and one of us would go up and give him a hand for a bit. The servery had a small stove, a fryer, a grill and a hotplate. The various starters and main courses were finished off prior to the waitresses taking them out into the restaurant.

In the evening, the Chanticleer Restaurant was completely changed and turned into the Chanticleer Taverna, billed as London's first authentic Greek taverna. The whole menu was Greek, and the dishes were made on the premises by us. Mons. Habert had gone to a lot of trouble and had researched all the dishes through library books to get the right ingredients, methods of preparation and cooking. Nikki, the boss, a short, fat smooth, middle-aged Greek, had contacts for all the supplies: herbs, olives, oil, cheese, some of the sweets etc, so we were able to do all the dishes exactly as they would in Greece. We made fresh taramasalata, melitzanes imam mbailitze (stuffed aubergines to you!), as well as avgolemono, a chicken broth finished at the last minute by adding egg and fresh lemon juice. We made the keftedes, moussakas, dolmades, vodino stifado (a beef stew with plenty of onions and peppercorns, wine and vinegar), okra in a tomato sauce, fried aubergines and so on. We had another six traditional dishes and six more from the charcoal grill, including the now famous ntone kebab which we made ourselves by layering slices of beef, pork and veal on a long metal skewer, well-seasoned with herbs, salt and pepper. It was then covered with, I think, pigs' caul and allowed to set for a few hours. Then it was fixed onto a rotary spit, slowly grilled and, as required, carved thinly and served with a salad and wedges of lemon. We also did baby lamb, suckling pig etc.

For the sweets (my favourite part of a menu!), we had galatomboureko (a light pastry filled with honey and cream – delicious, I've put on a pound just writing about it)! There was also baklava, kataifi and rhum baba, pagoto krema (choice of ice creams) and, of course, halvas to go with the Greek coffee.

Mons. Habert used to get all the meat in 'en block', whole legs of beef, veal, legs and shoulders of lamb and so on. We would butcher them out and cut them according to the dish required. We also had to clean and wash the squid, one of the messiest jobs I have ever come across!

Business was good. Most nights we were very busy and poor old Rudi was going 19 to the dozen upstairs.

Nikki was the evening manager, helped by a couple of Greek waiters and two dolly-bird waitresses (just to keep the customers happy, you understand!) Then one day Nikki felt we should be a bit more authentic and, on his insistence, the chef had to engage these two 'first class' Greek chefs, especially brought over from Greece. I think someone was onto a slight immigration rule-bending exercise, because dear oh dear, they turned out to be a right pair of plonkers (or dimbos). I think the only kitchen they had ever seen was their mother's (that's if they ever had one). They both looked and were built like navvies and they had about as much concern for hygiene. We knew more about their national food than they did – a right wool-over-their-eyes job this one! Oh yes, and they couldn't speak a word of English either, so trying to communicate with them was zeroed for a start.

Mons. Habert and Nikki had a few 'conversations' over these guys (or 'prize dicks', as they were known!) Nikki was the interfering type of boss and eventually Mons. Habert had had enough and proceeded to tell Nikki his fortune, nice and quietly, mind you, no shouting or raising of his voice, but Nikki knew he'd been bitten! (Mons. Habert never had to raise his voice, but you certainly got the message!) So Nikki started with the well-used complaints tactics, you know the sort: 'the soup is not hot enough', 'the cream has been whipped too much', 'is the fish fresh?', 'does my shit stink?' etc. Eventually we'd all had enough of this pompous little twit and first Mons. Habert upped and left, then I found another job (with the help of Mons. H again!)

The Bristol had a really beautiful restaurant in the basement, it was done out in subtle shades of pink, with really good china, cutlery and glasses. It was mainly for the use of residents in the Roebuck House block (I'm not sure but I think that part of the agreement for the restaurant was that the residents could use it or have room service from it if they wished.) It was a shame that the business was never really great, I think it was a combination of being out of the way and not enough publicity. Nikki concentrated more on the taverna. The Bristol menu was equal to most five star hotels and the service was on silver. The restaurant manager was Greek and good at the job. We did the occasional floor service party, but Nikki had not thought through how to get the food up to the various floors and keep it hot, as we did not have any hot cupboards or tables like you get in hotels. The waiters couldn't cope and we lost out on business because of it – a bit short-sighted, I think!

The Bristol menu had a wide selection of dishes: 18 hors d'oeuvres, ten soups, six ways of serving Dover sole, four ways of serving turbot, four different scampis, plus various fillets of sole and river trout dishes, four lobster dishes, plus 15 house specialities, 13 grills, five roasts (not including game), six different potatoes and 14 vegetable dishes. We had a sweet trolley and a good cheese board so, as you can see, the clients had a good choice.

One of the more interesting dishes on the special list was the surprise d'homard bristol. This was similar to a lobster thermidor but brandy was used and, at the last minute, stiffly whipped egg whites were folded in. Then the mixture was put back in the shell and baked in the oven, and it came out like a soufflé. It looked good and by golly, it tasted good!

On the day I was leaving, Nikki had offered the chef's position to Rudi, who asked me if I would like to stay on and become his sous chef. I said no, but we parted on good terms anyway; he knew what I thought of Nikki's interfering, but he had to ask.

Years later, as I was going home on my afternoon break, I saw this guy sitting in the train carriage who looked vaguely familiar. It was Rudi. He had put on a bit of weight but still had the same look about him. He recognised me and we got chatting. I asked how he had got on at the Bristol/Chanticleer after I had left and he told me that Nikki had filled the place with 'first class' Greek chefs (a bit like the first two!) As they all screwed up, the place went downhill and finally closed, so justice was done after all!

THE BRISTOL RESTAURANT

ROEBUCK HOUSE,
PALACE STREET,
S.W.1.

CARTE du JOUR

LES HORS D'OEUVRE

Whitstable Royals (6) 14/6   Saumon Fumé 12/6   Honeydew Melon Rafraichi   Crevettes Rosés 10/6   Pâté Maison
Foie Gras Truffé 17/6   Truite Fumée au Raifort 7/–   Potted Shrimps 5/6   Jambon de Parme
Le Cocktail de Fruits de Mer 10/6   Avocado Pear Vinaigrette 6/6   avec Fruits de Mer
Crevettes Cocktail 8/6   Caviar de Beluga 23/–   Escargots de Bourguignonne (½ doz.)
Half Grapefruit Cerisette 3/6   Asperges au Beurre Fondu 10/6   Pamplemousse Cocktail

Consommé Madrilène Chaud
Crème Portugaise 4/–
Minestrone Milanaise 5/6

NOS SPECIALITES

Scampi en Papillotte Maison 20/6
Suprême de Volaille Elizabeth 18/6
Côte de Veau Papillotte 18/6
Piccata de Veau au Marsala 18/6
Escalope de Veau Brownie 18/6
Filet de Boeuf au Poivre Maxim 19/6
Petit Poussin Souvaroff (2 cvts. 30 mins.) 30/–
Filet de Boeuf Tartare 18/6

Surprise de Homard Bristol Fashion 27/6
Soufflé à la Reine 17/6
Escalope de Veau des Gourmets 21/6
Caneton à l'Orange (2 cvts.) 37/6
Coq au Vin de Bourgogne 16/–
Entrecôte Christine 18/6
Diablotins de Sole à la Sauvage 18/6

Omelettes: Jambon
Oeufs Pochés: (2)
Oeufs en Cocotte: (2)
Spaghetti: Napoli
Canelloni au Jus de Ve

LES GRILLADES

Châteaubriand Béarnaise (2 cvts. 30 mins.)
Entrecôte Steak 15/6   Double 32/6
Côte d'Agneau 14/6
Rognons Grillés au Lard 12/6
Minute 15/6   Filet Steak 18/6
Côte de Veau 16//6   Pointe ou Rump Steak 15/6
Filet Mignon 17/6
Cotelettes d'Agneau 14/–
Côte de Porc à l'Ananas 14/6
Poussin Americaine (2 cts. 20 mins.) 25/–

LES ROTIS

L'Aile de Poulet Rôti au Lard 15/6
Carré d'Agneau Sarladaise (2 cvts. 30 mins.) 30/–
GIBIER (En Saison)
Grouse   Faisan   Perdreau   Civet de Lievre
Double Poussin Rôti au Lard (25 mins.) 25/–
Poulet de Grain (2 cvts. 35 mins.) 30/–
Caneton Rôti, Sauce Pommes 16/6

Sole Grillée (20 mins
Filet de Sole: Veron
Truite: de
Scampi: F
Homard: Cardina

Pommes:
Haricots Verts au Beurre 3/6   Nouvelles 2/6
Epinards en Branches ou à la Crème 3/6   Sautées 2/6
Brocoli Hollandaise 4/6
Oignon Frites 3/6
Aubergine Frite ou à la Grecque 4/6
Pointes d'Asperges 5/6

LES LEGUMES
Frites 2/6
Petits Pois à la Menthe 3/6   Purée 2/6
Céleri Braisé 3/6   Croquettes 2/6
Ratatouille 4/6
Champignons Grillés ou à la Crème 4/6
Lyonnaise 2/6
à la Française 3/6
Choufleur Mornay 3/6
Courgettes Provençale 4/6

Poulet:
Caneton Rôti avec Salade à l'Orange 17/6
Aile 12/6   Cuisse 10/6

LE BUFFET FROID
York Ham 12/6
Côte de Boeuf 12/6
Demi Homard Mayonnaise Selon Grandeur
Langue Froide 12/6

Suprême de Vol
Tournedos: R
Escalope de Ve
Rognons Saut

Laitue 3/–
Panachée 3/6

LES SALADES
Tomates 3/6
Endive

réchale
Diane
rogonoff
olmades

Choix de Glaces 4/6
Crème Caramel 4/6

84

LONDON'S FIRST AUTHENTIC GREEK TAVERNA

The CHANTICLEER TAVERNA

Roebuck House, Palace Street, S.W.1.   Victoria 5695

OREKTIKA (Appetisers)

Anginares à la Bolita 6/6
Artichokes cooked with shallots and lemon juice—served cold.

Sardelles me Lemoni 4/6
Spiced sardines with lemon juice.

Taramosalada 4/6
Smoked fish roe mixed with onions, garlic and lemon juice.

Melitzanes Imam-mbailtzi 7/-
Aubergines stuffed with onion, tomato and garlic—served cold.

Karivides 8/6
Fried Mediterranean prawns — served hot or cold.

Muala Mosharisia Pane 7/6
Calves' brains cooked in breadcrumbs.

Salami 5/-

SOUPES (Soups)

Avgolemono 4/-
Chicken soup with eggs and lemon.

Psarosoupa 4/-
Mediterranean fish soup.

PSARIA (Fish)

Kalamarakia Tiganita 12/6
Fried baby ink fish.

Barbounakia Savoro 14/-
Red mullet marinated in vinegar and fried in oil with rosemary—served hot or cold.

PASTES

Kanelonia me Saltsa 7/6
Greek dish similar to canelloni.

Makaronia Pastitsio 7/6
Greek dish, with baked macaroni, garnished with a meat and cheese sauce

TIS KASAROLAS
(Casserole Dishes)

Arni Fresko Atzem Pilafi 14/6
Pieces of lean lamb cooked with onions, tomatoes and Greek herbs and served with rice.

Arnaki Kapama 14/6
Chopped leg of lamb, sautéed in a casserole with onions, tomatoes, herbs and white wine.

Yiouvarlakia Avgolemono 12/6
Chopped beef with rice, onions, eggs, herbs and garlic, cooked in a casserole with egg and lemon sauce.

Keftedes 10/6
Chopped veal, onions and eggs combined, fried in butter and spiced with lemon.

Mousakas Melitzanes 14/-
National Greek dish made with minced beef, onions, herbs, aubergines and tomatoes. Covered with thick cheese sauce and baked in the oven.

Vodino Stifado 14/-
Beef cubes sautéed with onions and peppercorns in wine and vinegar. Served with rice.

Lagos Stifado 15/-
Hare cooked in the same way as Vodino Stifado.

Lagos Marinados 15/-
Chopped hare marinated for twelve hours in vinegar with onions, garlic and herbs. These ingredients are then fried in oil and cooked in a casserole.

Dolmades 12/6
Vine leaves stuffed with minced veal, rice, eggs, lemon juice and herbs. Cooked in a casserole and served with special sauce.

ABO TIN PSISTARIA (From the charcoal grill)

Arnaki Galaktos Fresko 18/-
Baby lamb.

Gourounaki Pseto 18/-
Young suckling pig.

Kokoretsi 16/6
Fillets of pork, seasoned with herbs and cooked over the charcoal.

Kotopoula 14/-
Young Surrey chicken on the spit.

Souvlakia 12/6
Young lamb cooked on a skewer and seasoned with herbs.

Ntonekebab 12/6
Beef, pork and veal, highly seasoned with herbs and cooked on a vertical grill.

Selection of chops and steaks cooked to order on the charcoal grill.

SALADES (Selection of typical Greek salads)

Maroulia (lettuce), Tomata (tomato), Koukia (Greek broad beans), Angourakia (cucumber), Rossiki Salad (Russian-style salad). Kolokithakia (baby marrow with olive oil and lemon)   each 3/6

GLYKISMATA (Sweets)

Galatomboureko
Light pastry filled with cream and honey.

Paklava
Wafer-thin butter pastry, layered with chopped walnuts, almonds and spices, and sweetened with Hymettus honey.

Kataifi
Shredded pastry with walnuts, hazelnuts, spices and honey.

Halvas
Eastern Mediterranean sweetmeats.

Rhum Baba

Pagodo Krema
Selection of cream ices.   each 3/6

TURIA (Cheeses)

Graviera Krete, Kasseri Krete, Feta
Cheeses from the island of Crete.   3/6

KAFÉ ELLENIKO
(Greek coffee)   1/6

(Cover Charge 5/-)

The Westbury Hotel (Take 2)
New Bond Street, London W1
Chef tournant, chef de garde, May 1965-February 1967
Head chef: Mons. Coudroy

The morning I started at the Westbury (again) was like coming back home; I was greeted like a long-lost relative. The head chef was new, Mons. Coudroy, a Belgian, but the rest of the team were still going strong: Mr Williams, Mons. Marco, Mario, David, Pannis ,Ted, Bernard, Lily and the two Joes. Some of the main kitchen staff had changed: there was Derek on the grill in place of George; Marco had a new helper called Terry O'Neill; and on the veg was an older Frenchman with a humpback.

Mons. Coudroy was one of the few chefs I would work for again. He was of the old mould: helping, showing you and generally guiding you along – lovely bloke! He had 'workers' hands', which showed he was not worried about getting them dirty, unlike some! He nearly always had a small cigar on the go, puffing a nice aromatic cloud over us. Apparently he was well known on the continent, as he had been the Executive Chef at the world famous Brussels World Fair, and been in sole charge of all the catering, plus he had been working in some of the more famous hotels and restaurants both in Belgium and France. He was a very fair bloke and when you first started, as you were working he would come onto the section and work with you for a few shifts, showing and telling you, in his broken English, how he wanted the dishes prepared. When he saw that you had it off pat, he'd leave you alone and wouldn't bother you again.

Mons. Coudroy had a good sense of humour and he often had Mr Williams and Marco in stitches with some quip or other. (He spoke mainly in French but gradually learned the English swearwords first, then conversational English, until he was quite fluent). He had struck a good deal with the management and boss of the Westbury: he lived in, but every Friday after lunch service, he'd shoot off and catch a plane back home to Belgium to his wife, then return on Monday morning – all paid for, not bad, eh! I think he was worth it.

The hotel was still owned by the Knott Corporation of America, and the boss, Mr Knott himself, used to come over every now and again to see everyone. The General Manager was Mr De la Rue, who was a true gentleman and very fair. I must say that every time I saw him, he always

86

spoke to or acknowledged me, as he did all the staff. One nice touch was that he would never enter the kitchen before asking permission. Imagine that nowadays! A poor old chef does not have any respect given to him in most establishments now, he's just a worker to gee up like everyone else. It was a sad day for the trade when Mr De la Rue collapsed and died while playing tennis.

The veg chef was, as I have said, a Frenchman who had 'been around' and was very good, not only on the veg but also on the sauce and larder. The reason he had not quite made his mark in life was probably that he was an epileptic – a bit dangerous in the kitchen, you must admit, but as his work was good, this little problem was overlooked. He used to be working along one minute and the next thing he'd be collapsed on the floor, twitching and moaning. You just had to leave him, not touch him and just let him come round in his own good time. He'd then sort of shake himself and just carry on as if nothing had happened!

Then, one day, just as he was lifting a large pot containing about four gallons of tomato soup off the stove, he had a seizure. Well, luckily he went one way and the soup went the other. It was doubly lucky because it happened at a busy period and, with everyone rushing about, it was really a miracle that no-one got caught by the boiling soup. So there we were, in the middle of a rush, with one bloke on the floor, tomato soup all over the wall and the floor, and us keeping the orders going out (after Mr. Williams had made sure the poor fellow was all right and had not burnt or hurt himself). Confusion reigned for about five minutes, then he stood up and asked, 'What happened, everyone OK?' I think the chef and Mr Williams had a word with him, because a couple of weeks later he decided to retire home to France. (I later learnt that he had actually gone into a hospice in France and that the ACF – 'Association Culinaire Francaise – was paying him a small pension to help him along – a very nice touch).

Just before he left, we were chatting one evening and he asked why didn't I join the ACF. I told him that I was already a member (Mons. Habert had enrolled me when I finished my apprenticeship). He asked me what my number was and when I told him, he didn't believe it. 'It's only for Frenchmen,' he said. As I used to carry the card with me, I went down to the locker room and brought it up for him to see. He was amazed that I could have an 'ACTIV' number (A274). That's when I realised it was not just an ordinary membership Mons. Habert had given me. Funny, but the guy was really polite to me for the rest of his time with us. (Only much later did I find out that it's only the ACTIV members who can vote or be on any committee, so I felt quite chuffed, especially as this guy was 'only' a participant!)

Mons. Coudroy and Mons. Marco used to have some friendly 'barneys' during service, each one trying to get the other going. I remember one day when it was fairly busy, Mons. Marco called over to Mons. Coudroy and asked if he would give a hand for a couple of minutes. Well, the chef was always willing to help so he came over to the sauce and asked what he could do. 'Finish this steak for me,' said Marco, handing the chef this cremated steak from the shelf. 'It needs the chasseur sauce.' Now Mons. Coudroy was dead against meat being served well done. 'Philistines', I think he called people who liked it that way. Anyway, he looked at this black thing in horror. 'How was it ordered?' he enquired. 'Saignant [rare],' said Marco. 'Wot!' the chef cried. 'Are you trying to get me the sack'. He started to get 'warm' and his complexion was getting redder by the second. Marco, testing his luck to the utter limit, replied, 'It's OK, it's only for the prince [we used to have these Arab princes stay at the hotel on a regular basis, sometimes for a month or more, and they were good tippers], he won't know the difference!' Well. Mons. Coudroy was about to have triplets. 'How can you call yourself a saucier!' he shouted, adding some French swear words just for luck. (I have left these out due to sensitive eyes.) The chef called Mr Williams over from the hotplate to show him this 'thing' and to verify that the things that he was calling Mons. Marco were true. Marco looked at the chef, smiled sweetly and said, 'Oh sorry, that was the wrong one, here it is', and gave him a lovely rare steak. Mons. Coudroy realised he'd been had, started to laugh and patted Marco on the back with enough force to shake loose his dentures, then tried to strangle him (friendlywise, of course!) Everyone had a good laugh on the chef and it helped to ease the tension of a hectic day.

The first commis working with Mons. Marco was a Liverpool lad called Terry O'Neill. Before he came to the Westbury he had worked in France for about eight months, so he was fluent in French. He had the typical Scouse humour, trying to wind up all and sundry, especially the waiters. Terry was very good and confident in all that he did. Most of the staff of our age (mid-20s) – the waiters, chefs, porters etc – all got on well, taking the mickey out of each other, but all in good spirit.

Our Jeffrey was a young commis chef, about 18, who thought he was a stand-in for Mick Jagger. Mind you, he could strut his stuff just like Mick and he knew all the words to their songs. He was a nice lad, a bit overconfident (he believed all the girls were in love with him), but OK in small doses. He was a hard worker and could take the stick and give it back without getting upset.

Our George had gone from the grill. (I'm not sure whether he had retired or got fed up with the previous head chef). Anyway, we now had dear old Derek in charge of the grill section. Derek was a different kettle of fish from Terry and the others, he was about our age, a Geordie but without much sense of humour. He could enjoy a joke on someone else but when it was on him, well, that was different. He took it personally and got quite upset. As you may have gathered by now, this sort of behaviour was like a red flag to the other chefs, so more jokes were played on Derek than on anyone else. Derek was a 'my job' chef: you've met the guy; this was his job and if you got in the proverbial, don't expect help from him. But if he was busy he would expect you to help him out.

I remember one day when Derek had one of his moods on. We were all quite busy but he wasn't; he was reading a newspaper! Well, I got a bit peeved so I crept up quietly, put a lighted taper to the bottom of his paper and rushed back to the veg and carried on working. It took about a minute for the flames to gather momentum and start devouring the pages, and another ten seconds before it registered with Derek that his paper was on fire. By this time, all work had stopped as we looked and wondered what Derek would do. He gave a sort of hop and skip followed by a strangled cry, dropped the by now charred paper onto the floor and started to jump up and down on the ashes. By now everyone was falling about in hysterics; the waiters came out of the restaurant to see what all the commotion was about. It took about five minutes before order was restored. By now Derek was in full throttle, up on cloud 27, threatening all and sundry. I think he invented some new swear words that day, and if he could have shot us all and got away with it, he would have!

But deep down, Derek was a softie and he was always in good form at staff parties after he'd had a few beers. The last I heard, he'd gone back home to Ashton under Lyme and had opened a clothes boutique. Are you still there, Derek?

It was about this time that we discovered the pleasures of egg whites in beer. Take a pint of beer (someone else's!) and, while they are not looking, slip a fresh egg white into it. Then stand near the beer and, when the owner *is* looking, have a good coughing fit right by the glass. 'Sorry about that,' you say, wander off and wait patiently for the beer to be drunk. As the egg white is swallowed, it feels like phlegm and invariably the drinker will spit out the offending mouthful and hopefully change colour. 'Sorry, I wondered where that had gone,' you say apologetically. Another trick was to add salt to a cup of tea and stand back. Many's the time some innocent person has been covered with tea!

One of the most effective jokes I have ever seen was played on the restaurant manager, Mr Ernest, by our Jeff. Mr Ernest still sampled the wines during the afternoon break and, come five o'clock he was getting peckish and would eat anything he could find, usually the sandwiches from the lounge waiters' tray, or a cake that might be lying about. This particular day Ernest came out and was hunting around for something to eat. 'If you'd like to come back in a couple of minutes, I'll get you some sandwiches made up,' said Jeff. 'Lovely,' said Mr Ernest, 'I'll be back in a few minutes.' Jeff nipped out and got four slices of bread, well buttered them, killed some flies that were idly flying about, stuffed them between the slices of bread, cut them up dainty with garnish and left them out on the table by the cashier's office. Mr Ernest came out, grabbed the sandwiches and wolfed them down. 'Lovely!' he said, and went off for a shower and change ready for the evening service! Later that night he complained of not feeling well, but put it down to the afternoon session. Absolutely true!

The pastry still had the old crew on board. Aldo had just returned from a stint at the Savoy but it was business as usual: home-made petits fours, all the old sweets. Ted, Bernard and Lily were still 'on form', Mario, David and Pannis still inhabited the grill room. Mario used to have a Sunday job for a Jewish company to provide chefs for the Sunday 'dos' at the Cafe Royal in Regent Street and nearly all the lads helped out on their Sunday off. It was quite a long day. We used to meet at Mario's house just off Caledonian Road (the Kings Cross end) at 8 am. Pannis would come by and pick us up in his Austin Cambridge and off we would go. In the Cafe Royal, we'd get changed then set to work on the menu for the day. Mario would split us up, and some would do the canapes for the arrival and the others would get on with the main meal. We often had whole salmon to decorate and sides of smoked salmon to carve.

The Bernards (the bosses) had large 'cages' locked and stored in the basement of the Cafe Royal, filled with all the pots and pans, marked 'meat' and 'milk'. They had their own knives (we were not allowed to use our own), also marked 'milk' and 'meat', and woe betide you if you used the wrong pot: they would literally cry! But I fully understood why one day, when Ted, who didn't like their knives because they weren't too sharp, brought his own in. Well we had a surprise tour by the Shoma; normally we had a warning that he was on the way and had a couple of minutes to check that all was well. But today he just turned up, grabbed Ted's knives and called out 'Stop work!' It transpired that all their knives had been blessed and were 'legal' for the job. The Shoma called the bosses and threatened to close the place. As we were expecting about 300 people, that would not have been easy. Mario, a quick-thinker, told the Shoma he was sorry, but Mr Bernard had told him to buy some more knives for them; as they had been busy, he'd not had time to have them blessed, but he assured the Shoma that they were only milk knives. After a lot of sweet talk, smoked salmon sandwiches and bubbly, the Shoma relented and agreed to let the food prep go ahead, but the offending knives had to be locked away until they had been properly blessed at a later date. Poor old Bernards had to go out and buy some new knives so that they had them ready for the blessing. That really brought home to me the importance of different religions and styles of conduct.

All the kraploks (I think that's how you spell it) and the rest of the various garnishes were made by a group of 'old witches'. No, not really, but if you looked quickly, you could make that mistake. What with them all huddled in a circle in their long aprons, talking at the same time (typical women eh!) and stuffing chicken necks, they did remind one of that scene from Macbeth, the 'bubble bubble, toil and trouble' bit! On a dark night they were frightening; in daytime they just made you nervous.

As I have said before, the day at the Cafe Royale was a long one. Snacks had to be prepared first for the guests' arrival, then after they had consumed these, they went on to the main course, which always consisted of traditional chicken broth with all the garnishes, then sometimes a fish course followed by a chicken dish with veg, then a sweet with coffee and petits fours. The Shomas would turn up and bless and cut the cholla (I hope that's the right spelling). Then a bit later, they would have the evening snacks: sandwiches, bridge rolls, fancy cakes and the inevitable Jewish ice-cream. It was one of the best ice-creams I have tasted. We used to have a quick break before the main part of the function started. The women used to offer us some of their lunch but we declined with many thanks and ended up with toasted rollmop sandwiches that we did ourselves – very nice.

The Bernards were the father, mother, son and son-in-law. The father, in his day, had got the business going by sheer hard work and now he was the 'front man'– the greeter who toured the room looking for compliments! The mother was a bit of a busybody (aren't all mums, especially Jewish mums!), and she would be parading about in her long dress with her jewels flashing and her red nails waving, organising all and sundry. During the service, she always stood at the end of the hotplate, inspecting all the dishes lined up to go. (Bear in mind that they were all different numbers, some tens, some, say, 11s and eights etc.) Her habit was to start changing the services just as they were about to go out. 'Oh, Mario', she would say, 'give this dish to table five, it has my best friend on it', or 'Give this one to the top table, it looks better than the one you have ready for them'. So for the first five minutes all hell broke loose as Madam Bernard, in her own inimitable style, strove to screw up the whole system by switching the services around, and Mario and the head waitress tried to get the services out in order and still convince the good lady that they were in her new order. Wot a day!

The son was a bit of a ladies' man, smooth, dapper and full of chat and promise, despite being married with children. He did not seem to do much, just followed the old man around and basically did nothing in particular. I remember one of these functions when one of the waitresses was French. She could not speak much English and did not seem to have done any waitressing before, but she was young and a very good looker with 'da bigga boobies' (just like the fallen Madonna). Anyway, everywhere she went, the son would follow, 'trying to teach her English', Mario said. All the girls and the head waitress complained to the son-in-law but he couldn't do much about it, so he put the French girl out back with us so she could help clear the plates as they came in and help with the coffee. Our David tried to be friendly but she obviously had better targets in mind. The last we saw of her was when the son took her out to the staircase to 'talk' to her (oh yeh!)

The son-in-law was the real worker, but he never seemed to get any credit for it. He organised the food, the girls, the whole caboodle. He was quite good and sometimes had time for a laugh and joke with us, but most of the time he was nipping around all over the place sorting out this problem and that problem.

The worst part of the day was when we had finished. We had to play hide and seek with the son-in-law, trying to get our money. If we saw him across the room, we'd signal to him; but he would just wave, move to another spot and start chatting to one of the customers. But if Mario got fed up and went to get hold of him, he'd come over quickly; he didn't want a chef having a go at him in front of a roomful of interested guests. He'd take us out by the back stairs and start the ritual: 'Sorry to keep you waiting, but I got held up'. 'OK,' we would all say ('Bloody liar,' we'd be thinking). 'How much?' he'd say, 'four wasn't it?' 'No,' we'd say, 'five!' 'Oh yes, that's right'. Then he'd pay us. I asked Mario why he always came out with this spiel. 'It's just their way,' he would say. The Bernards was hard work but I enjoyed it. The money wasn't too bad in them days either, and as you all know, every little helps!

The menu at the Westbury this time around had changed quite a bit. Whereas Mons. Dutrey's menu had been mainly classic dishes, Mons. Coudroy's was a mixture of classic and his own special dishes. There were 18 different appetisers, 11 soups, six egg dishes and six different ways of serving omelettes; 23 different fish dishes, including four lobster; 26 entrees, 18 grills and roast dishes, including a large T-bone steak dish for two, a double entrecote and a chateaubriand, and 16 cold buffet dishes. There were 17 sweets apart from the ones on the sweet trolley and eight different savouries (where do you see them nowadays?) On top of all this, Mons. Coudroy used to have a 'gourmet' section as well. Quite a lot to remember, don't you think? And this was apart from the Grill Room menu and the function menus!

(Mons. Coudroy once told us, via Mr. Williams as interpreter, about a particular speciality he had served up during the war when Belgium was occupied by the Germans. He was at the time a head chef in one of the best hotels in Brussels and when the German generals took it over for themselves, he and his staff were required to cook for them. Every now and again an outbreak of the 'running chocolate' – the shits, in plain

English – would occur and when questions were asked, Mons. Coudroy would always blame the poor quality or lack of freshness of the food. But the truth was, he was grating bars of soap, mixing it with cheese or in some highly seasoned stew and serving it up to the generals! By the time the 'cheese' had worked its way through the system and given them the runs, it was too late to find out what food it was. 'My way of putting the shits up the Germans,' he'd say – a lovely feeling, I bet!)

The waiters in the restaurant were the same ones as before, only some of the commis had changed. We had dear old Willie who was, I think, second in command after Andreas. Though he didn't have much of a sense of humour, now and again he'd be full of fun and jokes. I think he was more shy than anything. He was still there when I last saw him in 1994/95, and was head waiter then. One of the others was a small Greek called George, who later went to the Carlton Club as manager. The wine waiter (or sommelière, as he should be called) was a small, rounded 'Pickwick' man from Belgium. He really knew his wines and if pressed, could probably tell on which vine and what part of the vineyard the grapes for a particular wine were grown. He used to wander from table to table with his silver wine-tasting bowl around his neck, looking like an oenophile Peter Lorre (yes, him again!)

The commis and chefs de rang had a habit of invading the sweet trolley as it came out of the restaurant to be returned to the pastry and, like a swarm of locusts, they picked it clean. Mons. Coudroy gave out the order that the waiters should ask the pastry before taking anything, but they ignored it and carried on with their 'cleaning operations'. Then one day, Mons. Coudroy happened to catch a young German commis in the act of cutting a large piece of gateau. He called the pastry chef, enquired whether the commis waiter had asked for the piece. Negative, was the reply. He called Ernest over, then gave the commis the whole gateau. 'Now charge him for the whole thing at restaurant prices,' he said. It worked out at quite a bit of money, roughly eight shillings a portion for about 12 portions – £4, 16d (old money) and as the poor little bugger probably only got about £10 a week, it hit him hard! It was amazing how much sweet was returned after that, a visual smack works wonders don't you think? (Good job all these human rights people were not around then, he'd have probably been had up for cruelty to Germans!)

During this period we had a little old Frenchman (or maybe he was Italian) called Albertini in the larder as the buffet chef. He was about five foot nothing with thick glasses perched on the bridge of his nose, and he always looked over them when he talked to you. This chef used to come trotting up to the kitchen, go to the lift, take out his pâtés, place them in a bain-marie and put them in an oven, wrap a cloth or piece of paper around the door handle and say, 'Don't touch'. Then he'd toddle off back to the larder. At a certain time he would reappear, take the pâtés out, put them in the lift and send them down to the larder to be cooled and then presented on the daily buffet. He made a variety of pâtés, some en croute, some fine, some rough, and they always turned out perfect. Apparently Albertini was well-known for his buffet decorations and the ones I saw him do lived up to expectations. His favourite decorations seemed to be assorted types of flowers with butterflies or bees landing on them, really remarkable when you think that he used to cut out everything by hand, no cutters or any new fangled mixers for him. His hams and beef joints used to look like a picture, the flowers almost real, and when he did the whole salmons, they looked like they were floating on the water.

Around this time, the people from British Gas decided to use chefs from some top class hotels to promote the uses of gas – how quick and versatile it is etc. Mons. Coudroy was asked if he would like to do one; he agreed and the hotel thought it was a good idea as well. The day came and Mons. Coudroy went off to the studios to give the performance of his life. But he came back not at all happy. When Mr Williams asked how he had got on and what dish he had made (the chef and Mr Williams had spent a couple of days trying to decide which of his special dishes would come out well on the telly), Mons. Coudroy exploded, 'They wanted me to make a bloody omelette!' Apparently he had spent the entire day making omelettes until they had got the right shots! Still, he was paid something like £30 for his trouble, but as he said, 'People will think I can only do omelettes and nothing else.' After four or five of these commericals, they stopped. Maybe the other chefs weren't too happy either and no-one else wanted to do it!

During this time the still room was going through a dilemma. Our Tony had gone up the still room in the sky and the hotel was having great difficulty in finding someone else as good as him (there'll never be anyone that good, that's for sure!) For a few weeks we had a pair of 'transies' working the late shift (transvestites to you!) One was about 5'6" and the other over 6', both with bleached hair. They weren't very good as they kept arguing between themselves. If a waiter wanted an order while they were having a tiff, they just told him to piss off and come back later! I must admit they did take some stick from the chefs and waiters. Once they were seen all dressed up in frocks and long wigs, touting outside one of those funny joints (sorry, clubs) in Berwick Street! Shame about the stubble. Yes, you certainly used to meet some funny people in those days.

The old potwash guy really deserves a mention. He must have been the only pot man to clean a multitude of pots in a broom cupboard. Imagine a room about six foot wide and ten foot long with a large double sink at one end surrounded by racks for the pots. He just about had

94

enough room to swing half a cat! But to my knowledge he never complained, just came in and got on with the job – a real trooper!

The Westbury had a floor service whose department was run by a large men called Fred. He nearly always had a weary look about him as if he'd been on the go for the past three days, but he was good and knew his job. Like the others, he had a good sense of humour, so there was always a running insult between the kitchen and floors. All in good fun of course, although sometimes a casual passer-by might think war had been declared! The second in command was a chap called Ross, who hailed from the 'hills' (Wales) and was the main instigator of many of the jokes we played on each other. A girl used to answer the phone and take orders for room service, writing them down and then giving them to the kitchen, and one trick I remember was played on a new girl before she had time to learn about us and the number of rooms the hotel had. One of the larder commis had managed to get though to the floor service, gave her a really good order (good spender, good tipper) and a ghost room number. Well, she gave it to Mr Williams to call out, 'Excuse me,' he said, 'the hotel does not have this number room, does it?' Well, it was possible that the guest had given the wrong number, because it had happened before. Anyway, after about 15 minutes of searching, phoning the combination numbers it might have been and drawing a blank, Mr Williams called Fred over and said that he thought the kitchen was ahead on points. Well ahead! The guys took it in good spirits and the girl was relieved it was not her fault after all, but the room numbers were always double checked after that!

One of my favourite stories from the floors was the time (so I was told) when Bridget Bardot, the French film star and sex symbol, stayed at the Westbury (as did quite a lot of celebrities). She used to have a large dish of caviar with all the trimmings delivered to her suite each morning. This particular morning one of the floor waiters, a Greek, took up the caviar and Miss Bardot opened the door starkers! Well, the waiter, being young and healthy, forgot about the caviar and had a good eyeful. Apparently she was well-known for walking about in the nude in her suite and Fred had forgotten to warn this new chap that you just had to look in front and serve. Miss Bardot complained and Fred had to go up and apologise to her, explaining that the waiter was new to the job etc. He was never allowed to serve her again, but old Ross did, and thoroughly enjoyed it. Wonder why!

Another time some pop stars had a party at lunchtime and some of us were sent down to help with the serving. (They had about three hot dishes and wanted chefs behind the buffet.) I remember serving Dusty Springfield amongst others, though I only knew it was her by the blonde hair and the black eyes. We were kept too busy to take much notice of the people. The Rolling Stones were supposed to be there but I never saw them, though our Jeff said he did and thought he was much better than Mick Jagger! The next day we were told that the party had gone with a swing and everyone had enjoyed themselves. Then they found that the toilets had yards of toilet paper stuffed down them and it took a while to unblock the drains – one for the first 'pop incidents', I think.

When I started back at the Westbury we had a black guy as the chef de garde. He used to come in at 2.30 pm and work till 11.30 pm, getting the mise en place ready for the evening service, putting the ribs of beef in with the chateau potatoes, topping up the stoves – anything the veg or sauce wanted en place. He'd also cook something for the lads' supper and, during the afternoon, do any floors orders that might come along. It wasn't a bad job really: he used to have an hour's break around 8 pm, then when Mr Williams or Mario went off about 9 pm, he was in charge, with just the commis 'on board', then he had to lock up. Still, he was not really up to the job, kept forgetting to do things and so on. When he left, Mons. Coudroy offered the job to me. Well, a bit more money, a lay-in in the mornings and I got to see the kiddies a bit more. Once I got into the swing of it I quite enjoyed it.

At the back door we had two timekeepers, one was 'Big Jock' and the other was a small Italian. They used to share early and late turns. The early turn meant checking in deliveries and checking visitors etc. The late shift was just generally seeing that no strangers entered and no 'shopping' went out. Big Jock was about 60 and about 6'1", well-built but his muscles had slipped down a bit, know wot I mean! He used to smoke Clan baccy, a lovely scented aroma. The Italian, also about 60, was always giving me different Italian cigars to try (I smoked then). They were both pleasant blokes, always cheerful, and enjoyed the fun of the kitchen.

My favourite memory of the timekeepers was when, one night about 10 pm, the front hall porter phoned to say that a really good-looking girl would be coming down the floor service lift and would he make sure she got the taxi that was waiting outside the back door. A couple of minutes later a young woman came out of the lift and the timekeeper duly put her into the waiting taxi, and that was that. Or was it?

About five minutes later this really gorgeous creature came out of the service lift and asked the pop-eyed timekeeper where the taxi was. 'It's gone with a woman in it already,' he said. He phoned the hall porter to find out if there was more than one woman wanting a taxi, then chaos reigned. The first girl turned out to be the new cashier who had just finished her shift; as she had started before the timekeeper came on, he had not met her yet, so she had a good finish to her first day. The other poor creature had to wait while the hall porter called another cab. 'I thought she wasn't quite as pretty as I'd expected,' said the timekeeper, 'but I just thought "Each to his own taste!" '

By now I had been at the Westbury nearly two years and I was thinking I should perhaps move on. But as I was enjoying my stay I was a bit slow in the moving. Then one day, out of the blue, I got a phone call from Mons. Habert, who told me he had just got himself a new position as head chef at the Turf Club. Would I be interested in the sous position? (Praise indeed!). Yes, of course, I said. I duly gave my notice. Mons. Coudroy and Mr Williams were both sorry I was going but understood why. I received a very good reference from Mons. Coudroy and left some good friends behind.

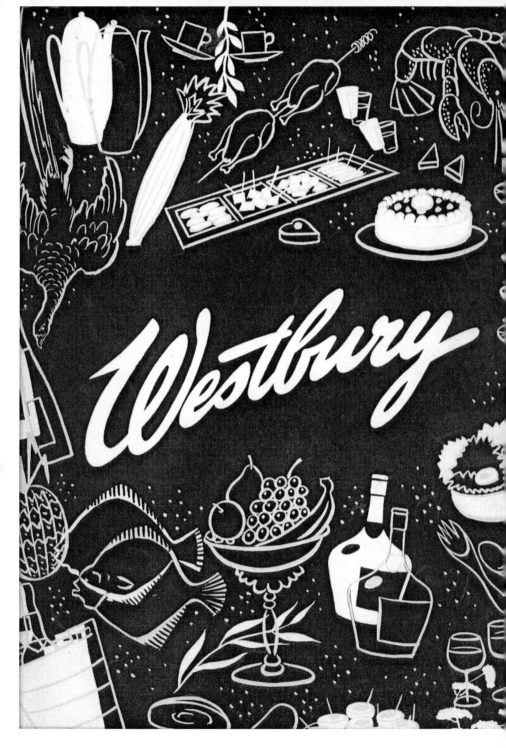

Appetisers

Caviar 32/6	Foie Gras de Strasbourg 18/6	Corn on the Cob 5/6
Smoked Scotch Salmon 14/6	Smoked Eel 12/6	Smoked Trout 10/6
Pâté Maison 8/6	Melon	Avocado Pear Westbury 10/6
Potted Shrimps 6/6	Dressed Crab 10/6	Shrimp Cocktail 10/6
Lobster Cocktail 14/6	Parma Ham 12/6	Escargots de Bourgogne (6) 9/6
Fondu Bruxelloise 6/6	Grapefruit Cocktail 5/6	Hors d'Oeuvre Riche 14/6

Soup

Consommé Madrilène 5/6	Onion Soup and Parmesan 5/-	Cream of Mushroom 5/-
Chicken Consommé 4/6	Minestrone 5/6	Vichyssoise 4/6
Crème St. Germain 4/6	Gazpacho 4/6	Petite Marmite 5/6
Mulligatawny 4/6	Bisque of Lobster 7/6	

Eggs

En Cocotte:	Ribeaucour 10/6	au Jus 8/6	la Crème 8/6
Poached:	Béarnaise 8/6	Florentine 9/6	Bénédictine 10/6
Omelettes:	Mushroom 10/6	Spanish 10/6	Tomato 10/6
	Ham 10/6	Westbury 13/6	Richemonde 13/6

Fish

Fried Whitebait 10/6

Scampi:	Fried 18/6	Meunière 18/6	Grilled 18/6
Sole:	Meunière 18/6	Grilled 18/-	Colbert 18/-
Fillets of Sole:	Frits en Goujons 17/-	Westbury 18/6	Bonne Femme 18/6	Walewska 18/6
Turbot or Halibut:	Grilled 15/6	Poché Mousseline 15/6	
River Trout:	Meunière 13/6	Philippe 15/6	Luxembourgoise 13/6	au Bleu 13/6
Lobster:	à la Hollandaise 35/-	à l'Americaine 35/-	au Whisky 35/-	Thermidor 35/-
Salmon:	Poached 22/-	Grilled 22/-	au Champagne 25/-

Entrees

Supreme of Chicken:	à la Parisienne 21/-	à la Kiev 21/-	Maryland 21/-
Sweetbreads:	des Gourmets 20/-	en Cocotte Clamart 20/-	Brillat Savarin 20/-
Fillet Steaks (Tournedos):	Rossini 25/-	Escoffier 23/-	Helder 23/-
Calves Liver:	Lyonnaise 16/6	Grilled à l'Anglaise 16/6	Meunière 15/6
Escalopes of Veal:	Viennoise 18/6	au Marsala 18/6	Cordon Bleu 18/6
Veal Cutlet with Mushrooms 18/6	Veal Cutlets Archiduc 18/6	Braised Ham, Madeira Sauce 16/6
Curry of Chicken Madras 18/6	Lamb Cutlets Favorite 18/6	Chicken à la King 18/6
Saddle of Lamb or Best End of Lamb Bouquetière (for 2) 50/-		Shaslick à l'Orientale 17/6
Entrecôte Minute Diane 20/-, Provencale 20/-		Veal Kidney Beaugé 18/6

Turf Club 1968 Sous-Chef

Avocado Restaurant 1969, Single Handed Chef

Piccadilly Hotel 1970-1, Sous-Chef

Mansion House 1969-70, Head Chef with Lord Mayor
Sir Charles and Lady Trinder.

1981

Royal Westminster Hotel Victoria 1979-85, Head Chef

Royal Westminster Hotel Victoria 1979-85, Head Chef

Thatchers 1984

Fisherman's Wharf 1987

A welcoming salute at the Royal Westminster Hotel

Frank Stalley

For Le Gourmet

Consommé Germiny 5/6

Suprême de Turbot Paiwa 18/6	Tortue Claire au Jerez 7/6
Filets de Sole des Fées 18/6	Délice de Sole Sans Nom 19/6
Lobster au Whiskey 35/–	Chateaubriand en Papillotte (for 2) 60/–
Gratin de Homard Mauresque 25/–	Soufflé Glacé au Grand Marnier 7/6

Grills and Roasts

Entrecôte Steak on the Bone Villette (for 2) 45/–   Scotch Porterhouse (for 2) 60/–   Chateaubriand (for 2) 50/–

Fillet of Beef 21/–		Rump Steak 20/–
Entrecôte Steak 21/–	Tournedos 19/6	Entrecôte Minute 20/–
York Gammon Steak 12/6	Lamb Cutlets or Chop 15/6	Pork Chop 15/6
Mixed Grill 17/6	Lamb Kidneys Brochette 13/6	Sweetbreads 18/6
Veal Kidneys 15/6	Veal Cutlet 15/6	Grilled Chicken Americaine (for 2) 30/–

Roast Duck à l'Anglaise or with Oranges, Peaches or Pineapple (for 2) 42/–

Cold Buffet

Ox Tongue 14/6	Veal and Ham Pie 12/6	Steak Tartare 18/6	Eggs in Aspic 8/6
Lobster Mayonnaise 25/–	Norfolk Turkey 16/6		Aylesbury Duck 18/6
Surrey Chicken 15/6	Assiette Anglaise 18/6		Scotch Beef 16/6
York Ham 14/6	Chicken Mayonnaise 15/6		Salade Lorette 6/–
Salade Niçoise 10/6	Half Lobster Salad Mayonnaise 35/–		Chef's Special Salad 15/6

Vegetables

Garden Peas 4/6	French Beans in Butter 5/6	Leaf or Creamed Spinach 4/–
Brussels Sprouts 4/6	Cauliflower au Gratin 4/6	Céleris à la Moëlle 5/6
Creamed Sweetcorn 4/–	Brocoli Mousseline 5/6	Buttered Carrots 4/6
Artichoke Hearts Favorite 10/–	Artichoke Mousseline 10/– Celery Milanaise 5/6	Braised Endives 5/6

Potatoes: Sautées, Lyonnaise, Croquette, Purée, Chips, Paille, Frites, Allumettes 2/6

Sweets

French Pastries	Dame Blanche 5/6	Fruit Salad 5/6
Crème Caramel 5/6	Pineapple Marquise or Marouf 8/6	Crêpes Normande 5/6
Crêpes Georgette 5/6	Crêpe Suzette 9/6	Soufflé Glacé à l'Orange 7/6
Soufflé au Citron 8/6	Soufflé Rothschild 9/6	Soufflé au Grand Marnier 9/6
Orange à la Turque 5/6	Zabaglione al Marsala 8/6	Ice Cream 4/6
Poires Fine Bouche 8/6		Lemon or Tangerine Sorbet 5/–

Savouries

Canapé Diane 4/6	Canapé Westbury 4/6	Canapé Baron 4/6
Pig in Blanket 4/6	Mushrooms 4/6	Welsh Rarebit 4/6
Scotch Woodcock 4/6		Sardines 4/6

Coffee: Continental   American   Hag   Sanka   2/6

6.6

100

The Turf Club
Carlton House Terrace
Sous chef/saucier, February 1967-January 1968
Head chefs: Mons. Habert, Mons. Campanna

Mons. Habert and I both started on the Monday morning with an Indian chef called Chadouri (I think that's how his name was spelt) who was going to be the veg chef. We went in 'blind'. Mons. Habert had organised a menu and placed the orders. We spent most of the day going through the fridges and store room sorting out the crap that the last brigade had left. If the state of the food and general hygiene was anything to go by, no wonder they had been given the big E! I remember that after we had got the lunch service out of the way and got en place for the evening service, we started to clean the kitchen properly with the help of two kitchen porters. We didn't have a break that day but just worked through. The old pigs must have thought all their birthdays had come at once!

After a few days we seemed to be getting the hang of things and were doing well. Already some customers had asked if the club had a new chef! The menus were a mixture of English and French dishes; we had an à la carte that changed about every three months and two menus for lunch and dinner that changed daily. We also had party menus, although the members seemed to like to see the chef and make up their own.

The à la carte consisted of eight cold hors d'oeuvres, five soups, omelettes to order and one other egg dish, four fish, six entrees, six grills, nine cold buffets, ten veg and salads, four sweets, seven different ice-creams and sorbets and three savouries, plus the set menus. These were a choice of five cold, one soup and one egg dish, three different main courses with a choice of vegetables and potatoes, two hot sweets, one cold and a cheese board with coffee, all for the grand price of 15 shillings and sixpence –

about 75p in today's money. Not bad, eh!

The kitchen was situated in the basement and from the larder window you could look up into the street. The store room was outside the larder under the stairs from the street, in what looked like a disused coal hole. On the whole the kitchen was not too bad; we had enough room to work fairly comfortably. 'Charlie' (that was what Chadouri was called) and I had a medium-sized double fridge to use, half each, and the main fridge for the 'overflow'. Charlie was quite well-known in the West End, he was a good chef, one of many that never quite made the 'big' time. The standards, although I say it myself, were high. Mons. Habert used to make all the pâtés, cold game pies, fresh pork brawn (made from pigs' heads – lovely! But it sold quite well.) The chef did the larder, butchery, salads etc, I did the main courses and Charlie did the veg, pastas and egg dishes.

Charlie and Mons. Habert both had a good sense of humour and as I liked a laugh as well, it made the kitchen a friendly place to work in. The two porters (Jock, a Scot, and Billy) both liked a tipple and sometimes they told us they had 'lost weekends'. Still, it made the time pass.

The club restaurant was on the first floor and at the end of the kitchen we had two lifts for sending up the orders. At lunchtimes I used to go up to the small servery kitchen just outside the restaurant and do most of the service from there, as most of the orders were off of the table d'hôte menu. In the evening I worked downstairs as most of the orders were à la carte. It certainly kept you moving!

Most of the other staff lived in and on Bank Holidays and weekends we had to leave a certain amount of food for them in the fridge in the server. Most of the staff were pleasant enough, though there were a couple who thought that, as they'd been there a few years, they were better than the others. Mons. Habert soon put them right.

The club secretary was called 'the Commander'; he was in fact a Lieutenant Commander called Franklin. He was not a bad bloke, didn't really interfere with the running of the kitchen. He used to come down most mornings and have a quick chat with the chef. Some of the chambermaids also popped in now and again to have a chat and a tease, we all got on well. Sometimes my father-in-law would come in after work – he worked for the Government in security and was often stationed at the far end of the terrace in one of the Ministry buildings. He and Mons. Habert were about the same age and shared the same sense of humour, so they got on like a house on fire.

During the summer the Horse Guards Parade takes place, and the Turf Club had a large 'patio' at the back which overlooked the Mall. Every year on this day, they used to lay on a buffet lunch for members so that they could watch the Queen's procession down the Mall after the march past. The Queen Mother's brother, Mr Bowes Lyon, was a member, as was

102

Lord Spencer Churchill. He was as tall as Mr Bowes Lyon was short. The club had quite a few distinguished members from the aristocracy and the racing fraternity. I remember seeing Vera Lynn (now Dame Vera) at one of the lunches. The summer I was there, the 'parade buffet' went off very well. Mons. Habert had put on a traditional cold buffet: decorated hams, joints of beef, whole decorated salmons, supremes jeanettes, minted lamb cutlets, six different salads and about four cold sweets, including fresh strawberries with whipped cream. We received a lot of compliments that day, everyone said that the whole thing was absolutely wonderful! We had a good time as well. This was the only time we had to work on a weekend, as the club, like all the others, only opened Monday to Friday.

While we were there the film The Charge of the Light Brigade was being made and some of the location scenes were shot outside and along the Carlton House Terrace. The road markings were covered over and the people in the buildings were asked not to look out of the windows as it spoilt the shots. We often heard a director using a loud hailer to ask someone to move away from a window! If you ever see the film, look carefully at the outside house shots and now and again you can faintly see someone looking out. Trevor Howard was one of the main stars and while he was just sitting around waiting to his bit, he must have been bored out of his mind, so someone in the club had the brainwave of offering him the club to 'rest' in. Well, someone offered him a drink of club port, and after about two bottles he was just starting to enjoy himself. I think shooting was postponed for the rest of the day and we were told that Trevor had palled up with a few of the members and was standing his round with the best! A good time was had by all that day (except maybe the producer!)

I spent a very enjoyable year at the Club. Business was going very well, we seemed to be doing more customers than when we first started. Then one day after evening service, Mons. Habert was called up to the Commander's office. I don't know exactly what happened, but he was sacked! He had to gather up his stuff and leave. I was then called up to the Commander's office and he explained that Mons. Habert and himself had disagreed about how the kitchen was run and Mons. Habert had been asked to leave. I wasn't very happy about this because if there was a problem with the kitchen, then it reflected on me as well, as I was the sous and helped Mons. Habert to run and keep up standards.

From that day I started to look around for another position.

On the Monday the new chef arrived (quick or what, I thought?), Mons. Campanna, who was Italian or Spanish with a big, droopy bloodhound face. Charlie had already told the Commander bye bye and the guy had got in a small Italian as the veg chef. The first couple of days Mons. Capanna did nothing except sit in his office and receive 'friends'.

I found the guy quite lazy in his attitude to work, and when he did come out of the office to 'work', he was as slow as Mons. Habert was quick – so slow that a snail beat him up the kitchen one day!

All in all, a bit naff!

I'm not sure whether he'd had an accident at one time or what, but Mons. Campanna had no eyebrows, so he used to mark them in with eyeliner! I'm almost sure he also wore make up! (If not, why did he always have a lovely peachy complexion? Cor!) I got out within a month of him arriving!

HORS D'OEUVRES

Smoked Salmon	10/-
Smoked Trout	5/-
Potted Shrimps	4/-
Pate Maison	3/6

Egg Mayonaise	3/6
Melon	3/6
Hors d'Oeuvres	5/-
Prawn Cocktail	5/-

SOUPS

Clear Soup	2/-
Consomme in Jelly	2/-
Turtle Soup	5/-

Pea Soup	2/6
Tomato Soup	2/6

EGG DISHES

Omelettes: (To Order)	5/-

Poached Egg Florentine	5/-

FISH (15 Minutes)

Scampi (To Order)	11/6
Fillet Sole Mornay	11/-

Grilled Sole	12/6
Lobster (when available)	M/P

ENTREES AND ROAST (15 Minutes)

Tournedo Chasseur	14/6
Braised Ham Madere	9/6
Entrecote Bercy	11/6

Roast Duck, Apple Sauce	10/6
Roast Chicken and Bacon	9/6
Roast Best End Lamb (2) (30 Mins.)	17/6

GRILLS (15 Minutes)

Fillet Steak	14/6
Sirloin Steak	12/6
Minute Steak	11/6

Lamb Cutlets	8/6
Mixed Grill	10/6
Kidneys and Bacon	7/-

All Grills with Mushroom and Tomato

COLD BUFFET

Roast Duck	10/6
Roast Chicken	9/6
Roast Game (when available)	
Roast Beef	7/-
Roast Lamb	7/-

Ham	7/-
Tongue	8/-
Steak and Kidney Pie	7/-
Veal and Ham Pie	7/6

VEGETABLES AND SALADS

Grilled Mushrooms	2/6
Garden Peas	2/-
French Beans	2/-
Spinach Leaf	2/-
Braised Celery	2/-

New Potatoes	2/-
Saute Potatoes	2/-
Lettuce Salad	2/6
Mixed Salad	2/-
French Fried	2/-

SWEETS

Meringue and Ice Cream	2/6
Fruit Salad	3/-
Cream Caramel	1/6
Peach Melba	2/6

Ices: Vanilla, Strawberry, Coffee	
Chocolate	1/6
Biscuit Neapolitan	2/-
Sorbet: Lemon, Orange	1/6
Fresh Cream	2/-

CHEESES

Selection	2/-

Stilton	2/6

SAVOURIES (Dinner)

Welsh Rarebit	2/-
Soft Roes	2/-

Mushrooms	2/6

CAFE	1/-

Table Charge—Guests 5/-

SET LUNCHEON

Friday, 10th March 1967

Hors d'Oeuvres : Melon
Smoked Salmon : Potted Shrimps
5/- extra   1/- extra
Paté Maison : Cream of Vegetable Soup
Poached Egg Provencale

. . . .

Poached Salmon, Hollandaise Sauce
Roast Rib of Beef with Yorkshire Pudding
Fricassée of Chicken and Rice
Buttered Cabbage : Carrots Vichy
Rissolees Potatoes : Parsley Potatoes
Baked Jacket Potato

Cold Buffet : Salad

. . . .

Baked Jam Roll
Semolina Pudding and Apricots
Fresh Fruit Salad : Ice Cream
Cheese Selection

Coffee 1/-

Luncheon 15/6d.   Table Charge - Guests 5/-

A LA CARTE
PLAT DU JOUR

Avocado Pear	4/-
" with Prawns	5/6
Coquille of Salmon Mornay	9/6
Roast Duckling Normande	11/6
Plovers Eggs.	4/6

Annabels
Berkeley Square, London
Sauce chef, January-August 1968
Head chef: Don Smith

Next I managed to get a position as saucier at Annabels in Berkeley Square. At this time Annabels had a very good reputation so I was pleased I had got in. The hours were a bit unsociable, from 5 pm to 11.30-ish, depending on business, five days a week. (The restaurant was open from 8 pm until the early hours.) The kitchen was in the basement and consisted of a large-ish room with a passage from the back that led past the larder – a couple of shelves and tables in the passage. Up a flight of stairs was the tiny pastry room, which you passed through to reach the changing room.

The head chef was a guy called Don Smith, who was not too bad. He had to produce daily menus with variety and also keep seasonal 'goodies' on the menu. You know the sort of things – milk-fed lambs, suckling pigs, fresh lobsters, asparagus, caviar, langoustines, salmon, trout etc.

The daily menu consisted of, on average, 19 starters, five different egg dishes, six soups, 13 different fish dishes and 12 meat dishes, not counting the cold buffet. Apart from the sweet trolley there were about seven different sorbets and ice-creams, all made on the premises – quite a lot to sort out on a daily basis. Everything was fresh and came in on a daily basis, and the standards were high: if you needed brandy then you got brandy, not a substitute.

The sous chef was a guy called, I believe, Mr. Bayley, who was a very dapper dresser. He used to do the cold buffet work and the cold starters; his decoration of the dishes were very good indeed. As far as I can recollect he used to come in a bit later than the rest of us and stay on until the place closed, doing the guard, as they say! I would say that Mr. Bayley and the French guy in the pastry were the best blokes for standards in the kitchen.

The larder chef was an Italian called Franco. I had previously met him briefly when he did a few lunches to help out at the Bristol, together with his nephew Carlos who was on the sauce at Annabels. Franco did the butchery and general larder prep, always moaning about the amount of work he had to do – shame! (He later took over from me as head chef at the Hertford Club, but that comes later!) We had a young lad on the veg called Malcolm (am I right?). He was Jewish and told us that one of the English footballers, a bloke called Salmon, was related to him. Wow! I hear you cry. Yes, that's what we thought as well. He was quite good as veggie but was one of those super-confident types, OK in small doses.

Another guy was called Steve Pullman. I remember he always smoked little thin roll ups and seemed to spend most of his time rolling them and putting them in a tin for later. Steve did not really do too much; he was classed as the chef tournant but just seemed to drift around the kitchen doing bits and pieces. He was another super confident guy, and later he and Malcolm went as chef and sous to the newly opened Frederick's Restaurant in Islington. The last I heard of Steve was that he had gone to Oz and was doing well in, I think, Sydney. Malcolm faded away – if not, tell us, Malc!

The pastry guy was French and he turned out minor miracles each day from the small area that was set aside for the pastry. All he had was a three-tier pastry oven, a couple of gas rings and a medium-sized fridge. The pastry was situated in a smallish room that staff were always walking through to get to the changing rooms, but for all this he turned out some lovely sweets.

On the sauce was myself and our Carlos (I heard a little while ago that he was now the head chef at Annabels, well I'll be buggered!) Now our Carlos was a super, super-confident bloke. He really only knew the ways of the club, but you'd think he'd travelled the world to hear him. Don Smith had taught him to do the sauce in his style and Carlos followed it to the letter – very good for Don but not so good when we had special requests from members for dishes that were not on the menu! Then he'd have trouble.

Carlos and I got on fairly well, though we only worked together for about three nights each week, so we didn't have much time to get on each other's nerves. On those days Carlos had a very annoying habit: he wanted to do all the orders and didn't seem to think anyone else could do sauce work, which was a bit frustrating. Every time I had a day off I came back to a virtually empty fridge, as Carlos had used up the mise en place but not bothered to replenish it. As his day off was the day after mine, I was left to build up the mise en place as well as do the service single-handed. I told the chef but it didn't make much difference; Carlos kept using me as the 'mise en place man'. So one night I just did enough to get me through the night. The next evening when Carlos arrived, his face was a picture; he was very upset that I had not topped up all the mise en place for him! 'Now you know how I feel,' I said as he moaned to all and sundry. When he complained to the chef, to his credit Don told him to stop moaning and get on with topping up the supplies.

Most of the waiters were the 'friendly' type (know what I mean?), but they certainly fussed over the members. The disco booth backed onto the front of the kitchen and all the DJs were these lovely mini-skirted females with blonde hair and plummy voices. They were completely enclosed in a sort of bubble, and could be seen but not touched. Many was the time that a young (and not so young) member strolled into the kitchen, casually asking where the entrance to the booth was. They would be politely guided back to the dance floor.

While I was there we did a charity event on a Sunday night and the stars on the cabaret were Ike and Tina Turner. Didn't think much of him but she was a real cracker! That night was an eye-popping night, starting with a fashion show, so we all got the menu ready early so we had time to peek behind the curtain and watch the show. We also got our own private show as the girls got changed, and we got paid for it!

By the time I finished and got changed after work at Annabels, I had missed the last train and had to make my way to the Charing Cross bus stop for the night bus. This used to take me as far as the Pond at Thornton Heath, about a mile from home, so I had to walk the last bit and didn't get in till about 2 am. About the only two really good things about working at Annabels were (a) I got to see the kids for part of the day and (b) the reference. Apart from the sous chef, the kitchen really was not a very happy kitchen; there was no sort of comradeship that I'd found at other places. What with this and the long haul home, it all became a bit of a drag for me, so in the end I called it a day.

During my last few weeks at Annabels I had been doing a little lunchtime job at the Avocado Restaurant and the woman boss offered me the job as chef. As it was for lunch and dinner, I would have to leave Annabels, which was what I wanted anyway. She offered me the same money as I was getting for the two jobs, so I thought: why not give it a try?

Annabel's

Cover Charge 5/-

FRESH ASPARAGUS 25/-
Beluga Caviar 42/- Smoked Salmon 25/- Croute Rothschild 25/-
Lobster Cocktail 21/- Smoked Trout 16/6 Dressed Crab 21/- Truite au Bleu 21
Mousse de Jambon 21/- Caille en Aspic 21/- Smoked Turkey 21/-
Prosciutto di San Daniele 27/6 Avocado 10/6 Fresh Sardines 18/6 Melon 18/6
Caviar Tartare 42/- Crespelle Fiorentine 18/6 Gnocchi Verde 18/6
Croquettes of Lobster 21/-

Oeufs en Cocottes   Oeufs Poches
Portugaise 12/6   Florentine 15/6
Perigourdine 12/6   Nantua 15/6
Oeufs en Gelee 15/6
Beef Tea 9/6 Bisque de Homard 12/6 Turtle Soup 9/6
Vichyssoise 9/6 Scotch Broth 9/6 Petit Marmite 9/6

LOBSTER A L'AMERICAINE (2 CVS) 80/-
Sole Bonne Femme 27/6 Sole Colbert 25/-
Sole Meuniere 24/6 Sole Normande 27/6
River Trout with Almonds 19/6 Haddock Monte Carlo 19/6
Brochette de Fruits de Mer 30/- Lobster Thermidor 40/-
Lobster Newbourg 40/- Quenelles de Langoustines 21/-
FRESH SALMON TROUT

CARRE D'AGNEAU ROTI BOULANGERE 30/-
STEAK DIANE 27/6
ESCALOPE DE VEAU ARCHIDUC 30/-
MEDAILLONS DE BOEUF PERIGOURDINE 30/-
CANETON A L'ORANGES 32/6

Filet 30/- Entrecote 27/6 Minute Steak 23/6 Chateaubriand (2 CVS) 59/-
Rib of Beef (2 CVS) 59/- Lamb Chop 25/- Lamb Cutlets 22/6
STEAK TARTARE

Fresh Fruit
Strawberries, Fruit Salad, Fraises Romanoff

White Coffee Ice, Bitter Chocolate Ice, Biscuit Glacee a l'Oranges
Marmalade Ice, Lime Sorbet, Granita al Caffe
Crepes Vefour

110

Avocado Restaurant
Charlwood Street, London SW1
Single-handed chef, August 1968-February 1969

It was hard work at the Avocado, compiling the menus, ordering supplies, preparing all the dishes, making the starters, main and sweets. I was kept out of mischief, I can tell you! As the restaurant was only a few minutes' walk from the station, I used to go home for a couple of hours each day, see the wife and kids, have a cup of tea and a sandwich, then toddle off back to work, so it was quite good. I had a fairly free hand with the menus, which gave me chance to experiment with various dishes and food stuffs. To reflect the restaurant's name, I created quite a few avocado dishes, both hot and cold.

However, my boss, Miss Butler, was a bundle of nerves. She always knew best and as it was her place, I agreed!

We had a few regulars, but most of the customers were 'off the street'. Our most regular lunchtime customer was 'Steptoe' (Wilfred Bramble). I always expected him to take his teeth out to eat but he never did!. In fact he was a very snappy dresser, always smart in a suit with a rolled up umbrella. He always ate alone, and we used to feel sorry for him. The manageress Pauline used to chat with him and try to get him to laugh as he always seemed so sad.

The boss had another restaurant, the Aubergine, in Westminster and was always comparing our place with the other. This was a bit unfair really, as the Aubergine was a bistro and we were a French-style restaurant, two completely different types. The former was near the main road with offices around, and we were a little bit off the beaten track. Miss Butler did a few adverts to try and get business going and slowly, slowly the customers started creeping in.

Then one day Madam received a phone call from Sammy Lohan's secretary to say that he would be coming in for lunch the next day. Mr Lohan was at that time the restaurant critic for the Evening Standard (Fay Maschler does it now), and he was very well respected(?) Well, she went absolutely to pieces! She started phoning up her friends, offering them a free lunch, just to make sure the place was buzzing when the great man came. I made up a super-duper menu incorporating some of the house specials mixed with some classics, a nice balance I thought.

The day dawned and we served a few free meals to her friends and our

111

few regulars as we awaited the arrival of the 'man', who eventually turned up with his secretary. The first thing everyone noticed was that he was three sheets to the wind! Pauline sat them down and offered them a drink (as if he needed more!), then said she'd like to show him round the restaurant. More like carry, I thought (but I mustn't be catty).

A couple of drinks later Mr Lohan looked at the menu and after great deliberation and conferring with his secretary, Pauline and Miss Butler, he chose – a fillet steak, *well done with chips!* A gourmet indeed!

I went off him straight away, especially as he only ate a quarter of the steak and, after another few drinks, left with his praises ringing from the rafters, telling us to keep an eye out for his column the next day. To be honest we did not think he would even remember where he'd been, let alone what the food was like! Oh yea, we thought!

Next day Madam rushed out and bought the first edition of the Standard. Sure enough, Sammy Lohan had written about the Avocado. We could not believe our eyes. It was a brilliant piece, full of praise for the attentive, friendly service, saying how good the food was, how much thought had been put into creating the house specials and so on. If we hadn't seen his condition the day before, we could have believed him and felt proud. As it was, we felt quite let down; we had done our best but had he really noticed?

Nevertheless, from about midday the phone was melting – it rang so much that Miss Butler just sat next to it and took booking after booking.

Now panic ensued as the boss started frantically phoning round to get in extra girls for the evening and I topped up all the mise en place. I didn't go home that afternoon, just stayed on and built up my service stock. We ended up with a full booking (about 35 covers) from 7 pm, with another wave due in at about 9 – brilliant! The only trouble was, although the restaurant was topped up with staff, the poor old kitchen was left to fend for itself (where have we heard that one before – ring any bells, folks?)

The evening dawned (funny expression that!) and the first wave came at us with a vengeance. A multitude of starters, same with the main courses and only me to do it all: take the checks from the lift, read them, get the starters going, get the mains on, send up the starters, then the mains, plus the various vegetable orders to go with them. Bloody hell, I didn't know whether I was coming or going, it was really a bitch of a night. Customers had to wait a bit because I could not be in six places at once and do eight jobs as well. Most of them understood and were OK about it, as they could see we were really under pressure, but you always get the odd one or two who don't or won't understand and they spoilt the evening for us. Madam got her knickers in such a twist that we thought (or rather hoped) they would strangle her. Come the end of service I was completely knackered. All the mise en place had gone, the fridges were empty, and the only thanks I got from the boss was moans because I could not turn out the orders quickly enough! That really turned me off her.

From that night on business was much better, though obviously the numbers dropped as Sammy Lohan's faithful moved onto his next write-up! But after a few weeks of Miss Butler regurgitating the fateful night and all of us getting uptight because of it, the standards started to suffer. Pauline and the girls lost a bit of interest because whatever they did, the boss was looking over their shoulders, and I was finding it hard to get motivated and create new dishes.

Anyway, one Friday evening after service, Madam called me in to her office and paid me off, just like that (they could in those days). I must admit it was a bit of a relief because I was getting ratty at home with the hassle and frustration at work. So I went on the trail of another position!

While I was trying to sort myself out I was offered a couple of weeks at Chez Solange in the West End by one of the agencies. It was supposed to be a very good restaurant but boy was I surprised! Though it was a French restaurant, all the chefs were Italian and didn't speak much English, so I was a bit buggered from the start. They were all friendly enough, but they seemed very 'clicky' to me, and I could not seem to get into their ways. (French dishes done the Italian way does add some confusion to one's memory for style and garnish.)

The kitchen was on the top floor with the lower three floors as the restaurant. Every night after service, the chefs used to hoist the pig bins out of the back window and lower them into the back alley to be collected by the 'pig man' first thing in the morning. As a porter went down to guide the bins down the last few feet and unhook them, I waited with baited breath for one of them to come off the rope and the contents to fall out and cover the poor porter, or even better, a passer-by. (It never happened, not at least while I was there.) I wonder what the Health and Safety experts would say about this now, and I still wonder how they got away with it then!

The restaurant was supposed to be well-known for good food, but in my humble opinion it was poor. They used fillet steaks, jumbo scampis, mostly fresh veg, but they served them it up in cracked and chipped Le Creuset dishes, sometimes even cooking in them. I was 'brought up' with silver (well, sometimes stainless steel) dishes and I though this method lowered the standards quite a lot. I was used to garnishing the dishes and making sure they looked good, but here was just a case of slap it in a dish, make it hot and serve. Yet the place was always busy so they must have been doing something right, I suppose.

The boss, a well-known French chap, seemed nice enough, never bothered the kitchen, just let them get on with it. When my time was up, he asked if I wanted to stay on but I politely declined. You may be wondering how I could judge a place within such a short time. Well, this was only my personal impression of the place. Maybe it got better (I know the answer you're ready with – yes, 'cos I left!) Anyway, I had been offered a position as sous chef at the famous Overton's Restaurant and I was looking forward to starting there.

.

Overton's Restaurant
St James' Street, London W1
Sous chef, March-June 1969
Head chef: Mons. Lehener

Entering the restaurant of Overton's was like going back 20 years. The room was long and narrow with banqueting seating and a few tables along the middle. As you came in the door, just to the right was a long counter. This was the Oyster Bar. The customers used to sit on bar stools and have their oysters and champagne. The bar was staffed by a couple of guys who had probably been there since the place was built (they weren't that old really, they just looked it). At the far end of the restaurant there was a large smoky glass window/partition through which you could see the hazy figures of the chefs doing their 'thing'. Fancy sending in a near impossible order during a very busy time and watching the chef have an attack! Wicked!

The restaurant was very light and airy, painted in lovely pastel colours. The waiters all wore 'penguins' and the commis wore traditional long white aprons. The restaurant manager was a dapper Italian, very good with the customers, treated them like gods, especially the regulars. 'How are you today, Sir? Your usual drink, Sir? Your usual wine, Sir? The chef has your favourite fish, meat etc in today, Sir!' and so on. The clients were treated better than royalty, which always made a great impact on them. Shame not many places do it nowadays.

I remember there was one regular who came two or three times a week and always sat at the same table (handy, 'cos we could peep though the crack in the service door and see him). He always had a lovely young girl with him; there were three or four different ones. I don't know what his attraction was, as he was short, about 60 and plump, with a white monk's haircut and a flowing moustache. It was either his wallet or he was incredibly sexy! Nowadays the girls would be called 'bimbos' but then they were 'secretaries' or 'daughters'.

At the side of the restaurant there was an alley that led into a small square. This was used, so I was told, for duelling in the days of yore. When two guys had a dispute over something, they would come here to settle it (just a little bit of useless information to bore people with at parties!)

The hours were split, we used to start at 9 am till about 2.30 pm, then return at 5.30 pm till about 11 pm. The restaurant was shut Saturday lunch and all day Sunday, plus all the Bank Holidays. Not bad really once you got into the rhythm.

The kitchen was quite small for the amount of work produced in it: about 30 feet long by 20 wide. In this space we had a medium-sized hotplate, fridges, stoves, grill, salamander, worktops and, of course, us! So it was quite compact and we didn't have far to go to get things. At the back of the kitchen was a flight of stairs going up and down: down was to the store rooms situated in caged off, disused coal cellars (remember coal?); upstairs led to the chef's office, the prep rooms and the wash-up areas for both the kitchen and the restaurant. This room was not much bigger than the kitchen below. In it were two or three pot boilers for cooking crabs, lobsters etc. The wash-ups were staffed by … you've guessed it … Pakistanis! They were a friendly lot who minded their own business and got on with the job. Sometimes as you climbed the stairs the atmosphere took on the appearance of a foggy day back in the middle ages. What with the steam and the fishy smells, I used to think Billingsgate had moved in! The chef's office was on this floor and it turned into a Turkish steam room some days.

The amount of fish we got through in the course of a week was amazing. The chef never ordered by the number or pound (sorry kilo, must keep in touch with Europe, mustn't we?) but by the stone. (By way of explanation is for our younger readers, this is not a lump of rock, but a term for a weight in the good old days.)

The fish and meat was all prepared on the premises. Overton's menu consisted mainly of fish dishes (it was famous as a fish restaurant, and had a sister restaurant in Victoria for many years, which has now been turned into a standard class restaurant – shame!) The hors d'oeuvres were mainly served from the Oyster Bar so the two guys used to stock up before services with whatever they needed from the kitchen. There were 17 types of hors d'oeuvres on offer, together with eight different soups, 26 fish and shellfish dishes, 14 entrees, 15 grills, six cold buffet dishes, 20 specialities, 16 veg, seven potatoes, 14 different sweets and nine savouries. (You don't find these on menus much now, but they used to be popular). The cheeseboard always had at least six different types on it, and the wine list was extensive. So as you can see, we had our work cut out. The only thing I was a bit disappointed about was that some of the soups were powdered and some of the veg was frozen. But when you consider the size of the menu and the amount of room we had to work in, it was understandable.

The chef, Mons. Lehener, was a German who still had quite a strong accent ('ve have vays of making you talk,' sort of thing!) A very nice guy and good at his job, he was very fair and always had time for a joke. If you were under pressure, he'd be there helping – great bloke. He used to like a bet on the gee gees, and always picked out the ones whose names were connected with food or cooking. I remember one was called Asparagus and he made a few bob on that one (though some of the others should have been sent *to* the kitchen, not named *after* it!)

Although I was the sous chef I still had to work mainly on the sauce with the sauce chef, a Hungarian. Though he was quite sturdy, running to fat, I swear that he used to lose thee or four pounds each service. The amount of sweat he let loose would probably have helped Yorkshire Water nowadays. He was very good, confident but good. The other chap was a small Spaniard who did most of the sweets and the veg prep and service. He'd come in a bit later than we did and stay on later to take care of the last orders. He had been at Overton's since, I think, the Magna Carta was signed and knew the place backwards (SSEMAJ TS 'SNOTREVO. Oh no, I've done that one before, never mind!)

Most of the staff there were good for a laugh, though you had the odd one or two that seemed to live in a world of their own. Most of the waiters were ... that's right, Cypriots, with a few Italians thrown in for luck.

Our Spanish guy was a great one for practical jokes, he was always up to something or other. I remember he used to buy plastic spiders and flies and sprinkle them on the staff lunches. His favourite was to flour and breadcrumb fillets of fish, deep fry them, then carefully slit the covering and remove the fish, pipe mashed potato inside and then serve it with chips to some unsuspecting waiter. Sometimes if a waiter was hanging about and getting in the way, he would fill a pot with cold water, turn round quickly and 'accidentally' splash – well, a bit more than a splash – drown the poor bloke. This worked especially well on new waiters; they soon learnt who was boss! Another favourite was to get a palette knife hot, lean over to take a check from a waiter and sort of catch him on the hand with the tip. I can seem them now jumping and cursing. 'Sorry,' you would say with a sweet smile, 'an accident.' If you did it casually enough, they would believe you.

The days when the Spanish guy was off on holiday I used to cover for him and work the late shift. Not bad, but I had to move quick to catch the last train home. It was all right for the Spaniard; he used to bring his

Volkswagen back in the evening, so it didn't matter what time he finished, but poor old me didn't have a car then, so I had to hoof it.

The guys in the Oyster Bar would always come out and tell us of bits of gossip they had just heard, or give the chef red hot tips, 'Can't fail!' they'd cry. The chef knew the horses would not come in, but as he could not take the chance, he had a bet, and sometimes they did pay off.

One day Mons. Habert phoned me and said that a friend of his had a job I might be interested in – head chef at the Mansion House, the Lord Mayor of London's residence, no less! I phoned his friend and, lo and behold, it turned out to be Mons. Cippola, who was now the executive chef at Fortes! He arranged an interview for me with the general manager of Ring and Brymer, the outside caterers.

On the appointed day I turned up at the head office. Three men were sitting behind this huge desk, one of them the general manager and the other two managers. Mons. Cippola introduced me to them in the most glowing terms (I was beginning to think he was talking about someone else!), then the general manager asked me how many salmon I would buy to make cold supreme of salmon with mixed salad for a party of 200. I replied, 'Ten times ten to 12 pounders.' He said 'Fine' and that was that. Mons. Cippola took me outside and made arrangements for me to see him again. A few days later I went up to see him, sorted out the bits and pieces, and we agreed that after I had proved myself in six months, I would get a good rise. Fine by me! Mons. Cippola said that I would get a confirmation letter from him in a couple of days, then we sorted out a starting date.

Mons. Lehener was not very happy when I told him I wanted to leave, but he agreed that it was too good an opportunity to miss. He gave me a very good reference and we parted good friends.

OVERTONS OF ST. JAMES'S

THEATRE DINNERS AND SUPPERS SERVED FROM SIX O'CLOCK UNTIL MIDNIGHT ARE OUR SPECIALITY

Hors d'Oeuvre

Caviar 35s
Foie Gras de Strasbourg 21s
Smoked Salmon 15s 6d
Smoked Trout 9s 6d
Special Hors d'Œuvre 15s 6d
Smoked Eel 10s 6d Pâté Maison 6s
Lobster Cocktail 15s 6d
Crab Cocktail—Prawn Cocktail 9s 6d
Jellied Eels 6s Potted Shrimps 6s
Grapefruit 4s
Jambon de Parme 12s 6d
Fruit Cocktail 3s 6d Melon
Escargots (Doz.) 17s 6d
Avocado Pear 6s 0d with Crab 13s 6d

Soups

Oyster Soup 8s 6d
Turtle Soup, Sherry 6s 6d
Mushroom 4s 6d Vichyssoise 4s 6d
Chicken Consommé 4s 6d Onion 5s
Tomato 4s 6d Minestrone 5s

Fish

Sole
Fried Grilled or Meunière 17s 6d
Colbert 18s 6d
Fried Fillets 17s 6d Mornay 18s 6d
Bonne Femme 18s 6d
Véronique or Walewska 18s 6d
Plaice
Fried or Grilled on the bone 15s 6d
Grilled Fillets 13s 6d
Lobster
Newburg 29s 6d Salad 32s 6d
In the Shell 29s 6d
Cardinal, Thermidor
  or Mornay 27s 6d
Crab
Salad 16s 6d
Dressed (20 mins.) 17s 6d
Turbot
Au Choix 16s 6d

Fresh Salmon
Haddock Monte Carlo 14s 6d
Curried Prawns 17s 6d
Halibut 16s 6d
Moules Marinière 10s 6d
Scallops Varies 14s 6d Whitebait 9s 6d

OYSTERS

	doz	half doz
Overtons Royals	40s	20s
Whitstable	30s	15s

Specialities

Oysters Mornay 16s 6d
Fried Oysters and Bacon 16s 6d
Bisque de Homard 8s 6d
Cannelloni Maria Louis 10s 6d
Coquille de Homard Overtons 27s 6d
Sole Overton 18s 6d
Scampi Alexandre 22s 6d
Scampi Maison 22s 6d
Scampi en Brochette 22s 6d
Turbot en Brochette 17s 6d
Blue Trout 12s 6d
Côte de Boeuf Grillé (2 cvts) 30 mins 40s
Carré d'Agneau 16s 6d
Caneton Rôti 17s 6d
Poulet Rôti 17s 6d
Suprême de Volaille De Vere 18s 6d
Paillard de Veau Overton 18s 6d
Brochette Overtons 16s 6d
Entrecôte Périgourdine 22s 6d
Poussin Grillé 16s
Apple Pie and Cream 5s

To-day's Recommendations

Egg Dishes

Omelettes, etc., au choix 8s 6d
Ravioli or Spaghetti Bolognaise 8s 6d

Entrées

Caneton à l'Orange 17s 6d
Suprême de Volaille
  Ambassadeur 17s 6d
Suprême de Volaille Maryland 17s 6d
Curried Chicken 15s 6d
Escalope de Volaille Holstein 18s 6d
Chicken Vol au Vent 14s 6d
Tournedos Chasseur 25s
Tournedos Rossini 27s 6d
Escalope de Veau Holstein 20s
Escalope de Veau Viennoise 19s
Steak Diane 22s
Ris de Veau Princesse or Madère 18s 6d
Veal Cutlet Sauté 18s 6d

Grills

Steaks
Fillet 27s 6d Tournedos 22s 6d
Rump 18s 6d
Minute 16s 6d Entrecôte 19s 6d
Entrecôte Double 39s
Chateaubriand (2 cvts) 52s 6d
Chops
Loin 16s 6d Veal 18s 6d
Crown 27s
Kidneys and Bacon 12s 6d
Mixed Grill 16s 6d
Lamb Cutlets 12s 6d
Calf's Liver and Bacon 16s 6d
Grilled Gammon 14s

Cold Buffet

Roast Foreribs of Beef 15s 6d
Steak Tartare 22s
Tongue 13s 6d Ham 13s 6d
Wing of Chicken and Ham 15s 6d
Salades Variées

Vegetables

Courgettes 4s
Artichoke 6s Haricots Verts 4s 6d
Spinach 3s 6d Broccoli 3s 6d
Peas 3s 6d Cauliflower 3s 6d
Endives Braisé 3s 6d Fried Onions 3s 6d
Braised Celery 3s 6d Carrots Vichy 3s6d
Brussels Sprouts 3s 6d

Sweet Corn 3s 6d
Grilled Tomatoes 3s 6d
Grilled Mushrooms 5s
Peas à la Française 3s 6d
Potatoes
à la Crème 2s 6d
Sauté or Lyonnaise 2s 6d
Boiled, Croquettes or Fried 2s 6d
Jacket 2s 6d

Sweets

Crêpe Suzette (3 pieces) 12s 6d
Crêpe De Vere 12s 6d
Fresh Fruit Salad with Cream 6s
Fresh Pineapple 6s 6d
Rum Omelette 7s 6d
Lemon or Jam Pancake 5s
Pear Melba 6s 6d Peach Melba 6s 6d
Meringue Glacé 4s 6d
Cream Caramel 4s 6d Cassata 4s 6d
Ice Cream: au choix 3s 6d
Fresh Strawberries and Cream
Compote of Figs 5s 6d

Savouries

Hot buttered Shrimps 6s 6d
Mushrooms on Toast 5s 6d
Sardines on Toast 4s 6d
Welsh Rarebit 4s 6d
Kidneys on Toast 5s 6d
Canapé Diane 5s 6d
Scotch Woodcock 5s 6d
Canapé Overton 5s 6d
Soft Roes on Toast 5s 6d

Cheeses

Camembert, Cheddar or Gruyère 4s
Brie, Wensleydale or Stilton 4s

Fruits

According to Season

Coffee 2s Fresh Cream 1s

Overton's Carafe Wines

(See also Wine List)

	Carafe	½-Carafe	Glass
Pouilly Fuissé	22s	11s 6d	4s 6d
Vin Blanc—			
Oppenheimer	18s 6d	9s 6d	4s 6d
Vin Rosé	18s 6d	9s 6d	4s 6d
Vin Rouge	18s 6d	9s 6d	4s 6d

Our chef will be pleased to prepare any dish you may wish to order

TELEPHONE FOR RESERVATIONS TRA 3774

Cover Charge 3s

Minimum Charge – Lunch 21/- Dinner 27/6

Overtons Restaurant outside Victoria Station is under the same direction and offers similar food

3/69

120

The Mansion House
City of London, E1
Head chef, July 1969-March 1970

I duly received my letter from Mons. Cippola, asking me if I would mind working for the first two weeks at the main depot in Sun Street and then start at the Mansion House. I didn't think much of that idea but I agreed to go anyway. I had to report to the executive chef of Ring and Brymers, a chap called John Witherick, I think – someone out there will know who I mean and will no doubt tell me. He was about 6'1" with gingery hair and a sarcastic manner, but I suppose when you are overseeing a number of outside catering functions every day without too many cock-ups, you can afford to be a bit sarcastic, can't you? Most days they had most of the livery halls in the City of London with a function of some sort, mostly lunches but also receptions and dinners. It made the place buzz.

There were six or seven(?) permanent chefs at Sun Street and they had their own livery hall to look after. If they did not have anything on, then they would be seconded to help out at another 'do'. Not a bad system, the only trouble was that the guys used to think they were better than they really were. Apart from that they seemed OK. Most of them started at 8 am but sometimes they had to be in even earlier, especially if they were 'doing' the races or some other large event. You would see them in the morning in their own little corner of the kitchen, sorting out and packing away whatever was needed for the menu. Each guy was responsible for the ingredients required to do 'the job', and this taught you to really check the menu and decide how you were going to serve it, what garnish you were going to do, what dishes you needed to make it look good etc, because after you had arrived in the back of beyond and found that you had forgotten something, it was too late. Also it was advisable to

121

check that your stuff was put on the right lorry as it was no good having a do in, say, The Leathermaker's Hall in the City and finding out that your stuff had been loaded onto a lorry going to the races. I give the chef his due, he always carried a back-up fridge so that if there was an emergency, they were able to do something about it. Also, the suppliers were very good and you could always get hold of someone to help, not like nowadays, when you have to give 24 hours notice and God help you if you need extra on the day!

At Sun Street they had a Polish (I think) chef who saw to all the sandwiches and canapes that were ordered. He had a fairly large room to himself and you could always see him beavering away, buried under a pile of sliced loaves. This guy was really amazing, he could knock out a couple of hundred rounds of cocktail sandwiches and a few hundred canapes in a flash. It seemed to be his vocation in life.

I went out on a couple of jobs while I was at Sun Street, but I must admit that I was not impressed.

The day I started properly at the Mansion House, the chef who was leaving was supposed to be there to help 'ease me in'. I was told to report at nine and this I did. I was met by the MD and Mons. Cippola, taken to the kitchen and introduced to the chef, the sous chef and Mary and Peter Drury, the Lord Mayor's butler. After Mons. Cippola and the M.D. had left, the chef wrapped up his knives, packed his bag and buggered off. Miserable sod, I thought! Then I found out that he'd just been told he was being relieved and would he stay on for a few days and show me the ropes. Then I understood why he buggered off at the first opportunity.

We had a lunch for 150 that day and I was left high and dry. The sous chef, a young German called Heinz (no, he didn't like baked beans!) was the only other one apart from me, so I said to him, 'You carry on with the style and standards that usually go on here, and I'll help you as we go along'. It took a few days but between me, Heinz, Peter and Mary, we won in the end. The four of us, I think, were a good team who all helped each other, none of this, 'I'm the chef and you're the waiter' stuff. We were all working for the same end, so we just got on with it.

Heinz was a good hard worker. (Towards the end of my stay at the Mansion House, more of which later, Heinz told me he had been offered the position as head chef to Princess Margaret. I wonder if he ever took it.) Peter Drury, who still attends the Lord Mayors, was a nice bloke, very friendly (if you know what I mean!), as were all the other footmen employed by the Lord Mayor. Every time a new Lord Mayor took office all the staff had to renegotiate their salaries and conditions of work with him as well as having new uniforms, usually in the colours of the livery company that the Lord Mayor belonged to. I was told that every Lord Mayor had to foot the bill for wages and the uniforms. Also, during their year of office they were expected to give quite a few private functions of one sort and another. This too they had to pay for, so becoming Lord Mayor is quite expensive.

Peter's job was to ensure the smooth running of the Mansion House, make sure the proper outfits were ready for the Lord Mayor to wear, and ensure that he and the Mayoress knew what was on the day's agenda. Every morning Peter met with the Lord Mayor to discuss the day's affairs. Sometimes the chef would be called up to help with the menus and suggest any ideas for dishes. Most of the large livery hall parties were organised by the managers at Sun Street and the finished menu was passed on to me to do, but in the case of the Lord Mayor's own parties, we used to make them at Mansion House. Sometimes Peter and I would discuss a menu and he would then go away and suggest it to them. At other times we would be called up to their private apartments to be told what they wanted or to go away and think of a special menu. More often that not, they were pleased with our suggestions.

When I joined, the then Lord Mayor was about halfway through his term of office and the reason for the change of chef was that he did not like the other guy's style of cooking. The Lord Mayor was called Sir Charles Trinder (no, not the brother of Tommy!) He was, so I was told, into cargo ships and had a fleet of them doing the Australian run. Sir Charles and the Mayoress were both very pleasant and treated me as an equal, not as a worker. They were quite considerate as well, for instance, if they were going to be late back and we didn't have any functions on that evening, they would ask me to leave a selection of cold meats or fresh cooked and decorated lobster. I used to set the shelled lobster onto a sockle surrounded by various lettuces and garnishes, so that it looked as it is was climbing up the sockle.

Cost was no object as far as the Lord Mayor was concerned; whatever they wanted they got. All their meals were served from solid silver antique dishes with beautiful scrolled edges. The silverware at Mansion House is really out of this world. If you ever get the chance to see this fabulous collection, I recommend you grab it with both hands. Most of it is 200-300 years old. It used to take, I think, three guys two days or more just to clean and polish all the silverware that was laid out for formal livery and other functions. When it was all displayed along the centre of the long tables in the Egyptian Hall, it was really a beautiful sight, with the lights picking out the various decorations and displays.

The chap in charge of the 'cleaning brigade' had been there for 20 years or more. (I think he was in the silver room cleaning as the Mansion House was built around him, but maybe not!) Peter told me to make sure I didn't let the dishes get too hot as they might melt, so I was always careful; I didn't want to face charges of melting down the 'family' silver!

One day when Peter and I were sorting out some dishes for a menu to present to the Lady Mayoress for one of their private parties, Peter told me of a dish he used to serve at his own dinner parties. It consisted of a fresh artichoke fond with pâté maison inside, warmed up, and a freshly poached egg on top masked with Bearnaise sauce and glazed. It sounded nice so we included it in our suggestions and they chose it. We did it individually in the sur plat dishes and called it Oeufs Poches Drury. It turned out very nice. I have used it quite a few times since then, on either a special dinner menu or an à la carte menu, and every time it has gone down well.

The Mansion House kitchen was one of the biggest I have ever come across, it covered nearly all of the basement area and must have been 100 plus feet long by 50 or 60 wide. In a small room at one end of the kitchen was the 'larder': a small walk-in fridge, just enough room for one person at a time, a couple of deep freezers and a medium-sized wooden chopping block. Considering the large amount of food that passed through the kitchen, the storage space was quite tight. Just beyond the larder was the stores room, really just a large cupboard. On one side of the kitchen we had the chef's office and at the far end there was the staff changing room. On the opposite side of the kitchen was the still room, where Mary reigned supreme! She was 40ish with a ruddy 'farmer's wife' complexion and was OK on the whole, though now and again she would get niggly. Mary was spotlessly clean and woe betide you if you left any marks on her tables. She ran her section like the army, everything in its place; you could go in blindfold and run a service without a hitch.

We had a 'divvy' manager who was seconded to the Mansion House. You know the sort: a know-it-all who knows bugger all! He tried to justify his position by interfering with things – a veritable pain in the butt! He and Mary were 'friends' and used to take tea and toast together (nudge, nudge, wink, wink).

In the middle of the kitchen stood a double bank of stoves, three either side, back to back, with a large double deep fryer on one side and a grill on the other with a bain-marie under it. At the far end of the kitchen we had one of the biggest ovens I have ever seen. It was about 7 ft high, 8 ft across and about 4 ft deep. If you took out the shelves you could stand inside quite comfortably, so if you were ever stuck for somewhere to stay it could be turned into quite a good bedsit! Its brother was at Sun Street and both ovens, so I was told, were built especially to roast the barons of beef, huge half sides of beef that were slowly roasted and served cold at the special banquets, mainly in the Guildhall, and carved in front of the guests by a team of chefs.

Next to this oven we had two large steam boilers, used to make the consommes, stocks, soups and sauces. Next to these was a medium-sized steamer, a bit too small for the amount of food we needed to steam at times. This was really brought home on the new Lord Mayor's Day. The traditional menu was home-made steak and kidney pudding with vegetables and boiled potatoes for 900! We had made up all these puddings over two days and had to start cooking the first batch at about seven that morning. When they were ready they were put into the large ovens in a bain marie on a low light, as we steamed tray after tray. There were two sittings, one at 11 am for 450 and the second at about 12.30 pm for the other 450. We had started work at six that morning and eventually finished about 5 pm, completely knackered!

We had to be available weekends. Though most of the time the Lord Mayors went home, we still had to cater for the live-in staff. Sometimes we'd leave cold meat and salads for their evening meal or steaks and cooked veg. Sometimes the Lord Mayors had to attend functions on Saturdays, either lunch or dinner, occasionally both. We would then be expected to provide the appropriate meals for them. The Trinders were quite considerate, most times they would just order cold meat or fish with a selection of salads so that we did not have to hang around waiting for them. We could leave it 'dressed up' in the fridge and Peter would take it out and serve them. The Bowaters were not quite so considerate. Quite often on a Saturday or Sunday evening they would order, say, grilled Dover sole with hot vegetables for two at about 7 pm, so whoever was on had to hang around all day to serve two people – a bit grating after a heavy week's work. The rule was that when Heinz was on he was paid overtime but when I was on, as I was the chef, I didn't get overtime; so over the year he was about ten per cent up on my wages.

The security guys were employed by Securicor, I think, and not by the City Corporation. A bit strange that, I thought, but never mind, eh! They did a good job as far as we were concerned, phoning to tell us when someone was on the way down, giving us time to get ready for the 'surprise' arrival. We used to look after them, give them tea, coffee, sugar and biscuits, and they were always included in the staff meals. Little things like this made for a good security system and they didn't mind helping us out at times when a delivery was left at the door; they would get a trolley and pop it into us, very handy, especially if we were busy. Occasionally when I was on over a weekend, my wife and kids would pop in to visit and the guys often gave them a guided tour of the house. Once, when a party was being shown around the vaults, they took my family on a personal tour.

I remember one particular accident that happened at the Mansion House. The security guys used to light up one side of the ovens for us so that when we came in we could get straight on with cooking the breakfasts. Well, this morning the oven failed to light properly and when I took the top off and went to light it with a taper, there was a big *whoomp*! The stove tops flew about three inches into the air; I lost my eyebrows and about six pounds in weight. The problem was that the chap had not checked to see if the pilot had lit properly. He had turned the oven regulator up and gone on his happy way. It was a near miss indeed!

Although I say so myself, we were always on the ball with the parties. All except one, that is. The managers at Sun Street had a bad habit of phoning you up and telling you of changes in numbers or dishes and not following it up in writing. Anyway, this particular week we were really steaming: lunch for 200 followed by a dinner for 300 on the same day, plus a couple of private Lord Mayor's parties – a wicked week! A couple of days before this particular party the manager had phoned up to say that it had gone up by 50. Normally I made a note of any changes straight away but, being under pressure, I said OK without jotting it down. Well, come the evening of this party we had got the menu sorted, portioned up and ready to go when all these extra chefs started to arrive. 'Why so many casuals?' I asked of the executive chef. 'Because the numbers have gone up,' he said. Shit! I remembered. And this was only a couple of hours before the dinner was due to sit! The starter was a soup, which was no problem; we could stretch that. The next course was, I remember, a supreme of turbot with a sauce – and I was 50 portions short! I was on the verge of having a baby, and it really screwed up my confidence, I can tell you! Anyway, the executive chef made a call to the fishmonger and managed to get him to deliver the fish. We shot over to the main kitchen at Sun Street and managed to raid the 'spare' fridge and sort out the rest of the dishes, so saving the day.

From then on, I insisted that they put everything in writing and I always double-checked the menu, numbers and times the day before. This kind of disaster never happened again, I'm pleased to say!

The worst thing that happened while I was at the Mansion House (yes, worse than being 50 meals short!) was the time that a dinner was being given in honour of Andre Simon, a well-known food and drink gourmet. He'd written books and books on the subjects. It was Sun Street's 'do' and I was told to keep out! Fine by me, so I caught up with my bookwork. Later in the day the food started to arrive, together with the Sun Street boys, I looked at the starter, which was meant to be a salmon mousse, to be served hot with a light creamy sauce. It was, as the Japanese would say, 'rubbery', but I was told it would turn out light when it was warmed up (they had cooked it earlier). The evening was screwed up because this 'bouncing mousse' was still rubbery after warming and, to make things worse, Mons. Simon refused to eat it! This made me feel a bit better about my cock-up. Wicked, I know, but at least my food was edible!

Working at the Mansion House was hard but it was an experience I was glad I didn't miss. I still have quite a few of the menus from my time there, plus a book in which I kept all the details of the amounts I ordered for each party – interesting to look back on. I also recorded numbers of guests, the menus, different wines with each course. I could probably write another book just on the menus I have worked on and the special dishes I have created over the years.

One of the 'divvy' managers, a guy called Brown (or something like it) used to hassle me from Sun Street, together with the other guy (Mary's 'friend'). These two were responsible for the standards, general hygiene and smooth running of the services at the Mansion House. Well, Mr Brown was a right pain in the arse! He used to send me letters with the function sheets telling me in detail how to make, say, an apple and blackberry pie, what I should put into a sauce chasseur, the exact weight of a slice of cold beef, how long a veal escalope should be and so on. I got so cheesed off that I asked him if he thought I was stupid or what? ('What!' I hear you cry!) He replied that as he was responsible for the service and for whatever happened, it was his business to make sure the dishes were served correctly. Cheeky bugger, I said, what a load of crap!

This guy admitted that he had to look in the repertoires to find out what the dishes were. When I created a special dish for the Lord Mayor he would wander about making out that he knew what the dish was and generally being a bighead! Once we had sussed him out, I used to get a medieval dish from an old book and casually ask him to get me the recipe as the Lord Mayor had asked for it. Or I would think up a name for a dish and send him off in search of the recipe. Sometimes he would succeed in finding it; then we would tell him that the Lord Mayor had changed his mind and wanted the other dish. This kept him occupied and out of our hair for a while.

The other thing that nearly drove me up the wall was the time when Lady Bowater wanted a lemon mousse for one of her private parties. 'No problem,' I said, but then the rub was put in. 'Can you make a sample of your mousse and we'll have it for supper.' Well, the first one wasn't quite right, nor the second or third. In the end I got paranoid and started phoning friends for their recipes and looking in countless books. Mons. Habert gave me about three different methods but all to no avail. Finally, as the world was running out of lemons, Lady Bowater said, 'Here, try this recipe, we use it at the Waterside Inn' (they owned the place at this time). So I followed it to the letter (or should that be lemon!), let it set and presented it to her. 'Lovely,' she said, 'we'll have this one for our party.' I could have cheerfully strangled her, but she was obviously trying me out. I must admit her recipe was good and I have used it quite a few times over the years.

Heinz and I had worked out a system for serving banquets at the

Mansion House. We would get all the dishes prepped up, the soup or starter ready with any garnishes, the meat trayed up, seasoned and ready to cook, the bouquetiers of veg blanched, seasoned, buttered and ready in the dishes, so that when the casuals came in to help, we would just supervise. This made it easier for us to keep tabs on what was going on, and we used to split the menu between us. One particular evening we had roast fillet of beef as the main course, the fillets had been counted, seasoned and buttered ready to cook. The casuals duly arrived, got changed and I assembled them to go through the menu and how we were going to serve it, numbers, who was doing what etc. Suddenly we noticed that a whole fillet was missing. The guys all suggested that we had miscounted, but I was sure of the number of fillets we'd had to start with and that there was one missing. So I told the casuals that I was going for a smoke (I did in those days) and when I came back I wanted to see the fillet back! If not, I would ask security to search everyone. Off I went to the office, shut the door and had my fag. When I returned, lo and behold our fillet had come home! The annoying part is that after each party the lads were given the chance to get something before it was 'shot' or put away, so this was just greed.

All of the City livery clubs used to have their main function at the Mansion House. It was, I think, a tradition and more often than not they had fresh turtle soup as the starter or soup course, which they ordered direct from Lusty's, giving about three days' notice to the company. The soup arrived in large steel containers on the morning of the function; we just took off the lids, boiled the soup up in the containers then sealed them up again and sent them upstairs for serving straight from the containers into the soup tureens.

Every year the Lord Mayor threw a party for deprived youngsters so on that day there would be something like 300 kids roaming the place noshing on chocolate biscuits and guzzling soft drinks, while being entertained by various children's entertainers.

The highlight of the year for the staff occurred when the Lord Mayor was near the end of his office and gave a staff party as a thank you for all the work the staff had done to make his year pleasant. All the staff were allowed to bring their families for the day, and we laid on a big cold buffet. The kitchen had to pay a little towards the cost. I still have the photos of my wife and me being presented to the Lord and Lady Mayor, and another photo of my in-laws being presented. It was all done in the time-honoured tradition. Everyone queued up and as your name was called out, you walked into the room and shook hands with the Mayor and Mayoress, something to remember. After the meal we had some speeches and then the party started, with a live band and everything. Everyone seemed to enjoy themselves.

The bit all my family remembers was when, after the meal and speeches, I took them downstairs to show them around the kitchen. While we were there a couple of the ladies wanted to go to the toilet, but the part where we were only had a gents. So as we fellows kept lookout and casually whistled, the ladies went in and did their thing. My father-in-law, bless him, was something of a joker and while the ladies were in the cubicles, he turned out the lights and made out he was a security guard checking that no strangers were about. I have never heard women be so quiet! It still comes up in the reminiscences.

During the August period, things tended to be a bit quiet as the Lord Mayor traditionally had the month off. We still had to go in and see to the staff feeding and do the occasional party, but it was a fairly good month for us, gave us a bit of a breather.

When I had first started at the Mansion House, I'd made an agreement with Mons. Cippola that after six months, if all was going well, I would get a good rise. Unfortunately, just before the time was up, Mons. Cippola left to go back to France to run the family hotel. After a couple of extra months, just to give the new guy time to settle in, I approached both our 'friends' and told them of the agreement. Would they see whoever was in charge about it, or ask them to come and see me? After a few weeks and no reply, I reminded them again. 'Oh yes,' they said. A few more weeks went by; still no news. In the end I collared one of the main bosses at Rings. 'Oh yes,' he said, 'I'll see about it.' Great, I thought, action at last!

I should have known better. Another couple of weeks passed with no news. Nobody knew anything. I got so cheesed off, I decided to leave, as I felt I was being given the run around. It rankled a bit; although I was in charge, with all the responsibility, because of the amount of hours we had to work, Heinz was making much more than I was in overtime. I was on basic money no matter how many hours I worked – not fair, I thought.

Anyway, I managed to get a position as sous chef at the Piccadilly Hotel under Mons. Martin, so I duly gave my month's notice. This apparently caused a bit of a stir as the Lord Mayor liked what I had been doing and was not happy about my leaving. I asked Peter to explain the reason. A few days later the bosses had the 'pleasure' of offering me a rise – a couple of quid a week! The cheeky buggers – I was going to earn more as a sous! It just showed how much they cared for their staff! I asked Peter if it would be possible for me to get a reference from the Lord Mayor, as I knew that if and when the Ring managers got around to writing one, I would probably be collecting my old age pension! Peter said he thought it was doubtful as they did not usually do that sort of thing, so imagine my surprise when their Lordships agreed! Although they did not normally give references to people not under their direct employ, as the Lord Mayor was happy with my work, he said he would get one drawn up. Very grateful I was too.

I had enjoyed my stint at the Mansion House, even though the work was hard and the hours long. The staff there were all friendly and I would really miss the place, but I had to go out and earn as much as I could for my family.

The day I was to leave, the Lord Mayor called me up to his chambers and wished me luck, which I thought was nice – it was more than Rings did! Peter and I had a couple of drinks with Heinz and Mary, and I left on good terms. I always look out for Peter every time we see pictures of the banquets that the Lord Mayor attends, to see if he is standing behind his Lordship's chair.

THE
WORSHIPFUL COMPANY OF BAKERS

ELECTION DINNER

AT

THE MANSION HOUSE

*(By courtesy of The Rt. Hon. The Lord Mayor
Lt.-Col. Sir Ian F. Bowater, D.S.O., T.D.)*

MONDAY, 24th NOVEMBER, 1969

THE MANSION HOUSE

The Master, Wardens and Court of Assistants of the Worshipful Company of Bakers express their grateful appreciation to The Rt. Hon. The Lord Mayor for the privilege of holding this dinner at the Mansion House.

The Mansion House is not only the official residence and home of the Lord Mayor. It is the focal point of all that pertains to the personality and office of the greatest municipality in the world. It is often the source of great national appeals. Included within its walls are a Court of Justice and a Prison.

It was completed in the year 1753 to the basic design of George Dance, the then City Surveyor, who in turn based his plans on the ...ks of Palladio, the 16th century Italian architect. Following ... Dance constructed the Mansion House with an ... This courtyard was later roofed in ... ...d lovely

Wines

Alsatian
Traminer Baumann-Schober, 1966

*

Claret
Chateau La Tour
Canon 1962

*

Port
Croft Commemoration
(Vintage Character)

*

Brandy
Sauvion Grand Fine
V.S.O.P.

At the conclusion of the Dinner, Grace will be sung,
'For these and all Thy mercies'
This will be followed by
The Loving Cup

Orchestral Music by
THE WALBROOK ORCHESTRA
under the direction of Herbert Lovick

Menu

*

Kaspin

*

River Trout Bourguignonne

*

Saddle of Mutton
Mint Sauce
Redcurrant Jelly
Roast Potatoes
Baby Carrots
and
Garden Peas

*

Deep Apple and Blackberry Pie
Devonshire Cream

*

Coffee
Turkish Delight

THE QUEEN

*

QUEEN ELIZABETH THE QUEEN MOTHER
THE PRINCE PHILIP, DUKE OF EDINBURGH
THE PRINCE OF WALES
and the other MEMBERS of the ROYAL FAMILY

*

The Rt. Hon. THE LORD MAYOR
and the CORPORATION OF LONDON
and the SHERIFFS

Proposed by . . . . Mr. Deputy Ernest A. Parker (Assistant)
Response by . . . . THE RT. HON. THE LORD MAYOR
Lt.-Col. Sir Ian F. Bowater, D.S.O., T.D.

*

THE GUESTS

Proposed by . . . . Mr. Deputy Percy T. Lovely (Assistant)
Response by . . . . Sir Glyn Jones, G.C.M.G., M.B.E.
(formerly Governor-General of Malawi)

*

THE WORSHIPFUL COMPANY OF BAKERS
root and branch may it flourish for ever
coupled with the name of THE MASTER

Proposed by . . . . Maj.-General The Rt. Hon Viscount Monckton of
Brenchley, C.B., O.B.E., M.C.
Response by . . . . The Master
Mr. Frank Hirtes

After the conclusion of his speech, the Master will invest the Master Elect
with the Master's Badge, and the new Master will invest his Wardens.

Piccadilly Hotel
Piccadilly, London W1
Sous chef, April 1970-January 1971
Head Chef: Mons. Martin

The Piccadilly Hotel was an amazing building and I suppose it still is. It had a maze of small banqueting suites, a large Versailles-style restaurant and a number of 'Lodge' rooms hidden in its bowels. I was only shown the doors of these rooms as we were not allowed in. Apparently in the old days, most of the West End Lodges used the hotel for their meetings and lunches or dinners, but during the time I was there I don't remember ever doing one. At this time the hotel was more or less at the end of its hey day and, due to lack of investment, the general appearance and service were declining.

The hotel basement was a rabbit warren of corridors, very spooky at times. I remember that the stores office was at the end of a long, narrow, badly-lit corridor. You had to knock on the door and, like something out of a horror movie, you waited with baited breath for the 'man' to open up and serve you. If you were a Hammer House of Horror fan, you would have loved working there!

The main kitchen was behind the restaurant, but on the floor above were the remnants of a large kitchen which, I was told, was the old banqueting kitchen. It was quite long with fridges all along one side. A couple were still in use, one as a deep freezer, the other as a general equipment store. Also up here the chef had his office. Until shortly before I arrived, the chef had a secretary but due to cutbacks (where have we heard this before?), they had to let her go.

Mons. Martin, the head chef, was in the mould of the great chefs, and what he said was law! Every week he would, without fail, go up to the offices and have a go about the stock sheet costings and percentage figures, as the office wallahs couldn't seem to add up properly. When he was in a good mood he was brilliant, when he wasn't (he was a ginger top), then watch out! He nearly always managed to reach the right percentage each week. When he went on holiday I took over the main running of the kitchen, the ordering, bookwork, timesheets etc, but I always had trouble getting near the required figure. Then he explained to me. In the freezer he had about 20 pounds of veal bones and trimmings 'salted' away, so that when the stock looked down, he'd include the veal and when it was OK, he'd forget the veal. Nowadays they call this 'hidden assets'.

The first sous was an English chap called George who had been here umpteen years, part of the building, I was told. He wasn't bad, a little lax but he was on a 'wind down', so things were all OK unless there was a complaint. He was very brash and a little bombastic but if you didn't take him to heart he was OK. George didn't want to know about bookwork or the organising of the menus and orders, he was happy just sorting out the staff and services, hence the reason why I used to do the orders etc when the chef wasn't in.

The breakfast section was run by two chefs, one was an old-stager, 50-ish, slim and always neatly dressed. He never seemed to rush around, but the work was always ready. He'd done 'the rounds' and now he too was on a 'wind down'. The other guy was black, and he too was always nattily dressed. He was not quite so on the ball, but still turned out the goods on time. On the days when one of them was off, one of the commis used to come on and cover, and the sous on duty used to help out by doing the staff lunch if they were busy.

In the larder, Jim was king. He was about 60 then, a Newcastle man who had arrived in London with the Jarrow marchers, found a job at the Piccadilly and stayed there ever since. Jim knew the business backwards, inside out and upside down. He could tell you to within two portions, how many of such and such a dish would be sold: amazing! The first few weeks when I was checking the various orders (each section filled in their own order sheet for the next day), I would ask Jim, 'Is four pounds of fillet sole enough for the table d'hôte?' 'Yes,' he'd say, 'and you'll have some over.' Well, he was right 98 times out of 100, and in the end I just accepted whatever he ordered as sufficient.

Also in the larder was a large, rounded Egyptian who was the second larder. He was very confident except when he made a mistake; then it was someone else's fault. (I know, you've met him as well!)

I'll always remember the day that I came for my interview with Mons. Martin. I was waiting by the hotplate to go up to his office when this guy came over and asked if I wanted to see the chef. 'Yes,' I said. 'What job are you after,' he said, 'commis?' 'No, not quite,' I said. He was very surprised when I started as sous. (I didn't think I looked that young!)

On the other side of the stove we had the sauce and fish section (combined) and the veg. On the veg there was a German called Charlie. He was very quiet for a German, timid even! No matter how much work we had, Charlie was always ready with the orders, no rush, no fuss. He had been there about ten years and always knew how much mise en place was needed. Charlie was always polite and friendly. He had a sense of humour too, but didn't often show it.

On the sauce there was Ala – he was Maltese or Italian, I'm not too sure, but he was the spitting image of Mussolini – and acted like him! If you asked him anything he would sort of spit out the answer – not a very friendly bloke. I think that if he could have got away with whipping the waiters, he would have done so. His favourite trick was to give an unsuspecting waiter a red-hot plate, passing it over with his hand. The waiter, seeing him holding the plate, naturally assumed it was not too hot and took hold of it – with agonizing results. Ala used to leave just a corner of the dish cold and get the rest red hot, so the waiter's hand sizzled into a red mess. He would smile (like a crocodile) and wait for a comment. Despite that, he was a hard worker and a good chef.

Coming out from the kitchen proper you came to the pastry on one side and the still room on the other. In the pastry there was an English guy in his mid-50s who was very good. Some of the dishes he turned out were really effective. He was helped by a young Irish lad who was quite good. (When he went home to Ireland on holiday, he brought me back my first taste of poteen – not much taste but potent! 'Home-made,' he said with pride. 'Do they live long in your family?' I enquired gasping for air.)

In the still room we had this lady called Mary or Margie. Now I like my cup of tea and it was not long before we had a routine. As I arrived I made a point of saying good morning to her, so that by the time I had changed and got into the kitchen, she had a pot ready for me. Lovely lady!

Then we had Pepe, yes that's right he was a Spaniard! He used to be a sort of commis/chef tournant and was good on all the sections. I heard later that he was the manager of some company in charge of all the catering. I wonder if you are still around or if you have gone back home, Pepe? Please tell.

There were about three commis flitting around during this time, but I cannot remember much about them all. The two I do remember are the Irish lads, sent over from the Sun Hotel Group on a release scheme. They looked like they had been digging ditches all night, and didn't seem to have much interest in cooking or work in general. They treated the scheme as a holiday, always going out and getting drunk and coming in late with some tale or other. How they ever got on back home I will never know (or is someone about to tell me?)

A short while before I left we had this young ginger lad start as an apprentice. He was very keen, quite good and always took care to be presentable. He got on with everyone; even Ala seemed to like him! It was quite a few years later when, as I was sipping a pre-dinner drink at a council gathering, this middle-aged, sorry, youngish guy came up and introduced himself as the apprentice. It didn't register with me until he had gone away exactly who he was, so if you read this, my apologies for not recognising you then, but you had changed a bit.

There was one bloke at the Piccadilly who I never knew how he kept his job or indeed how he ever got his job. This was one of the porters. He had a dummy leg and he walked with a sort of jerky movement. As he was tipsy most of the time, it was difficult to know when he was sober or not, as he always staggered. He used to be in charge of the lift, getting the goods upstairs or fetching the stores orders and generally mooching around. I was told that the chef let him look after the dirty oil and that he made a bit of his 'liquid' money by this method.

The restaurant was looked after by a pleasant middle-aged Italian cockney, who knew his job having done the 'rounds'. We weren't all that busy in the restaurant; we dealt mainly with tours, mostly Japanese or Germans. They would have set menus so it was like banqueting work with a few à la carte customers thrown in for luck. The restaurant was called the Versailles and was decorated out in the French Louis XIV style. It was a lovely big, high-ceilinged room that made you feel quite lost in it.

The menu was a fair size, still in the required French with a choice of nine starters, the hors d'oeuvres trolley with 20-plus dishes to choose from, six different soups, two pasta, 12 fish and of course, the homard au choix. There were also four specialities, eight different grills, six cold dishes, a large assortment of vegetables, a fairly extensive sweet trolley with five other sweets to choose from, plus of course the cheeseboard. All these dishes were in addition to any party dishes, and we were often pleased to see home-time come along. George and I used to do straight shifts, as did most of the guys, though some did splits.

I enjoyed my time at the Piccadilly. As I was kept going all the time, it was good for me, stopped me nodding off (not really). George was a bit of a funny bugger, never seemed to want to co-operate, wouldn't change a shift over if you wanted to go somewhere. He was a strict 'black is black and white is white' sort, though he could be cheerful at times. I'm not sure whether it was sour grapes or what with him.

George was really the reason that I left the Piccadilly. It all started about September 1970 while we were sorting out the Christmas rotas. I suggested to George that, instead of us both working on Christmas and Boxing Days, how about we each did one long day and then the other could have a day off. 'Better see the chef,' said George, so off I went and put the suggestion to the chef, who seemed happy about it. As long as the shifts were covered with a sous chef it was OK by him. I was quite pleased because it meant I would have at least one day with my wife and family over Christmas. I could put up with working one day, but I thought two days was a bit much.

Anyway, with a bit of humming and hawing, George agreed to do all day Christmas Day and I would do all day Boxing Day. Brilliant, I thought, as I reckon Christmas Day is the best for family, especially if you had children. So that was that. We put the finishing touches to the staff rotas and made sure everyone was happy with their shifts. (I always liked to make sure people were happy with their shifts, especially over a Bank Holiday, as that way you were sure they would turn up and not suddenly go sick with some mysterious disease that's gone in 24 hours. I'm surprised the modern scientist has not been able to identify this particular germ yet!)

About two weeks before Christmas, George had a change of heart. He wanted to go back to the old system of me on early Christmas Day and him on late, then him on early Boxing Day and me on late. I was really peed off about this, as it screwed up all my family arrangements completely. I went up and saw the chef, hoping for a bit of support, but he was not very interested; his only concern was to have the shifts covered. 'You have to expect this' he told me. 'Like hell,' I thought (I have always been a 'family first, job second' man; it's the only way to keep your marriage together). So, very reluctantly, I gave in my notice. If you have to work with pigheaded people, it makes the job that much harder and therefore less enjoyable. The chef was not very happy about it and didn't speak to me much during my notice time. A bit daft really, I thought, as he knew who the problem was.

It was during my last few months at the hotel that the great Euro debate was boiling along. One day we were called to a meeting in one of the rooms and told that soon the old money would be no more. We were then given a selection of the new coins to look at, told about their value, how they would be brought in and so on. Bloody awful, I thought (and still do!) We were also told about the new weights and measures that were coming in (even now I still count in pounds and ounces, feet and inches, why did we have to change? Does anyone have a proper answer to this question?)

The day came for me to leave. All the lads wished me luck, George managed to say he was sorry to see me go, the old man said I did not have enough interest in the job and would not go far! Balls, I thought, if you had been a bit more understanding, then I would probably still be here.

The Versaille

The Versailles

Bon Appetit

Hors d'Oeuvres Riches 10/- (50p)
Selection d'oeuvres medley
Avocat Marie Rose 11/- (55p)
Avocado pear with prawns
Saumon Fumé d'Ecosse 16/- (80p)
Wild smoked salmon
Jambon de Parme et Melon 15/- (75p)
Parma ham and melon
Oeufs Brouillés aux Pointes d'Asperges
10/- (50p)
Scrambled eggs with asparagus tips
Truite Fumée au Raifort 14/- (70p)
Smoked trout, horseradish sauce
Terrine du Chef 8/- (40p)
Chef's special pâté
Tranche de Melon Rafraîchi 7/- (35p)
Fresh cool yellow melon
Omelettes à Votre Choix from 10/- (50p)
Made to your request

Les Choix des Courtisans

Crème de Volaille, Asperges ou
Tomates 5/- (25p)
Cream of chicken, asparagus or tomato soup
Crème Vichyssoise Chaude
ou Froide 6/- (30p)
Cream of vegetable with chives, served hot or cold
Tortue Claire au Xérès 8/- (40p)
Clear turtle with sherry
Consommé Madrilène 4/- (20p)
Cold soup with tomato
Ravioli 10/- (50p)
Spaghetti Bolognaise 10/- (50p)

Les Fruits de Mer

Scampi Provençale,
Meunière, ou Frit 21/- (£1.05)
Scampi, French style, fried in butter or deep fried
Sole de Douvres Grillée
ou Frite 21/- (£1.05)
Dover sole grilled or fried
Truite de Rivière, Meunière ou
Grillée 15/- (75p)
River trout in butter or grilled
Saumon d'Ecosse Frais, Poché ou Grillé
Fresh Scotch salmon, poached or grilled - when available
Turbot Grillé, Sauce Béarnaise, ou
Poché, Sauce Hollandaise 18/- (90p)
Grilled or poached turbot
Homard à Votre Choix from 10/- (50p)
Lobster, any style - when available

Specialitées

Escalope de Veau Eros 25/- (£1.25)
Veal escalope, lightly fried with ham and gruyère cheese, served oven-creamed wild mushrooms
Poulet sous Cloche Traiteur 25/- (£1.25)
Rolled breast of chicken filled with fois gras and truffles, cherry cream sauce and asparagus
Sole de Douvres au Vermouth 25/- (£1.25)
Whole sole simmered in vermouth with cream and Parmesan cheese
Pilaw de Rognons au Marsala 22/- (£1.10)
Kidneys flavoured with marsala presented in a border of savoury rice and button mushrooms

La Rôtisserie Royale

Rump Steak 21/- (£1.05)
Entrecôte Steak 21/- (£1.05)
Fillet Steak 23/- (£1.15)
Mixed Grill 20/- (£1.00)
Lamb Cutlets 15/- (75p)
Poulet Rôti - 2 persons
(30 mins) 35/- (£1.75)
Roast Chicken
Caneton Rôti à l'Anglaise -
3 persons (45 mins) 45/- (£2.25)
Roast Duckling

Le Buffet Froid a l'Ancienne

Aile de Poulet et Jambon de York 17/- (85p)
Chicken wing and York ham
Langue Ecarlate 15/- (75p)
Ox tongue
Jambon de York 15/- (75p)
Agneau Rôti 15/- (75p)
Roast lamb
Contrefilet de Boeuf 15/- (75p)
Roast sirloin of beef
Veal and Ham Pie 12/- (60p)

Les Délices du Jardin

Choux de Bruxelles 4/- (20p)
Brussels sprouts
Haricots Verts Frais 5/- (25p)
French beans
Epinards Sautés au Beurre, ou à la
Crème 4/- (20p)
Leaf spinach with butter, or creamed
Chou-Fleur au Beurre 4/- (20p)
Buttered cauliflower
Pommes à Votre Choix 3/- (15p)
Potatoes - as you like them
Céleri Braisé au Jus 4/- (20p)
Braised celery
Petits Pois au Beurre 4/- (20p)
Buttered garden peas
Pointes de Brocoli au Beurre 5/- (25p)
Buttered broccoli spears
Salades de Saison - Romain,
Cole Slaw, Orange, Sweet Corn, etc.
5/- (25p)

Les Faveurs de Madame de Maintenon

Sélection de Pâtisseries 5/- (25p)
A variety of sweets and pastries, from our trolley
Pêche Melba 6/- (30p)
Coupe Alexandra 6/- (30p)
Fruit salad, strawberry and vanilla ice cream
Glaces Assorties 4/- (20p)
Various ice creams
Cassata Napolitaine 5/- (25p)
Cassata ice cream
Fruits de Saison
Fresh fruit in season
Le Plateau de Fromage Assortis 4/- (20p)
Carefully chosen selection of English and Continental cheeses

Café d'Europe

Café Cona 3/- (15p)
Café d'Ecosse 7/- (35p)
with Scotch whisky
Café Bon Soleil 8/- (40p)
with Cognac
Café de The Verte 7/- (35p)
with Irish whiskey

Couvert 3/- (15p)
Cover charge

139

Jewish Old People's Home
Golders Green (where else?)
Single-handed chef, January-June 1971

I cannot recall how I got this job (funny, ain't it) but anyway, I started with Alf Bornstein for two weeks at his other place in Bishops Avenue (money!) Alf had the contract to supply the catering for the Bishops Avenue home and he had also been given the contract for the Golders Green home, but I had to work at this place until the handover.

It was obviously all Jewish cooking and as I had already had an insight into this by way of the Cafe Royal, it wasn't too bad freshening up. Alf employed a live-in girl who used to get up early and start the breakfast, make the coffee, lay out the cereals etc. Then I would do the lunch and afternoon teas and end with the supper. It was a longish day but not bad, and the wages were good, a bit more than the Piccadilly (though it cost me a bit more in fares, so it worked out about the same in the end). Alf got all the food stuff – fresh veg and meat, fish, bread and all the dry goods – and I used to cook and serve it.

The weekend prior to Alf taking over at Golders Green, he took me to meet the matron of the home and the two live-in staff he had inherited. They were housemaids/kitchen hands, and one was petite and pregnant, so she had already been given her marching orders. The other was a largish sort, a bit butch I thought. The pregnant one left within my first two weeks there and the other lasted about a month. I remember she was always moaning and miserable, so I did not really miss her when she left. Then Alf employed this German student, a slim 19-year-old who was a hard worker. Most nights she would be off on the razzle down the West End. Then Alf got this middle-aged woman to come in and help over the weekends, thus giving the girl weekends off (after breakfast service, of course!). I used to have Sundays off.

The matron seemed a 'homely' sort. She was a pukka matron (nurse wise) and was always friendly to me. I used to make up the menus a week in advance, then write out the orders and give it to Alf, who would go out to the cash and carry and return with the goods. Lunches tended to be light dishes, though still three courses: a starter, main with three veg and a sweet. There were about 30 residents of various ages, some really old, some still lively, but as they had to pay, they were mostly business people or their wives.

The home looked like an ordinary block of flats situated behind the main Golders Green High Road. All the residents had their own flats, then there was a large communal room and, of course, the restaurant. There was a fairly large garden out the back where they used to sit during the summer, very nice and peaceful.

Alf showed me how make some of the Jewish dishes and sweets. He was quite a good cook and he told me that prior to this, he'd had his own bakery. He was a cheerful sort and, typically, was always on the lookout for a bargain. He was very fair to me and a few times lent me his Mini for the weekend. I took my wife out in it a couple of times, so all in all not bad.

Dinners were a slightly more formal affair. The meal was a bit more substantial and the service a bit more leisurely. The residents could invite family and friends in for meals if they wished, obviously paying a supplement for it, so the numbers varied a bit, with some of them going out and others having guests in. When some of them missed a meal by going out, they often asked for a plate of sandwiches or a bowl of fruit to be left in their flats for when they returned. Talk about getting your money's worth!

Every Friday night we served up cold fried fish and salad. They'd have a large cholla (I think that's the right way to spell it) and I believe the local Rabbi used to come in and bless it. Friday nights were good for us as it meant we could have a relatively early night. I used to put a note out with the menu on a Friday night wishing them 'Good Shobbas'. This seemed to please them – a Gentile who could 'speak' to them in Hebrew.

The majority of the inmates (sorry, residents) were nice and never complained, but we had the odd two or three who always looked for something wrong. You know the sort, never happy unless they had a complaint. It seemed to make their day – sad really! There was this doctor who used to drive us mad with his complaints. I think he lived by the saying, 'A good complaint a day keeps the doctor happy!' Now and again we treated the residents with, say, steak for supper. This particular night in trots the doctor. 'I don't want to complain' – (but you will anyway, we thought) – 'but this steak is tough and not well done enough.' 'OK,' I said, 'I'll do you another one.' After he had gone back into the restaurant I got another steak, jumped up and down on it a couple of times, well singed it and served it up. My mother-in-law (who was doing some evening work for Alf) was laughing fit to bust. Later the doctor popped his head in and thanked me for a better piece of steak!

A couple of the residents caused a bit of a stir when they were seen coming in and out of each other's flats. Scandal! The guy was a professor of something, in his late 60s with a shock of bristly hair and glasses. He was supposed to be very brainy. She was a small (5'1") woman who always looked good. She must have been in her late 60s or early 70s but she was a lively sort, always well dressed and made up. Best of luck to them, I thought. One of the others I remember was a little 'homely' Jewish woman who seemed to be 'in charge' of the home. If anyone had a problem then they would see her and she would sort it out for them. She always gave me a smile and a little wave every time I saw her, nice old dear!

It was interesting working for these people, as I learnt a fair bit about their food. One of the best times was Passover. On the evening of this special day, they all sat down to a special meal cooked by Alf, with myself as helper. The starter was chicken noodle soup, followed by poached turbot with a Hollandaise sauce, three veg, new potatoes and a special sweet. They had cholla and, I believe, some wine with the meal. It all went down very well and everybody was talking about it for a few days after.

I also did a couple of outside catering jobs for Alf. I cooked and prepared the meals and Alf took them and served them in other old people's homes, another little sideline he had. He was always doing something, was Alf, mind you, a pound here and pound there soon mounts up. I remember on one occasion I did some stuffed poussins for him, cooked them in a wine and tomato sauce, served with a riz pilaf. He had trouble reheating them as he had to work in a garage and he only had a small bottled gas oven. But he managed it somehow and they were very happy. (Where there's a will there's a way!)

One of the interesting things about working here was the afternoon teas. I used to make marble, ginger, chocolate, sticky Jamaican, fruit and almond cakes, and a multitude of others. Alf always turned up with different Jewish cakes. I used to make up all sorts of choux pastry, buns, rings, eclairs and so on. When I had laid up the assorted cakes and biscuits for tea, I used to retire to the staff room and have a late lunch and a couple of hours' break, then back to do the dinner.

Although I enjoyed my time here I realised it was not worth a long term, as I was not really improving myself. So I started to look around in the direction of the West End again, which is how I arrived at the Royal Court Hotel.

The Royal Court Hotel
Sloane Square, London SW1
Head chef, June 1971-June 1972

The day I started here, the few staff left in the kitchen had already given in their notice, so that was a good start – straight into deep water without a lifejacket! Gradually over a few months, we managed to get staff together and establish some sort of routine.

The general manager was about 28, a ginger-haired, well-spoken sort of chap with a hint of what sounded like a Scottish accent. He used to drive around in a gold-coloured Mercedes Convertible – wow! Even if it was pouring with rain he'd still have the top down (whether he had never found out how to close it or was just a sheer poser, I never knew). He was quite good, and told me he had given me the job because he liked the way I had created dishes and formed them into menus. I was told later that he was something to do with the Cherry Valley company (it used to market duck dishes). He was a nice bloke but a bit fond of the 'juice'; he'd have a skinful and then go roaring off somewhere in his Merc. It's a wonder he never had any major accidents, at least not that I know of.

His second-in-command was a large Irish chap, about 6'1" and broad with it. He was always immaculately dressed and sported a large Victorian-style moustache. He was very good, firm but with a good sense of humour. I heard much later that he had been involved in a car crash and was badly injured. I hope he's OK now.

The actual boss was Mr Wild, the managing director. He had another hotel in Bournemouth, the Highcliff Hotel, and a large house near the coast with a big garden. Quite often Mr Wild would either bring or send in fresh vegetables that his gardener had grown, and as we weren't charged for them it helped with the percentages. Sometimes he would turn up with a salmon, pheasant or grouse he had been given, and ask us to put them on the menu. Mr Wild was always softly spoken, never seemed to flap – a true gentleman.

The kitchen was about two miles from the restaurant – a bit of an exaggeration, perhaps, but the restaurant was at one end of the building and the kitchen at the other. The kitchen itself was compact with a little side room, the larder, that looked more like an old coal cellar. Next door to the kitchen there was the pastry, which was nearly as big as the whole kitchen. As the hotel's budget did not run to us having a proper pastry chef, this room was wasted; either myself or the sous prepared and set up the sweets for the trolley. We'd buy in the gateaux and cakes and make the mousses, caramels, fruit salads and compotes, so all in all we had a good selection.

Business in the restaurant was fairly good and steady, as the hotel was in a good spot, right on one corner of the square, and most rooms had a view of the square. It had a steady stream of regular clientele which made it seem more friendly and homely.

We gradually got the brigade together. We had Philip Christodoulou as the sous, he was very confident but was one of those unfortunate chefs who, no matter what they did, seemed to get covered in food – 'a mucky pup', used to be the expression. Although Philip had a lot of problems at home he never let them get him down, he was always joking and what I liked about him was that he always had time to help others. We had commis come and go during my time there, as staff had to work long hours to cover and it didn't suit some guys. Others, such as chefs de partie, stayed for a couple of months and then drifted on. In those days jobs were easier to find, so the changeover was more frequent than now.

I remember we had a larder chef who looked like Popeye's friend Bluto, well-built with a bristly black beard. Unfortunately, he too had a 'juice' problem. He had been working on the cruise liners and was on one of the more well-known ones when it, I believe, caught fire and sank. We thought his problem stemmed from this incident, but as he kept his drinking out of the kitchen and did his work, I was happy. I remember he was an avid Chelsea supporter and that he and little Jock, one of our evening kitchen porters, had a standing bet each week. If Chelsea lost then he would buy Jock a quarter of scotch and if they won, Jock would buy him a quarter of scotch. Well, Jock picked the wrong year to bet like this, as Chelsea had a very good year that year and poor old Jock was soon moaning. In the end 'Bluto' felt sorry for him and called the bet off. But there was a sour note. One lunchtime, when passing through the larder, I noticed a carrier bag stuck under the table. I opened the bag and shock! Inside were three packets of jumbo scampis. Well, 'Bluto' went red and denied any knowledge of this light-fingered approach to my trust in him. I told him that either he gave me his notice or I would sack him and tell the boss why, so off he went.

It was during this time that I first met Carl Evans. Mr Wild and the manager both thought it a good idea to employ an apprentice, so we let the Labour Exchange know and lo and behold, Carl was interested. He turned up with his father to get the low-down on the trade and the sort of hours that would be required. He seemed a nice quiet sort so we took him on. From the start we knew he would be a good chef, as he was interested in the work. We also had a commis start; he was from Birmingham and was willing, if a bit on the slow side.

At this time the cellar of the hotel had been turned into a coffee bar, the forerunner of the brasserie. It was like an upmarket snack bar serving tea, coffee, wine, soft drinks, omelettes, burgers, grilled steaks with chips, various salads etc. This left the restaurant free to concentrate on the 'better' customers and to try and boost the parties. The only trouble was, the room for the parties was small and could only hold about 12, so we did not use it as much as we would have liked. Once, when we had the chance to do a large party, we had to 'fence off' part of the restaurant to accommodate them, so it was a losing battle with the parties.

The menu we had at this time was, I thought, a bit drab looking. It was a single sheet of brown cardboard with a gold crown on the top left hand corner and the name, Algonquin Restaurant, on the right hand side. (Apparently Algonquin is the name of a Canadian Indian Tribe. I must admit, I didn't think much of it, but the general manager, who had come up with it, was happy, so who was I to complain!) On the menu was crammed the à la carte list, comprising 14 starters, eight different soups, six fish dishes, 14 different grills and entree dishes. We carried a basic six potato and nine vegetable dishes, plus we put on a special dish every now and again. We had a pastry trolley in the restaurant and a choice of ten sweets from the kitchen, together with three savouries.

The kitchen porters were mainly employed on a casual basis as it was hard to get steady porters. One of the guys came from Aberdeen and one night, when it was quiet and we were chatting, I asked how come he had travelled this far to find work. He told me his normal job was on the fishing trawlers that operated from Aberdeen but he had been suspended from going to sea for two years (I can't remember why, can anyone out there jog my memory?) As he had always wanted to see London, he thought: why not now! He was about 30 and was always laughing, a great sense of humour. He said that as soon as his time was up he was going back home and off to sea again, I hope he realised his dreams.

Another one of the porters was also a Scot, from Glasgow (or 'Glasgay', as they say). His main job seemed to be fetching and carrying for the general manager (the first one), who had a motor launch moored somewhere. This porter used to clean it out and help stock it up with goodies.

Sometimes we did 'take-aways' for him. The tales that he used to come back with ... well! Being chased around the deck, being asked to stay the night ... He was a 'straight' guy, but as the GM used to tip him well, he put up with it, though he said he was always wary when on board.

Another of the porters was little Jock (yes, yet another Scot!) He was only about 5'2" and very slim. He looked like a miniature sergeant major, not your run-of-the-mill kitchen porter. In fact, he wasn't. He was a porter in a block of flats just up the road in Sloane Street, and used to do the live-in portering by day and then come down to us for two or three nights a week. He had a good sense of humour and fitted in with all the others. If you can't have a laugh at work, well, it's a bad thing!

Christmas was a busy time for us at the Royal Court as it is everywhere. Philip did all day Christmas Day, I did all day Boxing Day and the rest of the brigade we split between us. The same with New Year. Those who liked a lay-in to recover worked the night before and had New Year's Day off and the others had New Year's Eve off and worked New year's Day. Then we gave them another day off later to suit them, which kept them all happy.

I can't remember much about the waiters, sorry lads, better luck next time around. The people I do remember are the two maintenance men. One was stocky and balding, the boss type, a good shop steward, you know the sort. His mate was about the same age, a bit slimmer with all his hair and someone else's nose (WC Fields's, I think!) Once we got to know them and learnt how to handle them, they were quite helpful. Both had been there for years and, funnily enough, when I went for an interview for the chef's job with a new company a few years later, they were still there. I reckon they had got in touch with Madam Tussauds to 'cover them'. I bet when they pass on, their ghosts will still be going round repairing things!

Each day in the restaurant we used to lay up a small cold buffet table. This was handy because it gave the lads a chance to experiment with various dishes and decorations. If Philip or I had an idea for a cold dish, we would have a go and see what reaction we got from the customers – mostly good. It's like most things in life, you need stimulation to create. Sometimes a chance remark would send your mind off at a tangent and the dishes would come flooding in. We might be trying out a king prawn dish, and we would have a few good ideas in quick succession. We might go weeks without any, then right out of the blue ... BAM! they would come flooding in. I always wrote down the ingredients and methods for all my ideas and over the years I have quite a few 'jottings' that again stimulate ideas when I browse through them.

Although the work was hard and the hours long, I enjoyed my time at the Royal Court Hotel. I was left fairly well alone and left to get on with the work in hand. It gave me quite a good feeling to see some of my creations in print and to actually hear about people enjoying the dishes (who said 'Makes a change'?) We had entrecote algonquin, a sirloin steak cooked in butter (none of this cholesterol-phobia then), with a brandy, mushroom and cream sauce – tasty! Another dish was the riz de veau paradis – poached calves' sweetbreads sliced and served with a Pernod, cream and pimento sauce. I did and still do love to create dishes and while I was here I had the opportunity to create quite a lot of dishes that were used both in the restaurant and on parties (I feel a recipe book coming on).

It was during this time that I first met Dave French, who was introduced to me by my sous chef Philip. We were looking for a chef gardemanger and Philip reckoned that Dave would be ideal for the job. And well he was. We seemed to have an instant rapport that made all the hard work bearable. If you can have a laugh or two while you're sweating your balls off, then it has to be good for the general morale in the kitchen. We would take the mickey out of each other and no-one took offence. Carl was fitting in nicely and when he went to work in the larder with Dave it seemed to bring him out a bit more. Well done there, Dave!

After about seven months the GM left. I never did find out exactly why, but on the day he was leaving all the heads of department were invited to the bar after lunch service for a drop of 'shampoo'. Well, it turned out to be more than a drop, and the poor old barman was worn out keeping up with us. In the end, the number two took over the bar. 'Have what you like,' said the GM, 'I'm paying'. Well, we all had quite a skinful, but come 5 pm, we had to vacate the bar and go back to work (the work looked twice as much, if you get my meaning!) The now ex-GM got into his Merc and sailed off into the sunset. At least from the way he drove, it seemed that he was sailing – foot down, bonnet up and away!

After his departure, the restaurant was promptly renamed the Royal Court Restaurant (original or what!) and a more standard menu card was introduced, though I was still allowed to plan and execute the menu, which I enjoyed. It was a mixture of classic and house special dishes. We also started a small table d'hôte menu which gave us something more to think about.

The new GM was about 50 and sort of 'smooth', with his hair coloured and neatly combed – a bit poncy. We never got on well, something about him gave me the creeps, don't know what, but it was just a feeling.

The coffee bar was going well at this time. People were coming in off the street who just wanted a snack, not a full meal, and with its Victorian style booths, the coffee bar was quite comfy and homely. We upgraded the menu, gave them more of a choice, a better selection of salads and so on. Then one day after lunch I was called up to the GM's office for what I thought was a discussion about business. But instead, I was told 'walkies'. I must admit I was struck dumb: everything seemed to be going smoothly, the staff were good, business was good, what was the problem? The GM never told me properly, just muttered about complaints (what bloody complaints?) He asked me to wrap up and go just like that. I told him I would have to come back the next day (Saturday) and pick up all my belongings, which he agreed to.

Well, I waited on and saw Philip when he came back. When I told him what had happened, he was not very happy about the situation either. Next morning I went back, packed up all my stuff and left. I made arrangements to meet all the 'lads' in the pub the following Friday night for a drink. I was pleased to say that they all turned up and a good time was had by all. To this day I'm not sure how I got home that night, and David et al don't remember either! So we must have had a good time.

A few days later I got in contact with Mr Wild and asked him for a reference. He said he was sorry about my leaving, but as the new GM had his own ideas regarding the running of the hotel and restaurant, Mr Wild had to support him. Well fair enough I thought. I duly received my reference from the boss and it was a good one.

About six months or so later Mr Wild sold out both hotels and retired. Maybe that was why he had let the new guy get on with it, who knows?

For a while I was left in limbo, not having expected to be out of a job that was going along so well. I phoned around and managed to get a temporary booking as a relief chef at the Pastoria Hotel in St Martins Street near Leicester Square. Pastoria, here I come!

LES HORS D'OEUVRES ET POTAGES

Avocat Vinaigrette 35p • Aux Crevettes 45p • Terrine de Canard à L'Armagnac 40p

Jambon de Parme 55p • Anguille Fumée 45p

Demi Charentais au Porto • Saumon Fumé 85p • Artichaut Chaud ou Froid 35p

Crevettes Géantes 20p • Cocktail Fruits de Mer 50p

Escargots en Pâte Feuilletée 75p • Morilles à la Crème 60p

Oeuf sur le Plat Niçoise 35p • Omelettes Variées 55p

Minestrone au Parmesan 25p • Soupe de Poisson 30p

Consommé Chaud ou Froid 20p • Potage Cressonière 20p • Crème de Tomate 20p

Vichyssoise 25p • Tortue Claire 30p • Gazpacho 25p

LES POISSONS

Truite de Rivière aux amandes ou Grenobloise 75p • Filets de Sole Belle Aurore ou Frits £1 ·00

Homard selon la Saison • Darne de Saumon Pochée ou Bordelaise £1 ·10

Scampis à la Mode du Chef £1 ·25 • Sole de Douvre selon le Poid

LES ENTREES ET GRILLADES

L'Escalope de Veau Viennoise ou Nelson £1 ·25 • Ris de Veau Paradis £1 ·20

Tournedos Royale £1 ·15 • Noisette D'Agneau Judic £1 ·05

Poulet Rôti £1 ·00 • Suprème de Volaille aux Morilles £1 ·15

Côte de Veau en Papillote £1 ·25 • Rognons Bordelaise £1 ·15

Côte de Boeuf Villette (2 couverts—40 minutes) £2 ·50 • Entrecôte £1 ·10

Rump £1 ·05 • Filet £1 ·25 • Châteaubriand (2 couverts) £2 ·50

Sur la Voiture : Rôti Du Jour, Garni Complet £1 ·25

LES LEGUMES

Pommes : Nature, Croquettes, Purée, Sautées, Frites, Château 15p

Petits Pois, Boutons de Bruxelles, Epinards en Branches, ou Purée Crème 20p

Céleris Braisés, Petits Pois à la Française, Broccoli Sauce Hollandaise 30p

Haricots Verts frais au Beurre 35p • Endives Braisées 35p

LES DESSERTS

Le Choix Sur La Voiture du Patissier 25p • Coupe Melba 25p • Coupe Niçoise 25p

Coupe Belle Hélène 25p • Crèpes au Citron 30p • Crèpes Suzettes 75p

Soufflé Vanille (2 cts—35 min) 80p • Grand Marnier (2 cts) £1 ·10

Soufflé Fromage (2 cts) £1 ·10 • Glacé £1 ·10

Les Glaces au Choix 25p

Canapés Diane 25p • Champignons Sur Toast 25p • Welsh Rarebit 20p

Le Plateau des Fromages 30p

Service 12½ % • Minimum Charge £1 ·25 • Couvert 15p

LES HORS	Avocat: Vinaigrette 35p aux Crevettes 50p Melon de Saison
D'OEUVRE	Pâté de Canard à l'Armagnac 40p Jambon de Parme et Melon 75p

LES HORS D'OEUVRE

Avocat: Vinaigrette 35p   aux Crevettes 50p   Melon de Saison
Pâté de Canard à l'Armagnac 40p   Jambon de Parme et Melon 75p
Escargots de Bourgogne ($\frac{1}{2}$ douzaine) 60p
Cocktail de Fruits de Mer 55p   Truite Fumée 55p
Saumon Fumé d'Ecosse 90p

LES POTAGES

Consommé Chaud ou Froid 20p   Tortue Claire 35p
Crème de Tomate 20p   Crème à la Reine 25p   Crème Sénégalaise 25p
Soupe à l'Oignon Gratinée 25p   Minestrone au Parmesan 25p

LES OEUFS

Florentine 45p (*Poached with spinach*)   Bercy 45p (*Fried with chipolatas and tomatoes*)

Cocotte à la Crème 40p   Omelette au Choix 55p

LES POISSONS

Truite: Royal Court £1·00 (*Fried in butter, served with sliced avocado and prawns*)
Amandes 80p   Meunière 70p   Beaujolais 80p (*Poached with red wine sauce*)

Dover Sole: Grillée £1·20   Frite, Colbert £1·25

Filet de Sole: Bonne Femme £1·20   Frits en Goujons £1·10
Philippa £1·30   (*Cooked in butter with nib almonds and Madeira*)
Véronique £1·20   (*White wine sauce and grapes*)
Venture £1·20   (*With white wine, chutney and anchovy sauce*)

Scampi: Meunière £1·20   Provençale £1·30   (*With tomato and garlic*)
Frits £1·20   Anita £1·40   (*With rum, tarragon, mushrooms and cream*)

Saumon d'Ecosse (en saison)   Homard au Choix (en saison)

LES ENTREES

Escalope de Veau: Viennoise £1·20   Marsala £1·25
Catherine £1·40   (*with mushrooms, anchovy, tomato and red wine sauce*)

Côte de Veau Avocat £1·30   (*Cooked in butter with sherry, avocado, shallots*)

Châteaubriand en Papillotte (2 persons) £2·80

Tournedos: Choron £1·25   (*With tomato Béarnaise*)
Opera £1·25   (*With chicken livers and Madeira sauce*)
Royale £1·35   (*With chestnut purée and Madeira sauce*)

Rognons de Veau: Dijonnaise £1·15 (*Cooked with brandy, mustard and cream*)
Bordelaise £1·15   (*Cooked in red wine with shallots and bone marrow*)
Ris de Veau Paradis £1·25 (*Cooked with Pernod, pimentoes, shallots and cream*)

Poulet Rôti Garni £1·00   Caneton Rôti à l'Anglaise £1·00

HEAD CHEF

JUNE 71
JUNE 72.

150

THE
Royal Court
RESTAURANT

LES GRILLADES

Côtelettes d'Agneau £1·00   Côte de Boeuf (2 persons) £2·60

Rump steak £1·15   Filet £1·30   Entrecôte £1·20   Tournedos £1·25

Châteaubriand (2 persons) £2·60

All grills served with tomato, mushroom, straw potatoes, Béarnaise sauce

LES LEGUMES

Pommes de Terre: Nature 15p   Croquettes 25p   Sautées 20p
Allumettes 20p   Rissolées 20p   Purée 20p

Petits Pois Verts 20p   Choufleur Mornay 25p

Brocolis, Sauce Hollandaise 30p

Epinards: en Branches 20p   Purée à la Crème 25p   Carottes Vichy 15p

Haricots Verts Frais 30p   Céleri Braisé 20p   Milanaise 25p

Endive: Braisé 25p   Meunière 20p   Petits Pois à la Française 25p

Boutons de Bruxelles 20p   Salades Variées 25/50p

LES ENTREMENTS

Coupe: Melba 30p   Niçoise 30p   Belle Hélène 30p

Crepes: Suzette (2 persons) £1·50   Confiture 35p   Citron 35p

Soufflé Grand Marnier (2 persons) £1·30   Framboises Cardinal 30p

Les Glaces au Choix 20p   Chocolat Menthe Glacé 30p

LES SAVOURIES

Canapé Diane 30p   Champignons sur Toast 30p   Welsh Rarebit 25p

Le Plâteau des Fromages 30p

Café 15p

LES VINS EN CARAFE

Rouge, Blanc ou Rosé

le verre 20p $\frac{1}{2}$ Carafe 40p   Carafe 80p

Champagne le verre 45p

Service charge $12\frac{1}{2}$%   Couvert 15p   Minimum charge £1·25

151

The Pastoria Hotel
St. Martins Street, London W1
Relief chef, June-September 1972

The Pastoria was not an easy place to find, it was stuck away at the back of Leicester Square, on the corner of St. Martin's Street and Orange Street. The front of the hotel, apart from the doors and the sign, looked like an office block. The inside was quite nice – olde worlde effect – with an olde worlde service. Although the hotel was nice and had a fairly good name (so I was told by the hotel PR person), the kitchen was terrible. It really left a lot to be desired!

The head chef was a stewed Frenchman suffering from delusions of grandeur; the sous was an Italian who worked his nuts off and got no help or encouragement. The main kitchen porter was a permanently drunk Irishman, and his helper or second porter was a drunken Englishman – what a team, eh! With that lot we could have lost the last war!

The menu, however, was quite good, with a nice choice in the à la carte: it had 27 starters, including four soups and four different egg dishes; then there was a choice of 20 assorted fish dishes, 34 meat, plus six 'house specials', seven vegetable and seven potato dishes, plus, of course, the sweet trolley (consisting of eight or nine different sweets), hot canapes and the obligatory cheese board – not a bad selection eh! Considering the place was not in the top echelon of hotels (I think it came somewhere in the middle), and when you think of the small choice of dishes on most of hotels and restaurant menus today, it really was quite an offering, one which the poor old sous was fighting a losing battle with.

We did split shifts, and as far as I can remember, the restaurant shut on Sundays. I used to help out with the larder and the sweets, they had a small (I think) Italian on the veg, and the sous did all the main courses, plus some of the starters. The chef was lucky that the sous was a hard, quick worker who knew his job.

A typical day would start with us arriving about 9 am, stepping over one or both of the KPs in the locker room; they would be sleeping off a bender, *daily*! (I don't think either porter had a home to go to as their lockers were filled with clothes and nick nacks – no one was brave enough to look too far inside in case there was a lodger of some sort. It was strange how their lockers were on one side of the room and ours on the other – segregation or self preservation? I often wonder!) The sous would then rouse the 'sleeping beauties', and get them into some sort of working rhythm. This daily routine was straight out of a Mack Sennet comedy.

The Irish lad (he was only in his 20s) was always 'wobbly' and any time of the day would be trying his best to see the pots and find which one of the three he could see was the one to wash. On the *very* odd occasion when he was a bit 'dry', he had a good sense of humour and could converse quite intelligently, but when he was 'with sauce', he was argumentative, silly and lazy. It was hard work just getting him to sweep the floor, let alone mop it! We'd quickly realise of a morning that we were going to run out of clean pots, because the dirty pots from the night before had not been washed, but 'accidentally' left under the sinks, out of sight.

The English KP wasn't much better. When he got drunk he used to collapse on the locker room floor and nod off, snoring like a good un, bloody loud, with a gurgle. Sometimes we thought he had 'croaked' it, but no, he started again. The daily routine for the pair of them would be: wake up on the floor of the changing room, appear in the kitchen in a daze ('what day is it, is the war over?') After a couple of strong black coffees and maybe, just maybe, a slice of toast, they would be ready to squint at the day and try this thing called *work*! About 11.30, when the staff had their lunch, they would disappear to the local pub in Leicester Square and reappear at about one (maybe), feeling and, I must admit, looking better – hair of the dog and all that (more like the whole dog!) We used to finish lunch service about 2.30, clear down and go home or out (or in the porters' case, for a drink. They often brought some beer back with them ready for the afternoon break.) Then we would return about 5.30 and get ready for the evening trade.

The hotel used to do pre-theatre suppers, which were quite popular and most days this was our busiest period. About eight, our intrepid duo would slope off again, just to 'walk the dog'. They might come back before we left, but more often than not they would be found in the morning in the locker room, and so the routine would start again. Honestly, only seeing was believing these guys. To give them their due, they did change their shirts and jumpers on a fairly regular basis, but they seemed to forget about washing them. I am sure that part of the bar was quite a lonely place for them.

The head chef was, apart from his red 'glowing' face (also caused by 'the sauce'), quite good looking. He had this dream that the company would soon call on him to take over one of their hotels (dream on!) and that he was just marking time at the Pastoria, waiting for the call. (If he is still with us, then I expect he's still waiting). He really could not see that he had a drink problem. He'd arrive about 10 am, partake of a strong black coffee, and casually inquire if everything was OK, if the orders had arrived and been checked. He would then have a little chat and a laugh with us all before retiring to his office 'to do the paperwork'. He would then reappear about 12.30 and help with the service, calling out the orders and such like. Then it was back to the office to place any orders, then off he would go to the 'club'. He'd return oiled about 6.30 or 7 pm and try to help with the business a little, then he would toddle off home, a day's work well done! He really was convinced he was the 'greatest' and that his 'time' was coming soon.

One afternoon he invited me out to his 'club' for what I thought was a chat about some vacancies coming up that I might be interested in. The 'club' was one of those cellar jobs, and the 'barmaid' looked like a resting prossie. It was a bit of a dive, though this was not reflected in the price of their drinks. I only bought one round and left it to him to buy the rest, which he bought 'on account' (on account of what? I thought). As it turned out, the chef just wanted someone to listen to his boasting while he knocked them back, which he could certainly do: three drinks to my one. We returned to the hotel about 6.30 that evening and I must admit, I did not perform well that night!

The sous was one of the old brigade Italians: work hard, worry hard, moan hard. Still, he was a bloody good worker! All the orders were à la carte (done to order, nothing pre- packed like nowadays), even the individual Beef Wellingtons were done to order! The poor bloke really had a hard time of it, as all the managers used to come to him about any problems, and the staff as well, because the head chef was not usually in a fit state to deal with anything.

It was during this period that I met Frank Demauney again. We had met off and on over the years in various kitchens and got on quite well. Frank had been enlisted to help out with this sinking kitchen, but even with the three of us going flat out (that's me, Frank and the sous), we couldn't save it, all we could do was bale like fury!

After we had been there a short time the sous had had enough and departed to other pastures. An Irish chef took over from him. Now this guy was a cleaner version of the Irish porter, and he might have been his brother. You know what I'm about to tell you, don't you? Yes, another sozzled person to join the bridge! When he was dry, he was a good chef who worked well and kept on top of things. But when he was 'wet', he was bloody useless! Many was the night when it was just me and Frank doing the work, while the sous sat in the staff room, head in his hands, and sometimes even nodded off! The rest of the staff were OK, they took no notice of the chef or the Irish sous. They just seemed glad to have a couple of blokes who could cook the staff food without burning it, and would often chat to us during their breaks. Most of them had been there for years – born, lived and died Pastoria.

I will always remember the Saturday night my car disappeared. Usually on the Saturday evening I took my car into work (a Ford Popular, remember them?) It was originally my Uncle Bill's, but when he died, my aunt gave it to me and I used to park it with others, along the side of the hotel. Anyway, this particular evening, I had finished work about 11-ish, came out and – it had gone! 'I'm sure I left it here', 'Maybe along a bit, no!' 'Did I bring it today?' – you know the sort of thoughts that rush by while you're in a daze.

Eventually I decided that some sod had nicked it! But could I find a copper? Could I hell! Never around when they are needed! Eventually I found one in Trafalgar Square, told him what had happened and he called up on the blower. After a couple of minutes he told me my car had been illegally parked (yes, the same old excuse) and had been taken to the pound. 'Where's that?' I asked, 'Elephant & Castle,' he said. 'Bloody hell!' I said (I think it was a bit stronger than that, but I can't remember the exact words).

So I hailed a cab and was duly dropped off outside the pound. (Why they call it a pound and not the 'making moneyspot', I don't know.) I went up to the copper standing inside a cabin and when he eventually decided to open the small window so that I could talk to him and told him my registration number, he consulted a list very carefully and slowly, despite me telling him that I could see my car not 20 yards away. 'Ah yes,' he said, 'it was illegally parked on the corner of Orange Street, wasn't it!' (No it bloody wasn't, I thought, I never parked on corners) 'That's strange,' I said, 'it was parked about three cars from the corner!' 'Prove it,' he said, 'the officer's report is here'. So with controlled fury, I paid up. (I think it was about £20.) I was then allowed through the barriers and went to my car. My surprise was unlimited when I found that my crooklock had been taken off and slung on the back seat – what magicians these coppers were! I had securely locked it on to the clutch pedal and the steering wheel! On the way out I asked the officer how they had managed to get the crooklock off without my key. (They are supposed to be impregnable, aren't they?) 'It was not locked' he replied. 'It bloody was,' I said, and guess what he replied – yes, that's right: 'Prove it'. That really spoilt my night, as a good part of my wages had gone on this rescue operation.

I am sure to this day that the officer drove my car to the pound – it had not been towed – as the petrol seemed a bit down when I got it back! Maybe he had gone home for a cuppa on the way, but as I couldn't *prove it*, I had to swallow it and get on with life!

And then came the Hertford Club.

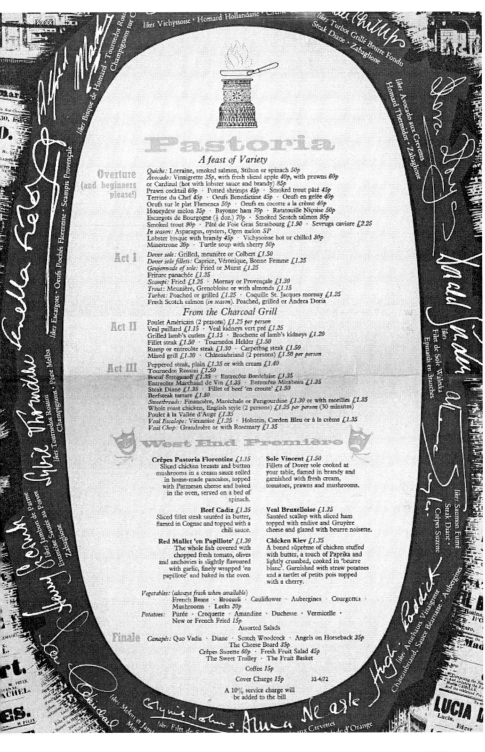

Pastoria

A feast of Variety

Overture (and beginners please!)
Quiche: Lorraine, smoked salmon, Stilton or spinach 50p
Avocado: Vinaigrette 35p, with fresh sliced apple 40p, with prawns 60p or Cardinal (hot with lobster sauce and brandy) 85p
Prawn cocktail 60p · Potted shrimps 45p · Smoked trout pâté 45p
Terrine du Chef 45p · Oeufs Benedictine 45p · Oeufs en gelée 40p
Oeufs sur le plat Flamenca 50p · Oeufs en cocotte a la crème 40p
Honeydew melon 35p · Bayonne ham 70p · Ratatouille Niçoise 50p
Escargots de Bourgogne (½ doz.) 70p · Smoked Scotch salmon 85p
Smoked trout 90p · Pâté de Foie Gras Strasbourg £1.90 · Sevruga caviare £2.25
In season: Asparagus, oysters, Ogen melon SP
Lobster bisque with brandy 45p · Vichyssoise hot or chilled 30p
Minestrone 36p · Turtle soup with sherry 50p

Act I
Dover sole: Grilled, meunière or Colbert £1.50
Dover sole fillets: Caprice, Véronique, Bonne Femme £1.35
Goujonnade of sole: Fried or Murat £1.25
Friture panachée £1.35
Scampi: Fried £1.25 · Mornay or Provençale £1.30
Trout: Meunière, Grenobloise or with almonds £1.15
Turbot: Poached or grilled £1.25 · Coquille St. Jacques mornay £1.25
Fresh Scotch salmon (in season). Poached, grilled or Andrea Doria

From the Charcoal Grill

Act II
Poulet Américain (2 persons) £1.25 per person
Veal paillard £1.15 · Veal kidneys vert pré £1.25
Grilled lamb's cutlets £1.15 · Brochette of lamb's kidneys £1.20
Fillet steak £1.50 · Tournedos Helder £1.50
Rump or entrecôte steak £1.30 · Carpetbag steak £1.50
Mixed grill £1.30 · Châteaubriand (2 persons) £1.50 per person

Act III
Peppered steak, plain £1.35 or with cream £1.40
Tournedos Rossini £1.50
Boeuf Stroganoff £1.35 · Entrecôte Bordelaise £1.35
Entrecôte Marchand de Vin £1.35 · Entrecôte Mirabeau £1.35
Steak Diane £1.35 · Fillet of beef 'en croute' £1.50
Beefsteak tartare £1.50
Sweetbreads: Financière, Maréchale or Perigourdine £1.30 or with morilles £1.35
Whole roast chicken, English style (2 persons) £1.25 per person (30 minutes)
Poulet à la Vallée d'Auge £1.35
Veal Escalope: Viennoise £1.25 · Holstein, Cordon Bleu or à la crème £1.35
Veal Chop: Grandmère or with Rosemary £1.35

West End Première

Crêpes Pastoria Florentine £1.15
Sliced chicken breasts and button mushrooms in a cream sauce rolled in home-made pancakes, topped with Parmesan cheese and baked in the oven, served on a bed of spinach.

Beef Cadiz £1.35
Sliced fillet steak sautéed in butter, flamed in Cognac and topped with a chili sauce.

Red Mullet 'en Papillote' £1.30
The whole fish covered with chopped fresh tomato, olives and anchovies is slightly flavoured with garlic, finely wrapped 'en papillote' and baked in the oven.

Sole Vincent £1.50
Fillets of Dover sole cooked at your table, flamed in brandy and garnished with fresh cream, tomatoes, prawns and mushrooms.

Veal Bruxelloise £1.35
Sautéed scallop with sliced ham topped with endive and Gruyère cheese and glazed with beurre noisette.

Chicken Kiev £1.35
A boned suprême of chicken stuffed with butter, a touch of Paprika and lightly crumbed, cooked in 'beurre blanc'. Garnished with straw potatoes and a tartlet of petits pois topped with a cherry.

Vegetables: (always fresh when available)
French Beans · Broccoli · Cauliflower · Aubergines · Courgettes
Mushrooms · Leeks 30p
Potatoes: Purée · Croquette · Amandine · Duchesse · Vermicelle
New or French Fried 15p
Assorted Salads

Finale
Canapés: Quo Vadis · Diane · Scotch Woodcock · Angels on Horseback 35p
The Cheese Board 35p
Crêpes Suzette 60p · Fresh Fruit Salad 45p
The Sweet Trolley · The Fruit Basket

Coffee 15p

Cover Charge 15p   32-4/72

A 10% service charge will be added to the bill

The Hertford Club
Hertford Street, London W1
Head Chef, September 1972 - September 1973

I had answered an advert for the club, which had not yet opened, and was given an interview with the manager, a Spanish guy called Rodriguez. He was slim, well-dressed, his grey hair combed back, as smooth and charming as an oily rag with a smile like a hungry shark – but enough of his good points. He told me about the style and the sort of services that would be required (it was going to be a gaming club, all the fashion at that time). He then took me down to the basement and showed me the empty room where the kitchen and store rooms were going to be.

A few days later I was asked to go back and they offered me the job. I was quite pleased as, apart from my reservations about Mr Rodriguez, it was quite a challenge to open, set up and staff a new place. The menu had already been 'sorted', understandable as they were due to open in about three weeks' time. Anyway, it was not too bad to start off with, and I was able to get my feelings into the table d'hôte menus, so at least I had a little say on the dishes.

So I got my roller-skates out of the cupboard, dusted them down and got zooming!

The main pieces of equipment had arrived and had been sited; it was left to me to sort out the rest of the equipment, the staff, the rotas of work, contacting and setting up the deliveries with the suppliers, the menu breakdowns etc. As you can see, I had a peaceful three weeks! The company put out various adverts for staff, and soon I was busy with interviews. It had been decided that we should have two brigades, one early and one late, then each week they would change about, as the manager hoped to get the lunch trade off to a good start and hold it.

It was at this time that I first met Geoff McKinnon, an Aussie who had just come over to England. He had spent about a couple of weeks at the Hilton, but wasn't too keen on the number of Germans that were working there. He was a confident guy (still is) who was on the same sort of food wavelength as me, so I took him on as one of the sous, in charge of one of the brigades. The other sous was foisted on me by Rodriguez (I knew why: in case I didn't work out, then this guy was ready to step in. This guy had apparently wanted the chef's job and had been second or third choice after me). I must say, we ended up with a good kitchen team.

The restaurant was called the Adam Room and it was to be run by a large Italian called Franco who was very good at his job, the old school, excellent! His second in command was another Italian, not so good as Franco (he joined Rodriguez as an oily rag type) and a right old creep, a tale-teller, you've all met one! The rest of the waiters were, yes, you've guessed correctly, Italians. The kitchen and the waiters got along very well, we were all in the same boat and rowing in the same direction. ('Makes a change!' I hear you say.)

In the kitchen I had two sous, two sauciers, two veggies and two commis. The ones I remember were Geoff obviously, and the other sous, a Spaniard who was not too bad but had a habit of *telling* what he could do, rather than actually doing it. One of the sauce chefs was a Portuguese bloke who thought he knew it all, but unfortunately didn't. The other was, I think, a Jamaican called Richard Mntdarbi (I hope the spelling's right!) who was much better, really knew his job. Another black guy was Tony Gill, one of the larder chefs. He was not the best larder chef in town, but he was good enough for us. Also I remember we had Henri Martinez, another veggie with the typical Spanish-thin moustache. He was good, though he used to get nervous when the pressure was on; but as he worked hard it made up for his nervousness. Then there was George Gorecki, a Pole (or was it Hungarian? Over to you, George!) The two commis were English ('Hooray!' I hear you cry; no, I wasn't racist!) They were both about 19 and very good, so I expect they've been head chefs for years now!

The grand opening day arrived, and all and sundry turned up for free 'bubbly' and food. So far so good! For the first three or four months things went well. The lunch trade was not much but the evening trade was picking up nicely, plus we had a few parties to promote the club more, so that created interest. Amongst the few dishes I created for the menus was one I called Supreme de Volaille Hertford (original, eh!) This was a breast of chicken, sealed off, placed in thin puff pastry (or 'poof pastry' as it was then known) with a good slice of fresh foie gras (remember foie gras?) and some fresh asparagus tips, wrapped up and baked, then served with a good sauce Perigourdine (remember the days when we had good sauces, not the gravies of today?). This dish was quite filling, so imagine my surprise when I produced this dish for one of the boxing promotion lunches and one of the star boxers proceeded to eat three with veg! Mind you, he was a big bloke so he had a lot of space to fill!

We used to serve the selection of fresh vegetables (changed daily) in oval copper dishes with lids, which looked quite effective when served at the table by the waiter.

The main à la carte menu was prepared 'earlier' with the agreement that we would change it in about six months. After things had settled down into a proper rhythm, I made up the daily menus and had a hand in the party menus. I managed to get some of my personality into things, so it was not too bad. The first menu we had to work from consisted of 13 various hors d'oeuvres, including Caviar Beluga at £2 per ounce and smoked salmon at £1.10 per portion – try and get them at this price now! There were five different soups, nine fish, nine dishes from the iron grill, 11 entrees and a choice of seven desserts. After a while I had planned and 'laid' out a new menu with (I thought) a better selection: 23 hors d'oeuvres, six egg dishes, five different pasta, ten soups, 29 fish, including five lobster dishes, 21 dishes in the grill and roast section, 27 entrees, a larger selection of vegetables and potato dishes. I also added canapes (hot) after the sweet trolley, which consisted of ten or 12 different dishes. So the punters had a much better and wider selection, which after all is what they want – to be spoilt for choice.

I was responsible for all the ordering, stock (the taking and control of), all the normal things that a chef does in the course of a day's work. I always remember one day when Mr Rodriguez had on one of his 'rags' (know what I mean! - if not ask someone). He came down to the kitchen and proceeded to have a go at me in front of all the staff (trying to make me out a c—t or what!). He was annoyed about the fact that we were paying too much for the fat around the veal kidneys (bear in mind that we had them on the menu roasted in their fat, sliced and served with a good sauce madere). He said that we should only allow a few ounces of fat per kidney (can't remember the exact figure), and that today's delivery was well over the limit.

Well, I let him get on with his serious drivel for about five minutes, then I got the scales and weighed each one. Lo and behold, each one was either on or below his prescribed weight! If we'd had any flies in the kitchen, they would have all disappeared down his open mouth! His jaw dropped so much that a flying pig would have had room to do a three point turn! Then with a huff and a puff ... (sorry, I got carried away with the Three Little Pigs story), he stalked away, his face much darker than when he had arrived! I think that was the moment I knew my time was up! Don't know why, just call it a hunch.

Maybe his antipathy towards me really started a few weeks earlier, when he had called me up to his office and told me we would not be doing lunches in the future and would have to get rid of one brigade; if we did any lunchtime parties, we would draft in a couple of guys on an early shift. He heavily hinted at the 'good merits' of his friend the sous, and that he thought he should be the one to stay, but of course it was my decision who would stay. After carefully taking note of his 'advice', I then promised to draw up a list of those who came second and would have to be given the big 'E'.

The sous who turned out to be the best was – yes, you've guessed it – Geoff! He was far better than the recommended one, not a poser. We had Richard on the sauce, Tony in the larder and Henri on the veg. The decision on the commis was much harder as both were good. This was one part of the chef's job I disliked intensely. It was OK if the guy was useless, but not if the choice was due to management decisions.

I remember one night just before service, Franco came down for his usual pre-service chat with the kitchen, and the conversation turned (as is normal) to sex. This time it was about who in the world had the biggest recorded dick. Gill was going on about how big the black guys were, how they were first in the queue when dicks were given out etc (apparently some of them used theirs as scarves in the winter! I wonder if that is in Trivial Pursuit). Anyway, Franco stuck up for the Italians, saying how good they were, then he said to Gill, 'Here, have a look at this!' He grabbed the fleshy part of his inner thigh and held it with both hands, so that it looked like a good '14-incher'. Gill's eyes popped. 'Christ, I've never seen one that big before!' he said. After we had all calmed down from our hysterics, we explained to Gill that he had been fooled, and that Franco had slightly cheated.

So everything seemed to be going well. The business was quite good, we were getting compliments on a regular basis and the lads all had a good laugh in the kitchen.

Then Franco upped and left. We never really found out why, but it seemed that his second in command had been doing some backbiting. (We've seen blokes like this before, haven't we!) We all knew he was 'close' to the manager, Rodriguez, and definitely in favour (or should that be flavour of the month?) It was a shame really, 'cos Franco was good, he had a good attitude and looked the part, whereas his second looked untidy, wasn't very friendly and didn't seem to care for the customers. Quite a difference!

As the guy took over from Franco, he seemed to think he had taken over the kitchen as well. He started to try and give orders to the lads in the kitchen, though luckily they took no notice of him. One day I invited him into my office and explained the 'facts of kitchen life' to him – nicely, of course! He was fairly sociable after that, but I had a feeling, you know the one you can't quite put your finger on, but you know that something is 'cooking'.

I really knew my time was coming when Geoff told me that he had caught this guy listening to my conversation outside the office door. Unfortunately the dividing wall between the office and the kitchen did not go all the way up to the ceiling and if you stood near, you could hear what was being said in the office. I cannot be sure, but I am sure that he had something to do with my leaving. I believe that if you have a problem, then speak up and let's sort it out, clear the air and no offence taken. Unfortunately, Rodriguez and the 'second' did not seem to share my beliefs!

Rodriguez called me up to his office one day, just as I had arrived, and after asking after my health and all the usual preliminary crap, he told me that I would be asked to leave as I was not up to the job. (Cheeky shit, I thought). He then proceeded to list all the so-called complaints about the kitchen which, considering all the compliments we received about the food, was a bit out of order. I said this to him, but his mind was made up. Rodriguez told me I had to leave at once; I told him to piss off, and that I would need a bit of time to pack up all my bits and pieces (and to make sure I took all my paperwork and menus with me).

As I was doing this the lads started to arrive. I imparted the news and they didn't seem very happy about the situation. Just before I had finished packing up, the new chef was brought in to the kitchen by Rodriguez's 'good friend'. Lo and behold, it turned out to be Franco from Annabels. I knew Franco was too soft to stand up to this pair and that he was only going to be the figurehead while Rodriguez and his mate turned the kitchen into just a subsidiary of the restaurant, under the control of the restaurant manager. And so it turned out to be!

I think it was about a year or so after this that The Hertford Club was shut down – 'under a cloud', I was told (a bloody big one, I'm sure!)

By now I was supplementing my income by doing a few hours at the Troika, a Russian restaurant in Queensgate, where I spent a brief but happy spell.

The Hertford Club

Les Aperitifs

Oppenheimer Goldberg 1970

Château la Croix de Millorit 1966
Côtes de Bourg
Château Bottled

Champagne Bollinger

Le Cognac et liqueurs

Crudités

Saumon fumé d'Ecosse
Les Huitres Natives
Le Caviar Beluga

La Coquille St. Jacques Joinville
Les Filets de Sole Venture

Les Noisettes d'agneau Cyrano
Le Medaillon de Boeuf Mireille
La Suprême de Volaille Hertford

Petit Pois a la francaise
Les Haricots verts au beurre
Les coeurs de Celeri Milanaise
Le Broccoli Polonaise
Les Pommes de Terre Nouvelles, Macaire, Delmonico

Les Fraises Mont Blanc
Les Peches au Pernod

Le Café

Les friandises

31st DECEMBER 1972

163

The Troika Restaurant
Queensway

The only thing really Russian about this restaurant was its name. The manager was Greek, the head chef was Spanish, the waiters were Yugoslavs, the barmaid was Polish and the two wandering musicians (one on the fiddle, the other on the squeeze box) were Hungarian. Then there was myself, an Englishman: a true conglomerate of nationalities!

The menu did, however, feature Russian specialities such as Beluga caviar, Sevruga Andketova caviar, traditional blinis served with various dishes and garnishes, pickled herrings and smoked salmon etc. They had about three different salamis (Russian, of course) together with 13 other hors d'oeuvres, or *zakouski*, as they called them. They had a choice of five classic (?) Russian soups: Ukranski, Borshtch, Bouillon pilimeni, Sielanka and Kourinnei bouillon. Try saying those quickly! There were 11 house specialities, including the classic beef stroganoff; one dish called Kaukaskie Golountse, which resembled Greek dolmades but with cabbage leaves instead of vine or spinach. Then we had seven recognisable dishes; escalope Viennoise, grilled fillet steak, etc; a choice of four basic fish dishes and a selection of seven sweets, the most interesting one being the Sernyk Alexandrovitch. This was a sweet pancake filled with cream cheese and sultanas, then quickly fried in shallow oil and served with a hot cordon of cream. Quite nice and different.

The restaurant was situated in an old disused hotel, and I used to have a few interesting 'mooches', during quiet periods, around the old kitchen that was in the basement and upstairs in the 'dorms'. Amazing how they used to work in such cramped conditions.

The bar had a hatch behind it that opened into the kitchen, and just below it in the kitchen was the famous freezer, where the vodkas and glasses were kept. Every now and again, bang would go the hatch, the barmaid would lean over, open the freezer, select the vodka or vodkas required, get the glasses, pour them out, put the bottles back and bang would go the hatch, with not a word spoken (just like watching one of the silent movies). The poor girl must have had frostbitten fingers and a set of bruised 'diddies' by the end of the night! She was quite brawny and used to wear dresses like Marilyn Monroe, but she had a bit more flesh to squeeze in than MM. I was never sure if the good business in the bar was because of the vodkas, or because of the shape of the barmaid!

The bar had three different 'authentic' vodkas as well as three special ones: Zoubrovk, which, according to the blurb, made your hair stand on end; Potzovka, which had a pink and pleasant 'kick'; and a liqueur called Spotekatch, about which they said that one mouthful made you think of a fruit, and every other mouthful made you think of a different fruit. The vodkas were all kept in an old freezer, as were the little 'shot' glasses . The idea was to take the vodka from the freezer, pour it into the frosted glass, then knock it back in one go. No wonder it took about four glasses to warm you up inside! Then it crept up behind you and whacked you over the head with an iron bar. (I was told this by one of the 'victims'.)

Once or twice a week the owners would lay on various cabaret acts, belly-dancing or men in boots with big fur hats kicking themselves into a hernia in the name of entertainment. They even once had a woman who performed a dance with a live boa constrictor wrapped around her. She was nice looking, but I think the main attraction was the question: will it squeeze or not?

The restaurant manager was always calm and composed, a true professional. The two Yugoslav waiters I remember were quite good and wore red, high-necked silky blouses with black trousers and a black cummerbund, Russian style. They both spoke good English, Italian and Russian: puts our education to shame, don't you think?

The two musicians were excellent. They dressed the same as the waiters and used to wander from table to table playing a variety of Russian and Slavic tunes, some lively, some sad. Every now and again they would do an impromptu cabaret spot – very, very good. Before they started and during their breaks, they used to retire to one of the back rooms to compose themselves and have a snifter or two from an unmarked bottle. I don't know what was in the bottle, but as the evening wore on the music became livelier and livelier. Even if they were 'on the way', they still played with gusto and never seemed to lose any notes.

The Spanish chef was about six foot and well built (for comfort not speed, is the proper description). He was quite a jolly type who was a caretaker at some nearby flats and used to moonlight here. He was fairly good, a little bit lax, but the work was done on time with no complaints, so at the end of the day and all that!

The Troika was a short but interesting period in my working life, something to look back on with a smile. In fact I have used some of the Troika's dishes to 'spice' up various menus that I have presented over the years.

Welcome to

TROIKA

120 QUEENSGATE, LONDON, S.W.7.
Telephone 01-584 9752

15. UKRAINSKI BORSHTCH
Carrots, Celery, Beetroot, Onions & Leek Simmered
for Hours in beef Bouillon with Russian Cream
Served Separately

16. BOUILLON PILIMENI
Small Meat Dumplings in Chicken Bouillon

17. SIELANKA
Russian Fish Soup

18. KOURINNEI BOUILLON
Clear Chicken Bouillon

£0.6

£0.25

CAVIAR
FRESH FROM RUSSIA

BELUGAVAIA IKRA	Russian Beluga Caviar	1 oz	£3.0
SEVRUGAVAIA IKRA	Russian Sevruga Caviar	1 oz	£2.7
KETOVAIA IKRA	Russian Red Caviar	1 oz	£2.00

The best Caviar comes from the "Beluga", the largest type of Sturgeon
and is fresh and lightly salted. Excellent Caviar is also produced out of
the "Sevruga" Sturgeon but it is smaller and slightly different in taste.
Red Caviar, made from Salmon Roe has a flavour of its own.

BLINI

BLINI, a typical Russian Speciality, very light, unsweetened thick
Pancakes served with salted or smoked fish or Caviar and thick
Russian Cream;

Blini with Sour Cream	
Blini with Pickled Herring	£0.50
Blini with Smoked Salmon	£0.80
Blini with Red Caviar	£1.25
Blini with Sevruga Caviar 1 oz	£2.00
	£2.75

166

HOUSE SPECIALITIES

£1.45

KURITSA KIEV
Breast of Chicken coated in Bread Crumbs
cooked in Butter

£1.40

KURITSA PUSHKIN
Chicken in White Sauce with Mushrooms and Cream

£1.35

2. **KAVKASKIE GOLOUBTSE**
Meat and Rice Rolled in Cabbage Leaves with Rice

£1.40

23. **SVININA PO URALSKI**
Smoked Pork Served with Kasha

24.

25.

26

2

ALL ABOUT VODKA!!!

Traditionally Vodka is served iced in a "RUMKA" a small liqueur glass and drank in a single gulp, followed by Russian Sweetmeats or Russian Hors d'Oeuvres. However if one prefers a long drink or a cocktail Vodka makes an ideal base.

We have three kinds of Vodka, apart from the usual colourless variety.

Zoubrovka (pale yellow) is vodka in which has been macerated a special herb which the Bisons eat in Poland. Bisons are strong . . . Zoubrovka should make your hair stand up on end!

Petzovka is also vodka but with Paprika in it, giving it a Pink tint and a pleasant "kick".

Another product made of vodka is the liqueur Spotekatch. One of the oldest known liqueurs in Russia. Each mouthful makes you think of a different fruit.

We would like to thank you for your visit to TROIKA and we hope that you enjoyed the food, music and atmosphere and that you will make the TROIKA one of your regular places for an evening out with a difference!

The Carlton Club
St. James Street, London SW1
Chef de cuisine, November 1973-October 1978

It's funny, but I can't remember exactly how I got the position of head chef at the Carlton Club. I seem to remember answering an advert, but I'm not positive. Anyway I was taken on as the head chef ... BRILLIANT!!

The first few days were taken up with meeting all the various staff and generally settling in. It was quite a good job as I was allowed a lot of artistic leeway with dishes and menus, so it was very good from a creative point of view. The house manager (or general manager, as he would have been called in a hotel) was called Mr Blackburn. He was the typical 'club' servant, always impeccably dressed in black jacket, striped trousers, white shirt, black tie, the usual undertakers outfit that all managers seem to wear – traditional or what! He was a Pickwickian type of chap in his late 50s and he always seemed cheerful. Nothing seemed to get on top of him, he always had a solution and knew his job backwards. We got on well and I like to think we made a good team. Mr Blackburn had been at the club for a few years as had a majority of the staff – talk about a job for life. He knew what most, if not all, the members' likes and dislikes were – a real mine of information was Mr B.

In the kitchen when I started was the sous, Fred Schofield, who had been a chef at the club for donkeys. He was quite fiery (he used to have red hair, now turning white), though he said he was now calmer. He must have been a right old burning bush in his youth! Once you got to know Fred you found out that under the 'fire', he was really a very capable and caring guy. He used to give blood on a regular basis during his afternoon break, and while I was there he was presented with a certificate for giving so many pints over the years. 'It's only extra blood that I don't need,' he

168

used to say. Fred knew the system inside out. 'What day is it?' he'd say, 'we'll sell more pie than fish today', or 'the cold buffet will take a hammering today'. And bloody hell, he was right 98 per cent of the time!

I must admit I found Fred a bit hard going at first, as he didn't see why I wanted to change things, introduce new ideas, different dishes, together with a new style and variety of menus. 'They have had it this way for years, why change?' he would say. But gradually, as he saw that business was getting better, he became more amenable and co-operative. Apart from being the sous chef, Fred was also the saucier, so he was kept quite busy. His pride and joy was his chestnut stuffing for the turkey which was one of the best stuffings I have ever tasted and I admit I have used his recipe ever since. Nice one Fred! All this, together with the occasional couple of hot starters, he managed by himself with a cheerful grumble. (He was one of those guys who had to have a grumble about something at least once a day, seemed to be his 'fix' in life.) Fred was a good working influence on the other staff.

In the larder was another 'old stager', Paul. He had not been there as long as Fred, so was a bit more flexible towards the different dishes and menus. Paul was a typical English chef, cool, calm and collected at all times. He ran the larder well and turned out the famous cold game pie that the members used to adore. Even after Paul had gone, we carried on with the same recipe – some dishes you just can't change, can you? The larder did its own butchery and pâtés etc, and we made most of the hors d'oeuvres 'on site', cleaned, filleted the various fish and shellfish, cooked our own gulls' eggs, quails' eggs, coloured the eggs for Easter etc. Paul always ran the larder efficiently and turned out the goods on time.

After I had been there a while Paul went sick. He had been complaining about his legs for a while, and unfortunately they just gave up on him one day. The last we heard was that he had lost a leg and was being admitted into a nursing home, then soon after, we heard he had gone to the 'big kitchen'. Shame, 'cos he was very knowledgeable and, with his sense of humour, a popular bloke.

In the larder, as a help to Paul, there was yet another old timer called Joe Kearns. He had done the usual rounds and was, like the others, a mine of information on the 'old days' – very interesting. Joe's main job was to do up the hors d'oeuvres, then go up and do the carving in the restaurant. We had about 20 different hors d'oeuvres on offer each day, and Joe used to change at least five of them daily. We had a revolving serving trolley, which went up into the members' and guests' restaurant on the first floor and another selection used to be laid out on two trays and put onto the large (bloody large!) table that ran most of the length of the club room (members only).

Joe only worked lunchtimes as it kept him busy in retirement and out of mischief. Though he was in his late 60s or early 70s, he was very fit and agile for his age. Joe had lots of stories about places where he had worked, some funny, some sad, but always interesting (like my little effort here, I hope!) He'd tell us how hard it was for an Englishman to get on in the 1920s and 30s in a trade that was dominated by French and Italians.

There is one story I will always remember. Joe was working in this London kitchen as a chef tournant. All the rest of the brigade were French, and they made life hard for Joe, ignoring him and speaking only in French. The sous chef seemed to delight in giving Joe all the crappy jobs, like making him work the afternoon shift, getting all the 101 things ready for the evening service so that the chefs de partie were in place as soon as they arrived back, then having to help them all during service time. After a while, Joe just let the mise en place 'slide'. When the chef arrived, Joe wrapped up his knives, told him to 'get stuffed' and walked out – after getting paid, of course. He got another job the next day (you could in them days, jobs were plentiful). He heard later that the chef had nearly had a heart attack when he found out what Joe had done just before service. The chefs de partie were so used to Joe getting everything ready for them, they hadn't checked out the sauces etc. Just a touch of English revenge, as Joe would say!

Also in the larder with Paul was a Moroccan who was the second larder. He was not very good but passable as a temporary measure when Paul went sick. I made him up to larder chef in the hope that with a bit of responsibility he would improve. Bad move! The guy used to go sick at the drop of a hat, and he was slow, christ was he slow! Even a tortoise in a coma was quicker off the mark. Then, to crown it all, he went sick again. After a couple of weeks chasing him up to find out what the problem was this time, what do you think? A message was sent in to say that he had suffered a heart attack! (Didn't think he was active enough for that sort of thing). The funny thing was that the doctor who signed the sick note was ... his brother! He was out for at least a month and we could never seem to get hold of him, strange eh! When he eventually came back he had such a list of dos and don'ts from his 'doctor' (no lifting, *regular breaks*, no stress, *regular breaks*, no late nights, *regular breaks*). He left soon after I had explained to him that his 'health requirements' would not allow him to work in a kitchen, and added couple of comments that I won't bore you with. So it was good-bye to him!

The breakfast chef was a Spaniard called Rikky di Castello. He had originally been a tailor in Spain and he used to make all his own outfits, as well as other people's, under his own 'Rikky' label. Rikky was fun and a good worker; apart from doing brekkies he also helped out with the staff lunches and wherever he was needed. He gave the impression of being gay, but no-one was really sure. (He and Janet, the still room lady, were

170

always together and as Janet liked her men, it left a question mark.)

One of the best things about working at the Carlton Club was the hours: Monday to Friday only, breakfast, lunch and dinner, plus parties. The dinner service finished at 9-9.30 pm. The club was closed bank holidays and for all of August (now, I believe, they stay open), so there was no worrying about who would work weekends and bank holidays. (Christmas and New Year are the worst times to cover.) I actually had time to see the kids (and the wife) and we could all go out or away at weekends without having to plan it months ahead – lovely!

Imagine my surprise when one day Rikky asked me to get his application for renewing his work visa stamped by the club When I checked that he had filled in the details correctly, I nearly fell out of my chair: he was only staying in the same flat where I had spent the first 20-odd years of my life, 86 Derby Lodge, Wicklow Street, Kings Cross! Amazing or what! Of all the guys in all the world ... (Sorry about that, I have just been watching 'Humph' in Casablanca.) But really, out of all the millions in town, one of the guys you work with living in your old flat. I wonder what the odds are on that? Spooky or what!

During my five years at the club, the staffing of the kitchen was pretty static, not many changes, and I like to think we had a good team ... in fact I know we did! We had many letters of thanks from members who had various functions at the club, praising the standards and the food.

Then Dave French joined us as larder chef (later sous) and Carl Evans became veg chef (later larder). I knew both of these guys from my Royal Court days, and as we all seemed to think along the same lines, it was natural that we should all get together again. Dave was (and still is) a good chef with a completely whacky sense of humour. Though he is small in stature, there is a brick wall inside so don't give him any hassle! When Fred retired it seemed logical to offer his position to Dave, and also to offer the larder position to Carl. So they both stepped up the ladder of life. As they had worked hard they deserved the promotions. Dave was a bit hesitant about taking over the sauce as well as the sous responsibilities, but he soon got the hang of it and settled in very nicely, as did Carl.

Carl was a bit on the shy side, but a bloody good worker, though he tended to worry about things a lot. Dave and I were always trying to 'calm' him down and boost his confidence, and I like to think that we succeeded. While Carl was with us he celebrated his 21st birthday. Normally I would have offered him the chance to have the day off, but as we had a few surprises in store for Carl, I asked him to work the lunch shift (rotten sod, wasn't I?) On the day, Dave and I arrived early and with the help of Rikky and Janet, we did up the kitchen and larder with streamers and banners etc. It looked like Christmas had come early that year. The main lights of the kitchen were turned off and the door shut, and with champagne on ice we waited for Carl to arrive. As he entered the kitchen, the lights came on, we all shouted 'Happy birthday!' and shoved a glass of bubbly into his hand. I think he enjoyed his day; I know we all did!

During the time I was at the club we had no pastry chef, so I used to do it. I made most of the trolley sweets, fruit salad, mousses, compotes, cheesecakes etc. The only things we used to buy in were the gateaux and flans. I like to think that we provided a good selection of sweets for the members. Also for lunch, we used to have a hot milk pudding of some sort: rice, semolina, tapioca etc.

When Carl moved into the larder, we had a guy called Bill (original, eh!) start as the veggie. Bill had served a lot of time in the merchant navy as a chef, and he had stories coming out of his ears about his days serving on various ships. The ones I remember were of the days during the last war when he was on the Russian convoys; how the waves would hit the deck and freeze solid in seconds, how they would wrap themselves up in umpteen jumpers and duffle coats, scarves, helmets, anything to stop the cold freezing their 'bits'. Then they would go on deck and try to chip off the ice before the ship got top heavy with ice and turned over. Apparently you could spit and watch it freeze before it got more than a foot away. Bloody cold!

'Old Bill', as he was affectionately called, was about 50 but still single and lived near the South Norwood Cemetery with (I think) his sister. Bill was a very good worker, and if he was en place, he would help either Dave or Carl out. That's what you call team work! He was a great guy, a good mixer with a zany sense of humour (the 'you don't have to be mad to work here, but it helps' type).

The main kitchen porter was a chap called Joe, whose dress sense harked back to the 1920s: hobnailed boots, heavy corduroy trousers, waistcoat and scarf. With his heavy overcoat and cheesecutter hat, he looked the spitting image of one of those 1920s photos of the 'good old British worker'. Joe was a right old cockney, not very bright in some matters (work) but well up front in others (money). He had a brother who was the 'spit' of him (two like Joe? Please!) Joe had been at the Carlton, like Fred, from the year dot. I don't think he had worked anywhere else. He was a methodical worker with two speeds, stop and slow (just joking, Joe!) He had his daily routine and you couldn't rush him, but at the end of the day the jobs were all done. Fred used to give Joe a rollocking on a daily basis, but I think it was just part of their daily ritual.

The other porter was called Albert (good old names, eh!) I never really found out much about him, as conversing with Albert was as easy as pulling a shark's teeth while it was swimming. He was about 5'1" and looked like a Pakistani, with his 'chin' beard and thin face. He had suf-

172

fered some sort of brain disorder (that's if he had one; sorry, that was very wicked of me!) Fred told me that Albert had survived an attack of meningitis when he was younger, but I never found out for sure. Our Albert was never very quick or 'with it' (except on paydays). He used to work mainly in the club room servery, loading and unloading the two lifts. I have to admit that on busy days (that is, most days) he would wind me up and I would finish off by shouting at him. His job was very simple: one lift up, one lift down, empty the dishes coming up and put them into the hot-plate, then put the dirty dishes in and send them down to the kitchen. Easy peasy, I hear you cry. But quite often Albert would keep both lifts up and go into a trance while we waited in the kitchen to send the orders up – really frustrating! Fred once told me that if Albert had looked better and was more 'with it', he could have his pick of the women as he was 'hung like a donkey' (Fred's words), although I never found out for sure. (Imagine: 'I say, Albert, would you mind showing me your dick, as I'm told you're hung like a donkey.')

We had a variety of porters in on a casual basis as and when needed. Some were best forgotten, others were a bit better. (This was during the time of 'Denmark Street', remember?) One guy that used to come fairly regularly was an old(ish) Italian with large glasses and a 'Groucho' moustache. He was quite good and seemed to enjoy washing the pots; he was at his happiest when he had a sinkful of dirty pots. Some of the other staff were: Jerry O'Connor, the maintenance guy, a jovial Irishman. He could do anything – no exaggeration – from knowing where the bends in the pipes were to tracing the wiring, to any building work, carpentry, etc. I remember once he transformed a spare room at the top of the building that was just used as a general store, into a library. He made and fitted all the shelves himself, put up the panelling and decorated it, it really looked great when he had done. He did a really marvellous job, just one of many.

There were a couple of hall porters who greeted members and their guests as they arrived, carried out various jobs and errands for members, and in general checked everyone who came into the club. One of them, Harold, had been at the club for years and years, ad infinitum. Harold had a marvellous memory, he knew all the members by sight and name, who their guests were etc. I sometimes thought he knew more about the members than their own parents. He looked a bit like Arthur Askey and was always flitting about doing something or other. I have a book about the history of the Carlton Club, written by Sir Charles Petrie, that old Harold gave me, and a very interesting book it is. I love history so it was right up my street.

The other porter was called Cyril. I was told that he had been in the navy for quite a number of years, but never found out for sure. These two porters really pampered the members, as the rest of the staff did.

Then we had Janet in the still room (if you knew Janet, you'd know this is a fitting comment). She came originally from Glasgow and was divorced (her second, I think). She was in her late 40s, petite and slim, and she lived in the staff quarters at the top of the club. Janet used to dress and behave like she was 20: she wore all the modern styles, short and skimpy, leather gear etc. Rikky used to make quite a lot of her clothes and I must admit she looked quite nice when she got 'dolled' up. Janet was on the whole (oops, there I go again!) a happy sort, always game for a laugh, good to give and take a joke. She used to have a moan now and again, but don't most women? Janet ran the still room with another woman, they were always busy whatever shift, with teas and coffees here, there and everywhere.

There was always some gossip or other about Janet and her latest 'boy-friend', and the antics they got up to. It sounded like she was the co-author of the Kama Sutra. On quiet days we used to get her to reminisce about her younger days in Glasgow. She had a good way with words and some of her stories were really hilarious. A couple of nights a week Janet did some part-time cashier work at the little cinema at the Piccadilly end of Piccadilly (you know what I mean!) and her stories of the 'raincoat' brigade were also very funny.

The club also had some chambermaids who lived in. The only one I really remember was called Nellie. Though she was old then, I recently heard that she is still going strong. Nellie had been at the Carlton for years and years and was a lovely lady, always cheery and full of energy.

All the staff at the club really got on well together. I really cannot remember anyone having a row – very unusual, don't you think?

There were about eight rooms at the club where members could stay overnight or for a longer period. I will always remember the time when Judge Argyle was staying and he claimed that he'd had some money taken from his room. He got quite stroppy, so I was told, and insisted that the police were called. All the staff were interviewed by the CID and had their hands put under a special infra red light to see if there were any tell-tale stains. It was finally concluded that the theft was the work of an opportunist thief from outside, but the episode upset quite a few of the staff, who thought their honesty and loyalty were being questioned. After a little while it all blew over.

In the members' bar, a large, dour-looking Irishman was in charge. He was always impeccably dressed, and I wouldn't be surprised to find out he had been in the guards. We got on well, as once you got to know him he was quite witty. He ran his bar very efficiently. As a member would hover in sight, he'd be pouring the chap's tipple for him.

During the season we used to put gulls' eggs into the bar for the members to eat with oriental salt. At Easter we would put some coloured eggs

174

to bring back memories of their younger days.

A barman called Barry, who was always cheerful and had some wise crack or other, ran the upstairs bar and was also the wine waiter in the 'mixed' restaurant. He too was still there when I last heard (1996).

Another guy was Jimmy Cassins, a jovial Irishman in charge of the wine cellar who was also a wine waiter (sommelière) in the club restaurant. Jimmy had a ruddy complexion (probably all the red wine he had to taste coming out) and was a bit of an 'old woman', but his heart was in the right place (round about the middle of the chest, I'm told). He knew his wines inside out, as well as all the members' favourite drinks. 'The usual, Jimmy,' they would say and before you could recite the Bible, there he was with the bottle or drink – bloody good memory. Jimmy left during my time there, though I was never sure if he jumped or was pushed. I did hear later that he'd had a nervous breakdown, but I never found out for sure.

Towards my last period at the club, the club committee decided to open an old store room in the basement as an evening supper room. The idea was that members not wanting a full meal could come down for a snack or just a quiet drink. The chef there was a Spaniard called Mike Campos, in his 50s, slim and always with a smile. I had met Mike before at one of my other jobs, and as he had a morning job and wanted a light evening job, he was ideal. Mike was one of those cool, calm and collected sorts who knew his job and was utterly reliable. He had his own little kitchen in a room next door to the supper room. They also employed a middle-aged waiter just to work evenings. He had a job as a butler in the city, so was very efficient. He and Mike got on well, a nice team, I thought.

Many a night Harold Macmillan was a customer, sometimes eating, mostly just coming in for a drink or two, and pleasant conversation with other members. He liked to have a bottle of port at his elbow (just to look at, you understand). Mr Macmillan was reputed to have a very good sense of humour, and to be full of amusing anecdotes. When word got round that he was 'holding forth' in the supper room, they used to crowd in to hear the great man. He was about 80 then, but his mind was still razor sharp, as was his wit. Often there would be roars of laughter coming out of the supper room.

It was about this time that Mons. Habert joined us. He had by now retired after being the head chef at the Hotel Russell for a few years. He took over as the carvery chef at lunch, as Joe had well retired by then. Mons. Habert used to come in about 10 am, set up his solid silver carving trolley in the members room, then give Dave a hand with the hors d'oeuvres and cold buffet for the club room. During lunch he would wheel the trolley around the room, carving at the table (you don't see this any more; no more personal service, all plated up ready now!). Mons. Habert seemed to enjoy the contact with the members and also getting back into the 'kitchen life' again. Besides, it kept him off the streets!

During my time at the Carlton, we were fortunate to be able to take part in the election night buffets – two, in fact. They are one of the most pleasant memories I have of the club. The buffets were strictly full decorated buffets, and we had to cater for about 400 members and guests. We provided such things as decorated pâtés, plain and en croute, glazed and decorated quennelles of sole, whole decorated fresh salmon, fresh lobsters, cold and glazed ham on the bone, whole cooked and carved sirloins, supreme jeanettes, potted shrimps, sides of smoked salmon, king prawns, cold duck with orange sauce glaze, a selection of at least eight different salads, fresh fruit salad, poached fresh pears, peaches, assorted gateaux and flans, baskets of fresh seasonal fruits, bowls of ripe strawberries etc.

We worked really hard the two days leading up to the evening. For the service (we had chefs on the buffets serving the members and their guests) we had to recruit three or four of our friends to come and help: Barry, Geoff, Mike, Mons. Habert. Although I say it myself, we did a very good job and received lots of compliments and congratulations from our members. One I remember especially came from one of the committee members, a Mr Senior, who was, so I was told, on the board of the great Cunard Line. He said that he had not seen such a good buffet for years, and it took him back to when he was younger and used to attend the 'old style' buffets.

The style of the service in the club started to change when a Mr Harvey joined the club catering committee. He was, I think, chief accountant for the then Rowten Hotels Group (originally the Rowten hostels for homeless men, who used to stay a night or week or even use it as their home address). They were about a two-star group, concentrating mainly on tourists and backpackers. Mr Harvey convinced the rest of the committee that he could make the catering turn a profit (hard to do when you buy a sky grouse for £2 and cannot sell it for more than £2.50, including all the proper garnishes, bread sauce, game chips, and brandy-flavoured game gravy!)

Anyway, he brought in his whizz-kid second in command, a woman who proceeded to say that we should buy in a lot of food ready made, buy cheaper cuts, not use so much cream or wine when cooking – in general, bring down the standards and quality of the menus. She also wanted to cut down on the selection we offered, so it really made life difficult for us, trying to please the management and the members.

In the offices there was an older lady who ran the secretarial department with a rod of iron. Most people didn't get on with her, but I found her quite good to work with. The main man was the club accountant Mr Woods, who seemed to be in a world of his own most of the time, but I suppose he knew what he was doing. He had an assistant called Philip Pitchen, a Mauritian, nice enough bloke but he didn't seem to get on with Mr Woods, so there was always a bit of an atmosphere in the office.

Then there was the club secretary. For a while Mr Blackburn had been performing a dual role as manager and stand-in secretary. I believe that for a time one of the members was a proxy (I said *proxy!*) secretary. One of the secretaries I remember had been, I was told, a captain of one of our battleships before retiring from the navy after umpteen years of service. He wasn't a bad sort, didn't interfere too much with the running of the club. He had a ruddy complexion (not sure if it was the fresh air or the booze) and he used to give me a 'shopping list' of his requirements at weekends, things like: two or three pounds of fresh sirloin, vegetables or salads, butter, eggs etc. When I inquired at the office if I was going to get credit for all this food going out, I was told he was not supposed to be having it. Oops!

Another secretary was called Robin McDouall who, I was told, had been the secretary at the Pratts Club and the Travellers before joining the Carlton. He was well-known for his books on food and was supposed to be an expert, but when he asked for the French name of Ogen Melon, you have to wonder. But Mr McDouall was friendly and didn't interfere much. He certainly had a passion for food and loved to come into the kitchen and see what new dishes we were trying out. It made a nice change to be able to talk about food.

About this time Mr Blackburn decided to retire, and the search for a new manager began. Among the applicants was a dapper little Greek called George, who had been one of the head waiters at the Westbury Hotel when I was there. I mentioned to Mr Blackburn that I knew him and thought he would be ideal for the position. George started about two months before Mr Blackburn retired, so that Mr B could 'run him in' and introduce him to the committee members and the rest of the members. Then George took over the reins and as far as I know he is still there. Found your niche in life, have you, George?

As the club closed every year for the whole of August, the last few days of July we were busy deep cleaning all the equipment and packing it away in the store room. We used to finish about 12 pm, then adjourn to the local hostelry, The Red Lion, for a couple of holiday 'jars'. We used to arrive back a couple of days before the club was due to open, unpack everything clean and wash down all the equipment (it is surprising how dusty things get when left), sort out the orders and generally get 'en place'. It was time off like this that compensated for all the split shifts that we did, although I used to stay on for one or two days so that I could plan the next week's table d'hôte menus and sort out any party requirements.

When I started at the Carlton, we were only doing a few parties a week and Friday evenings were absolutely dead – maybe four or five members would be in to eat. But when I left we were doing at least 20 plus on Friday nights and at least five or six parties per week, plus we had a regular political lunch once a month for 30-plus members. These were arranged with Mr Alex Macmillan, now Lord Stockton. I used to supply him with about four different menus, he would OK them and then all he had to do for the next four months was let me know the numbers that were coming.

The last secretary I dealt with was a Mr Linsley, who had also come from one of the other clubs. He seemed to be a pleasant enough chap, left us alone and seemed happy enough with the business.

But then we parted company, which was a bit of a surprise, to put it mildly.

It was a Friday evening and I had just sent the sweet up for a party when Mr Linsley phoned to ask if I would pop down to see him. I did so and was absolutely gobsmacked to be given notice to quit (to this day I'm not sure why!) I was told that I had to pack up and go that evening! The lads were not very happy when I went back and told them.

Within a couple of weeks all the lads had given notice and gone. Mons. Habert turned up on the Monday, packed his knives and walked out. Poor old Carl took it badly, I was told that he nearly cracked up. Dave told them what to do on the Monday, Bill did the same. I was quite touched by their loyalty. The club had to call Fred back to help them out.

Although the work was hard, I really enjoyed my time at the Carlton Club. The only reason I can think of for my having to go was that I was being made the scapegoat for Mr Harvey and his female colleague. They had promised to make the club show a profit, but in truth it never would if we were unable to sell anything at more than £1 over the cost price. Shame, but there you go!

This Menu is intended as a guide. The Chef will be pleased to
supply subject to due notice any other items required.

À la Carte Menu

Parfait de Fois Gras 30/-   Plovers Eggs.

Half Doz. Oysters 11/6.   Gulls Eggs.

Half Doz. Oysters Mornay 16/6.   When in Season.

HORS D'OEUVRE

ors d'Oeuvres Varies	8/6	Grapefruit Cerisette	2/-
moked Scotch Salmon	10/6	Honeydew Melon	7/-
moked River Trout	5/6	Pâté Maison	7/-
otted Shrimps	5/6		

POTAGES

lear Turtle Soup with Sherry	7/-	Crème de Tomates	3/-
isque de Homard	7/-	Crème du Jour	2/6
onsommé Yvette	5/-	Consommé du Jour	2/6
		Crème Vichyssoise	
		(Hot or Cold)	5/-

POISSONS

ried Fillets of Sole Lemon 10/6   ½ Lobster & Salad or
illet of Sole Veronique   12/-   Newburg, Cardinal, Thermidor,
illet of Sole Meunière Caprice 12/- American, when available.
over Sole Colbert   14/6
over Sole Belle Meunière   15/6

ENTREES

oast Aylesbury Duckling 3/4 47/6   Roast Surrey Chicken & Bacon
rilled Double Lamb Cutlet   (2)   25/6
rilled Fillet Steak   Duckling à l'Orange 3/4 52/6
ournedos Holder   Grilled Lamb Cutlets (2)
amb Chop and Kidney
ump Steak

Entrecôte Sauté Chasseur
Omelette Various

-:-

BUFFET FROID

ame Pie	9/6	Roast Chicken	8/6
ork Ham	9/6	Roast Duck	11/-
hicken & Ham	10/6	Roast Beef	9/6
x Tongue	10/-		

SALADES

ettuce Salad	2/-	Tomato Salad	2/-
rench Salad	2/-	Potato Salad	2/-
ussian Salad	2/-	Beetroot Salad	2/-

LEGUMES

auliflower au Gratin	2/6	Haricots Verts	3/-
raised Celery	2/6	Potatoes Boiled	2/-
etits Pois	2/6	Potatoes Mashed	2/-
pinach en Branches	2/6	Potatoes Saute	2/-
raised Fennel	2/6	Potatoes Fried	2/-

ENTREMETS

eringue Glace Chantilly	2/6	Glace Panache	2/-
repes Confitures	3/-	Peche Melba	3/6
oupe Jacques	3/-	Creme Caramel	2/-
ime, Lemon, Orange or		Peach Ambrosia	5/6
Strawberry Sorbet	2/6		

Cheese Souffle 8/-. Liqueur Souffle 8/6.

SAVOURIES

anape Diane	2/6	Soft Roes on Toast	2/6
cotch Woodcock	2/6	Angels on Horseback	4/6
ardines on Toast	2/6	Canape Baron	3/6

TABLE MONEY 1/6.

British Steel Corporation
Grosvenor Place, London SW1
Head chef, October 1978-June 1979

While I was trying to get over the loss of my job at the Carlton Club, I was asked if I would be interested in taking over as head chef at the main kitchen of the British Steel Headquarters in Victoria. I had never done this type of catering before (staff canteen/restaurant), but the hours were good (8 am until 4 pm, Monday to Friday, no weekends or Bank Holidays) and the money was near to what I'd been getting at the club, so I didn't lose much, plus I gained the challenge of sorting out the kitchen and the service.

The catering manager was a git called Triannis (I hope that's how you spell it), who was so smooth even butter wouldn't stick on him. He was not too bad on the whole, though he always had to have the last word. If you had a suggestion, it was no good: it wouldn't work, was absolutely useless, etc. But then a couple of weeks later it would be presented by him as a brilliant idea, and it had to be put into effect at once (creep!) Mr Triannis was, I think, Greek or Turkish, or maybe Algerian or Tunisian. He knew it all, a walking encyclopedia full of shit! Other than that he was a great bloke. He used to come down during the morning and check that all was well, make sure we had any party menus, have a chat with the lads ('Good morning, all right?' – short, sharp and sweet with the lower echelons.)

The kitchen was situated in the basement and served 200-300 every day, plus we had to provide for any buffet or cocktail parties for the middle management, as well as a separate lunch service for them. The kitchen was quite big and long, plenty of room to swing an elephant.

One of the other chefs was a small middle-aged Italian who could really laugh, but not very often. He knew his job (the sauce/fish) and turned out the goods on time with no problem, so I left him alone: no use trying to change a working system. He started at about 7 am and finished about 2.30; apparently these were the hours he was employed, so that was that. He had 'done the rounds' and was just cruising along until he could retire.

The guy on the veg was also an Italian, but I can't remember anything else about him, not even his name. (On his tombstone: 'here lies whatsisname'.) In the larder/salad section we had a young English lad who was due to come out (know what I mean, nudge nudge, wink wink). He only knew the British Steel way of doing things, so it was a bit hard to get him to change and uplift his style and quality of service. However, bit by bit we made it, and in the end he was quite good, showing a bit of flair in his presentation.

It's terrible, but I don't seem to be able to recall anything about the sweet and pastry section (been asleep since then!) The kitchen porters were a motley crew, they all used to slide off for a pint in the pub next door during the staff lunch break, but as they all pulled together during service and after, with the cleaning of the kitchen, I was happy. The manager tried to stop them going out for their daily pint (or fix!), but things got out of hand. They started to bring in the beer and drink during the service which meant that the work got a bit haphazard! After I had had a word with the manager and pointed out that the guys needed their fix before service, he did a Nelson, so I told the guys they could go back to the old system, but if they brought beer in they would be sacked. Peace then returned and apart from when someone had a birthday, they didn't abuse the privilege. (Funny but they always seemed to have a birthday at the end of each month, payday!)

The stores were run by a large black guy (or dude, as they say now) who was nice enough but I don't think he had much stores experience. It took him ages to do the orders, and as for the stock take, well, I often had to help him out. I tried to explain about stock rotation but gave up in the end, and just tried to be around when deliveries came, or gave him one of the more 'with it' porters to help him out. As the singer says, 'We will survive!'

Up in the directors' dining rooms there was a husband and wife team, he was the chef, she was the second. They were quite good and turned out some very good gear. They were about 23 and had only been married for a short time before British Steel. I met him a few years later and he told me they had broken up a couple of years before. Working together and living together doesn't always work out. Shame really, 'cos they seemed like a good couple.

There were two women who were the manager's seconds. One called I think, Joan, was in charge of the canteen staff, helping to oversee the service and generally keeping the girls in order. She always had a grim expression (a bit like our Italian sauce chef, could laugh but not often – very serious people at the B.S. you know!) The other woman was always very made-up with immaculate hair that could have been a rug ('bitchy, bitchy, where's the milk! I hear you cry.) They had both been doing the jobs for years and could do it with their eyes shut. I got on quite well with them both, once they saw that I was not going to be a problem to them.

They both thought that Mr Triannis was a right old plonker.

In those days I used to do a fair bit of pickling (onions etc,) and one evening as I walked to the station with four empty half-gallon jars in a carrier bag, I passed Mr Triannis and the two women who were going home, said hello and carried on. The next day I was summoned to his office and told off for taking the empty jars off the premises. 'Bloody hell,' I said, 'they were only going to be thrown away!' I was told, 'No matter, nothing was to be taken away'.

Unfortunately Mr Triannis seemed to have forgotten this statement a few months later when he gaily (not in the sense you think) went home with some 'goodies' from British Steel – funny eh! One law for the 'boss' and another for the poor old worker, so what's new!

Although my time at British Steel was fairly short, it gave me an insight into the other side of catering, the staff restaurant side. It was OK, I suppose, but apart from the hours, not really for me.

I was told a few years later by the director's chef that Mr Triannis (who knew it all, remember?), upon being told that one of the fridges was giving off electric shocks to all who touched it and needed attention, pooh-poohed this and casually rested his hand on the fridge door. Guess what ... yes, he got a massive shock! (It was as if the fridge was saying, 'I'll teach you to doubt me'). He had to be taken to hospital and it took him a while to recover.

This story is a fitting end to my account of my time at British Steel, don't you think! (The Lord does move in mysterious ways!)

The Cafe Royal
Wimbledon, London SW19
Sous chef, August-November 1979

While I was looking round to get back into the West End (and decent catering) again, I was offered a temporary position as sous chef in The Cafe Royal, situated at the top of the hill just before you got to Wimbledon Common, and more or less opposite The Dog and Fox pub.

The chef was a large Italian in his late 40s who still lived with his parents. He was not bad, a bit lax on standards, but on the whole a decent chef. The owner had inherited him and the other chef when she bought the place a few months earlier. We always got on well, so I found him bearable to work with. There was another chef (there were only the three of us) who did the starters, sweets and salads, a bit of an aging hippy who was really wrapped up in biorhythms and horoscopes. If he had a bad result with his early morning bio then he would redo it all day until he got a good result. (Me, I would have just cheated with the adding!) Amazing letting a set of numbers and figures rule your day, but it made him happy. Apart from his obsession, he was a very intelligent, capable bloke and didn't fall apart when the business got heavy. He also had a good sense of humour and all three of us got on well.

Although it was only a fair size place (about a 40-seater), it had quite a good selection in its menu: 20 starters (hot and cold), six different soups, 12 fish dishes, 13 different 'plats de gourmets', 12 entrees, five potato dishes, a large daily selection of fresh vegetables, seven salads, and 16 sweets plus the cheese board. There was enough on the menu to keep us out of mischief.

The trouble was, the chef did not seem to want to improve the turnover. He was quite happy with the small but steady number of regulars, while the boss obviously wanted to do much better – get well off the ground and breathe new life into the place. Business was erratic, lunches were up and down, as were the dinners, so no sort of pattern emerged to help with the planning of orders. Apparently the last owner had just let the place 'tick over', using the same menu all the time, so it was going to take a while for the news to spread.

Although I was only there for a short time, I enjoyed the experience. I could take the car and park it in one of the side streets, which meant I could get home for a couple of hours in the afternoon, so it was also good in that respect. The atmosphere was easy going, and I was sorry in a way to leave and head back to the West End, but there you go. Onwards and upwards, as they say!

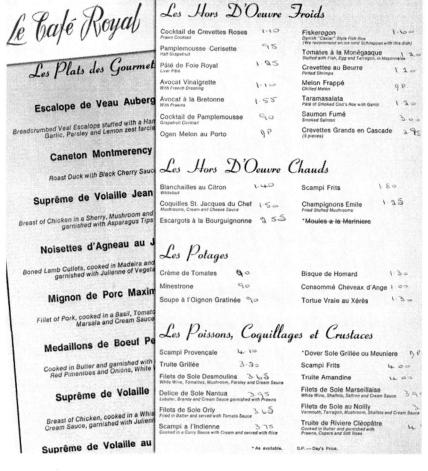

Le Café Royal

Les Plats des Gourmet

Escalope de Veau Auberg

Breadcrumbed Veal Escalope stuffed with a Ham Garlic, Parsley and Lemon zest farcie

Caneton Montmerency

Roast Duck with Black Cherry Sauce

Suprême de Volaille Jean

Breast of Chicken in a Sherry, Mushroom and garnished with Asparagus Tips

Noisettes d'Agneau au J

Boned Lamb Cutlets, cooked in Madeira and garnished with Julienne of Vegeta

Mignon de Porc Maxim

Fillet of Pork, cooked in a Basil, Tomato Marsala and Cream Sauce

Medaillons de Boeuf Pe

Cooked in Butter and garnished with Red Pimentoes and Onions, White

Suprême de Volaille

Breast of Chicken, cooked in a Whis Cream Sauce, garnished with Julienn

Suprême de Volaille au

Les Hors D'Oeuvre Froids

Cocktail de Crevettes Roses Prawn Cocktail	1·10	Fiskerogon Danish "Caviar" Style Fish Roe (We recommend an Ice cold Schnapps with this dish)	1·60
Pamplemousse Cerisette Half Grapefruit	95	Tomates à la Monègasque Stuffed with Fish, Egg and Tarragon, in Mayonnaise	1·20
Pâté de Foie Royal Liver Pâté	1·25	Crevettes au Beurre Potted Shrimps	1·10
Avocat Vinaigrette With French Dressing	1·10	Melon Frappé Chilled Melon	9 P
Avocat à la Bretonne With Prawns	1·55	Taramasalata Pâté of Smoked Cod's Roe with Garlic	1·20
Cocktail de Pamplemousse Grapefruit Cocktail	90	Saumon Fumé Smoked Salmon	3·00
Ogen Melon au Porto	9 P	Crevettes Grands en Cascade (5 pieces)	2·95

Les Hors D'Oeuvre Chauds

Blanchailles au Citron Whitebait	1·40	Scampi Frits	1·80
Coquilles St. Jacques du Chef Mushrooms, Cream and Cheese Sauce	1·50	Champignons Emile Fried Stuffed Mushrooms	1·25
Escargots à la Bourguignonne	2·55	*Moules à la Marinière	

Les Potages

Crème de Tomates	90	Bisque de Homard	1·30
Minestrone	90	Consommé Cheveax d'Ange	1·00
Soupe à l'Oignon Gratinée	90	Tortue Vraie au Xérès	1·30

Les Poissons, Coquillages et Crustaces

Scampi Provençale	4·10	*Dover Sole Grillée ou Meuniere	9 P
Truite Grillée	3·20	Scampi Frits	4·00
Filets de Sole Desmoulins White Wine, Tomatoes, Mushroom, Parsley and Cream Sauce	3·65	Truite Amandine	4·00
Delice de Sole Nantua Lobster, Brandy and Cream Sauce garnished with Prawns	3·95	Filets de Sole Marseillaise White Wine, Shallots, Saffron and Cream Sauce	3·9
Filets de Sole Orly Fried in Butter and served with Tomato Sauce	3·65	Filets de Sole au Noilly Vermouth, Tarragon, Mushroom, Shallots and Cream Sauce	
Scampi a l'Indienne Cooked in a Curry Sauce with Cream and served with Rice	3·75	Truite de Riviere Cléopâtre Cooked in Butter and garnished with Prawns, Capers and Soft Roes	4·

* As available. D.P. — Day's Price.

184

The Royal Westminster Hotel
Bressenden Place, London SW1
Head chef, November 1979-June 1985

This was one of the few jobs (the only one, come to think of it) where I actually got the interview from an agency. Does anyone really know exactly what an agency is really looking for when you go for the initial interview with them? (Form a queue to the left to answer).

I was told that the general manager, a Miss Fitzgerald, was a very demanding sort and wanted 'her' hotel to be the best in the group (EMI then Thistle, remember them?) Well that sounded good to me, because I have always tried to make 'my' kitchen, wherever I have worked, the best! I believe that you should have faith in your own ability and then 'go for it'!

When I had the interview with Miss Fitzgerald, I was impressed. She was a straight, to-the-point kind of person, so you knew where you stood with her. If you asked to do something or spend out on a piece of equipment, Miss Fitzgerald would say yes or no, and then tell you the reason. Fair enough. I could handle a no if I knew the reason behind it.

The day I started, I was introduced to Pip, the sous chef, and the other chefs, then most of the morning was taken up meeting the other members of staff: the restaurant manager and waiters, the front office staff, the guys in maintenance and so on. I told Pip to carry on as usual for the next day or so, while I got the feel of the place. Afterwards, we had a chat about the kitchen, the lads and the style of service that was in operation. This place had a strange staffing system for the kitchen, well at least to me it was strange. The main chefs worked from Monday to Fridays, and the weekends were covered by two casual chefs! These two guys worked from about 7 am until about 10 pm.

The menu I had inherited was a bit of a nightmare (sorry to my predecessor, but it was to me). Two of the dishes particularly bothered me: a stuffed veal escalope and a type of beef stew. The then system was to have both pre-cooked, but it took longer to reheat these dishes than it would have taken to do them from scratch!

After about a week or two, when I had found my feet (I know, I know, at the bottom of my legs, heard it before!), I started to change things – the menus for a start! I also changed the working hours and shifts. The system I came up with was, I thought, quite a good one, it went something like this (music, please): I set up two brigades. Miss Fitzgerald had OKd the plan of one week earlies, one week lates. Week one: Shift A, sous chef/larder, sauce, veggie and salad, 9-4, Wednesday to Friday, Saturday, Sunday, Monday, Tuesday off, then 3-11 Wednesday to Friday, and split shifts Saturday, Sunday, Monday and Tuesday, then start again. It gave the lads a good break after a long haul every other week, as they had four good days off together every other week: a mini holiday. Once the lads did the first stint they seemed to like the hours.

The original staff I had inherited were not a bad lot, though they had got into a bit of a rut. Pip was quite a good sous chef. Then there was Millie, a little Filipino woman who was married to one of the waiters and was also good. The breakfast chef was called Paul, he was a scruffy sod, a miniature version of ZZ Top or the wild man of Borneo. I seem to remember he was a devout Nottingham Forest fan (well, I suppose someone has to be – just joking, Nottingham Forest fans!) There was an oldish kitchen porter called Patrick in the plate wash, and another porter doing the pots, whose name escapes me.

For the first few weeks I worked weekends as well, just to get the feel of the services. The first week I was introduced to the two casuals, and I'll be buggered (not really!), it was ... Phil (Philip Christodoulou). By now he was really wrapped up in the Scientology religion and believed he had healing hands. Apart from that his work was just as good as before, and you could still tell the menu by his jacket, so nothing had changed there (mucky sod that he was!) Phil and the other guy turned out an enormous amount of work, mainly in the mise en place line, as business over the weekends then was not very good. The long weekend shift suited Phil, and it left the rest of the week to do the 'work' (as he liked to call it) for the Scientology sect. Once I had got the new shifts into operation, Phil and I parted on good terms. He told me he was going 'on holiday' to the sect's headquarters in America. I wished him well and asked him to let us know how he was doing, but from the day he left we haven't heard a peep from him. If you read this, Phil, let us know how you are!

As expected, we had a few changes in the kitchen staff. The first five months were tough, while I was trying to get a good compatible team together, but in the end I like to think we succeeded. We had some very good guys and apart from the odd commis coming and going we had a fairly stable team. Both shifts got on well, and helped each other with the mise en place. They all seemed to have a love of food and of serving it up well. I'm sure we had the best team in the group, in fact I know so! We must have been doing something right because the number of customers started to increase and the number of parties went up as well.

The chefs I remember are: Les Peat, my main sous chef for about three years. Les was really an excellent worker whose love in life (at the time) was motorbikes. He was the type of sous chef you could leave to get on with things and not have to worry. Our Les was a bit of a smoothy with the women, and he had quite a lot going for him. He was blond, blue-eyed, well-built and about 6'1". He was like a bee round honey when women appeared, and with the twinkle in his eye and a beaming smile, he'd melt even a stone figure! When he left us, he turned up at the May-fair Hotel as senior sous and from there, I was told, he went to California, I think. Anyone know how or where Les is now?

Adrian Allan was my other sous chef, a great guy in all senses. He was 6'4", calm, cool and collected, he got the work out without having to shout or get the 'whip' out. If they were getting in the proverbial, he would be there giving a hand like Les. Whatever work was needed, he made sure it was done. Adrian was with us for about 18 months and it was a pleasure having him working for us. He went on to be sous chef at the famous pub/restaurant in Wapping, then he was head chef at the Waverley Court Hotel in Southampton Row, Holborn. I lost track of him from there. How are you doing, Adrian? Let me know. (If everyone writes to me, I shall have writer's cramp in next to no time!)

Raphael Abela was a young man of Maltese extraction who came to us as a commis. He had not done much cooking before, but proved that he had the 'touch' and turned out to be quite good. He never clock-watched and had a real love for the job (a must in our trade). I think that Raph could have gone far. After he left the Royal Westminster, he used to let me know how he was doing – nice of him, I thought. Last I heard, he and a friend were going to set up in business designing and producing ties and scarves – quite a change of direction, eh!

Steve Millar came to us as a commis. A friend of mine, Miss Hobson, who ran a chefs' agency, asked if I would take him on as he desperately wanted to be a chef (no charge, of course). Anyway, I had a word with Miss Fitzgerald and arranged for him to start. He was about 16 when he came to work for us, but was already a big lad then, about 6 ft and wide with it. Steve had a good attitude to work and was eager to learn, what a change from some! He fitted in well and had a lovely disposition, always laughing, I never saw him get upset. (Mind you, if he ever had it would have been like stopping a bull elephant with a pebble.) After he left us he went to other places, but drifted out of catering. The last time we saw him was when he called round to the hotel driving this massive cream-coloured American car. He was a chauffeur to someone, he said. With his size, he seemed to suit the car. So, hi Steve, 'ow's you doing?

Mick Munnely (call and tell me, Mike, if I've spelled it wrong!) came as a chef de partie, mainly on the sauce. I remember he had a large tattoo of a panther on his left forearm, really well done. I think Mick's real interest in life was rugby, both playing and watching, with drinking coming a close second, or maybe a joint first. He never took time off and was always on time and raring to go. He had a cheerful disposition and got on well with all the others, even if he was a bit over confident sometimes. I put it down to being eager to get on. I seem to remember he took a job in the country somewhere. Is it true, Mick, and how are you doing?

Kevin Gibbons was about 30 when he came to us. He seemed like a well-informed sort of guy who'd certainly done the 'rounds'. Kevin was a sous, but unfortunately he didn't stay long because although he was fine while I was around, when I had gone home and he was in charge, he quickly cracked under pressure, which wasn't good for him and certainly not good for the lads. A shame really, because he was a very pleasant person. The last time I heard about Kevin was that he was going off to Canada.

Bill Harrison was a true character. He came as the day salad chef and though he was about 70 then, he worked like a Trojan. After all those years in the trade he still loved the job, which is how it should be. I always say that if you don't like your job, get out and find one you do like; it will increase your life-span and lower your blood pressure. Old Bill, as we used to affectionately call him, was willing to help anyone with a little job or two once he had finished his own mise en place. He used to be full of anecdotes about the 1920s and 30s. The lads had a hard job believing the hours chefs used to work in those days. A couple of years ago when pulling away from some traffic lights in Brixton, I was sure that I saw Bill going into a newsagents. I should have stopped but didn't. As far as I know Old Bill is still pottering around. If so, hello Bill, it was a privilege to have known you.

Carl Hayward was a young half-caste guy who came as one of the sauciers, he was very good and turned out consistently good work. Carl had a great sense of humour and a nice calm outlook on life. A good reliable bloke, he stayed six or seven months. The last I heard was that he was the head chef at a medium hotel in the country but he was looking to come back to town. Did you ever make it, Carl?

Richard Rayment was a natural saucier, he was good! He never seemed to rush or panic, the work was always turned out on time and perfect. Richard settled in well on Adrian's shift. He nearly always had a crooked grin as if he had a private ongoing joke. Rich was a little bit of a mystery man; on the couple of occasions I tried to contact him at the home number he had given us, the people who answered were always a bit hesitant in admitting he was there – funny! I heard that Rich had gone off to the States to try his luck, but I'm not sure. Anyone know where he is now?

Peter Terry was one of those reliable fellows that you meet, they just jog along through life getting the job done without tantrums or tears. He seemed a bit on the shy side when he started but we like to think we managed to bring him out of his shell just a bit. He was in his late 20s and solidly built, but wouldn't hurt a fly. With a bit of a helping hand Peter turned out to be a very reliable veg chef. The last time I saw him was when he was my breakfast chef at the Sloane Club, more of which later.

Towards my last couple of years at the hotel (although I didn't know then that they were my last couple of years), Dave French (yes, him again!) came as the senior sous. He was the same old Dave, good, reliable, solid, never prone to panic. I think he could have stood in the middle of an earthquake and not shed a drop of sweat or increased his blood pressure. Dave went on to be the head chef at the Cadogan Hotel in Sloane Street, and last I heard, he was working in a director's unit in the city. Keeping well, Dave?

One year we had a large group (about 120, I think) staying at the hotel over the New Year period, and we had to feed them with special themed menus for New Year's Eve dinner and New Year's Day lunch. Well Dave, with his zany sense of humour, came up with a cracking breakfast menu. I showed Madam, and she liked it so it was put into operation for all the customers on New Year's Day. Dave 'did' the break-fast and I did the dinner and lunch.

We'd had a party at my house for New Year's Eve and we didn't get to bed until about 3 am. My friend Ray said that he'd like to come in with us on New Year's Day to see how a kitchen works, so we were on the way before eight that morning, bleary-eyed and not very bushy-tailed! We dressed Ray up and gave him a couple of jobs to help out (under supervision, of course). He seemed to enjoy the experience, but I don't think he ever fully recovered from the mad, frenetic, zany morning he took part in. All the lads, despite going to parties the night before, turned up on time and gave their best. BRILLIANT! The two days of parties seemed to go off well, even though I do say so myself. (Well no one else will, will they!)

During my time at the Royal Westminster we had kitchen porters come and go, the usual thing in this trade. The ones that spring to mind are an Aussie guy who was a reformed alcoholic. He was a very good worker, always interested in overtime, but after he'd been with us a few months he went on a bender and went to pieces. He turned up a few days later, not too happy when I told him his job had gone, but there you go!

He said he was going to go back home, but I doubt if he ever made it to the travel agent's, let alone the airport.

Another porter was a young lad, about 20, who was a walking tattoo parlour; he had them all over! I remember that he had spiders' webs on both elbows! He was a good worker, reliable, punctual and always looking for overtime.

Then there was Paul, a Maltese who was a real case and a half. He was an excellent porter, always looking for work and overtime, but he was a bit of a mystery man. He always had a wad of £20 notes on him that any millionaire would be proud of. Apparently he had a good social life after work, connected to the 'girls' of Soho, and the money was used to pay their fines at the police stations. We never got to hear the whole story from him. He was a bit shady but still a lively, entertaining guy.

Another porter I well remember was Bill Phipps, or 'old Bill', as he was affectionately called (I know, he wasn't the only one!) His main job was in the plate room which he ran with ease. Bill was completely reliable both in punctuality and quality of work. When he laughed (which was often), his 'spaced' teeth seemed to glisten, Bill had a very good sense of humour, as I like to think we all had. He liked to bet on the horses and had a bet nearly every day. I think he gained more than he lost and the bookies must have been sick of the sight of him. Bill could take and give stick without malice or getting upset. Having guys like this around made working under pressure a bit more pleasant. Bill later joined me at the Sloane Club, but more of that later.

For about eight months we had in the staff room a lady called Holly, who used to set up the staff room for the serving of the meals to the staff, as well as keeping it clean and tidy, ensuring that there were enough plates, cutlery etc for the staff. Holly used to flit around them all like some mother hen, helping with the serving of the staff breakfast and lunches, and she laid up the room for the evening meals. She was a lovely lady with a great sense of humour who got on well with everyone. Imagine our sadness the day we heard that she'd had a heart attack and died. All the staff were shattered at the news. A lovely lady who was called far too early.

In the restaurant we had a guy called John Ioakim, a Greek who was the restaurant manager. He was a great bloke who knew his job, a bit soft on the waiters at times, but he got the job done and the waiters all seemed happy enough. (What they call a fair ship.) I don't think we had a cross word all the time we worked together. (Now that's something for a chef to say!) This has to be a record, don't you think? What do you say, Guinness Book of records?

John's main support in the restaurant was John Doyle, his second, who used to do breakfast and lunches, plus the occasional dinner service.

JD could sell anything, I reckon he could sell an ice maker to an Eskimo in the middle of a snow storm! Quite often I would have a few portions left over from the parties because numbers had dropped. I would tell JD what the dish was called, what was in it, and before you could pass wind, he'd sold it! Amazing! JD was a bit of a fiery one, but once again we got on well together – co-operation, it's called. Last I heard of him was that he was setting up a business in a fruit and vegetable shop. How's it going, JD?

Another head waiter who worked here for a while was called Ali Khan (no, not *the* Ali Khan, who is the religious leader of millions, and who gets weighed with jewels). Ali was a real smooth guy, very smartly turned out, nice black suit, brilliant white shirt, hair just so (cor, makes you feel sick, just joking Ali!) He too could sell. We also got on well, and I met Ali a few years later when he was the restaurant manager at the Waverley Court Hotel in Holborn.

Most of the other waiters were commis, and they were mostly Filipinos, a very friendly race of people, sometimes a bit fiery but on the whole good to work with. They all seemed to have a good sense of humour, very necessary in this business. They were always nicely turned out too, a clean and tidy race of people.

For the banqueting, a woman called Angela Kennedy was in charge. She used to get the 'girls' booked as and when needed for all the parties and a bloody good crew she had too! They all got on well with the lads and everyone worked together as a team, not like some places where the chefs and waiters/waitresses were at loggerheads. Angela used to liaise with us on the numbers, the type of service that would be best with each particular party, the number of services needed, the best way to serve some of our special dishes etc. The idea was that if we served certain dishes a particular way, then the girls would be able to give the customers a good smooth service with the least hassle.

I must say that we never had any tantrums or pinching from Angela's girls (just how I liked it!) We used to provide a meal for them prior to service, cold meat and salad, chicken curry and rice etc, and then after the party service was over, I would set out whatever was left at the end of the kitchen and give the 'girls' about ten minutes to 'see to it'. So as they all knew that they would have something to eat first and then possibly have something to take for supper, we never had any trouble with 'losing' food.

Sometimes if we had a problem, then Angie and the girls would help out to ensure that the customer never knew about it. If, for example, the main course was running a bit late (maybe due to a dropped service), then the 'girls' would slow down with the clearing of the previous course, maybe go round with more wine – a professional way of 'buying time' for us in the kitchen.

A sad time at the hotel was when one of Angela's young cousins (or was it niece?), a pretty, fun girl who used to work quite a lot on our functions, went on holiday to Spain and was found killed in a quiet lane, stripped of all her jewellery and money. Everyone at the hotel was really upset. She was only in her mid-20s; it's bad enough for an older person who has had a good run, but at that age it really hits home.

After her death, our Les was really 'out of it'. I hadn't realised it (funny how blind you can be when in charge), but he'd had a bit of a 'thing' going with her at the time, so he was really cut up and no wonder!

I remember Angela was very slim and petite – and smoked roll-ups! She looked like a strong wind would blow her away, but she was as strong as an ox (no, I didn't mean you looked like an ox, Angie, it's just an expression. Whew, got out of that one, eh!) She had a very good sense of humour, really vital when dealing with difficult customers. The last time I saw Angie was when she went to the Royal Horseguards Hotel with Miss Fitzgerald. Where are you now, Angie? Please write, phone or fax, or if any of her friends read this, then say hello for me, ta!

The last couple of years at the Westminster, we had a catering manager called Peter Pluck (I said *Pluck*!). Peter had a real love of food, and had had a bit of experience in cooking (more than some catering managers, eh!) He could be a bit of an old woman at times but on the whole he got on with the lads. He always liked to talk about food, how best we could serve our specials, the best way to promote and serve any sort of special weeks or themed menus etc. The only time we nearly fell out was when the office gave me the wrong menu for a party of about 80 people, and we didn't find out until about 20 minutes before 'kickoff', when the host came in to see the room (as they do), glanced at the menu and nearly had a fit when he saw that the menu was nothing like the one he had ordered. I thought that Angela was having a wind-up when she came out and told me. It wasn't just a dish, but the whole bloody menu that was wrong! Angela got hold of Peter, who started getting his knickers in a twist. I said that it was too late to change the menu: firstly, I didn't have half the ingredients, and secondly, even if I did, I did not have the time to do anything about it!

I suggested we offer the customer maybe a sorbet as a middle course and a brandy or port to go with the coffee, a 'buckshee' offer. The customer was a reasonable sort (thank Christ for that!), so Peter came back all relieved as the man had agreed. The only trouble was that Peter had offered him a tomato sorbet, and I had only about a half gallon of the stuff in the house so we had to start blending the other sorbets that we had, thankfully mainly lemon. A little bit of this and a little bit of that, and hey presto, a nearly good tomato sorbet for the use of! It was really something that we could have done without. We made sure that the party had 120 per cent service, extra vegetables, rolls etc, plenty of coffee at the end. Afterwards the client said he was very happy with the menu and with the quality of food and service (phew, we all breathed a sigh of relief!) I spoke to Peter and said that if it ever happened again, then he should check first instead of getting carried away with promises.

Peter later went on to become the GM at the Cadogan Hotel in Sloane Street. Are you still there, or have you gone onwards and upwards? Let us know.

While we are talking about Peter, it reminds me of an incident that happened at about this time. We had a small toilet just outside the kitchen that the lads used, and every day about late afternoon, one of the porters would go in and mop and disinfect it. Well, we had a spate of some dirty sod weeing all over the seat, floor and sometimes the wall. This person must have had the shakes quite badly, or they just shut their eyes and left it to luck. Anyway, we got a bit fed up with this, so one morning I cling-filmed the toilet top, put the lid down and told the lads not to use the toilet till further notice. We waited with infinite patience for a result. After a while Les (I think) came up to me and said, 'Chef, we have a complaint about the toilet.' 'Good,' I said, 'got the bugger, have we?' 'No, I don't think so,' said Les, 'it's Mr Pluck.' 'Shit!' I said, then went out into the kitchen and there stood Mr Pluck in all his glory, wet trousers and coat. Apparently he had nipped in for a quick jimmy and had got caught out. He understandably was not amused, and was very suspicious as to why the lads were trying hard to keep straight faces. 'What have you been up to?' I said in my best innocent voice. Peter started to be quite rude about whoever had played this practical joke. I promised to try and find out, but I'm afraid I never got to the bottom of it – no clues you see! Anyway if you read this, Peter, then I am sorry! Funny though, the word must have gone round, because the mysterious 'phantom spraying jimmy riddler' seemed to disappear!

When I first started at the Westminster, we had a woman breakfast chef. She was built like a man, but she wore skirts so she must have been a woman! The trouble was that items seemed to keep disappearing overnight, so to make sure we weren't mistaken, we began to count the items in the fridge last thing at night just before we locked up, then first one in next morning used to count them and note any variance in numbers. Once we had a few days of proof, I had a quite word with her and she left!

On the whole I enjoyed my time at the Royal Westminster. I was allowed to do my own thing with the à la carte, table d'hôte and banqueting menus, without too much interference. Now and again I would present a dish or menu that Miss Fitzgerald wasn't too keen on, so it was back to the drawing board to reach a compromise, no real hassle.

I think that the two most satisfying menus I created while there were the Royal Wedding menu (Charles & Diana, à la carte style), and the 'Taste of London' table d'hôte menus.

The Royal Wedding menu was, and still is, a source of great satisfaction to me, a job well done. It had taken me a couple of weeks of research to come up with the names that I thought were appropriate to the occasion, and much searching in the inner depths of my brain (what do you mean, what brain? Cheeky sod!) to come up with the dishes for the names, eg Gordonstoun School, Wales and Cornwall, (obviously), St. Pauls, Belviere, Caernarvon, Bonnington, Althorpe etc. (anybody know the reason for the last four names?) This menu has been reproduced in the book, so you can see what I have done, and maybe understand the thoughts behind the names.

It was hard work getting this mise en place sorted out, writing out the different dishes, with the methods for each of the sections. Miss Fitzgerald had a printer draw up a great border for the menu, really set it off. Well, I thought so! I really enjoy doing themed menus and dishes; I forget all about life when I get wrapped up in these. All the dishes on the menus were created by me and I was very pleased with the end result.

The other enjoyable menu creation was our involvement in the National Eating Out Week, organised by the Caterer. Our theme was 'a taste of London', so I made a list of all the well known places in London and proceeded to create dishes to fit the names. For example, Horseguards Parade was a selection of hors d'oeuvres; Mansion House was lamb cutlets; Smithfield was a ten-ounce rump steak with lots of mushrooms and tomatoes. I had enough dishes to make up five table d'hôte menus, plus a few over for daily specials such as smoked salmon Mile End (a large portion of smoked salmon with chopped hard boiled egg, mustard and cress with a lemon dressing) and Escalope St. Pauls (veal escalope stuffed with fresh spinach and pâté parfait, crumbed, cooked slowly in butter, served on riz pilaf with a brandy butter over, etc.)

If anyone is interested in any of my creations, I have a book with 150-200 dishes that I have created, so ask away.

At the end of this menu extravaganza I had five names over, so I had a word with Mr Pluck and suggested that maybe the barman could do something with them, fancy cocktails or whatever. He did a great job. There was Bloody Tower (three and you lose your head), consisting of Beefeater gin, tomato juice, Worcester sauce, Tabasco, celery salt, served over ice, wow! Big Ben (only one an hour) was Bacardi, apricot brandy, grenadine, sweet vermouth, squeeze of lemon, a blaster! We have been able to print this menu as well so you can see how good the layout and composition was. All the hard work was well received so it was quite satisfying.

Another time we had an inter-hotel competition, based on English fayre. Again I did some research with the names of the counties, roping in some of our suppliers to help by telling me what products were most associated with which county. I came up with three table d'hôte menus which ran for a week each: Cornish Cream (fresh crab soup with mushrooms, sherry and cream); Cambridge Don (thick Cambridge sausage wrapped in pork fillet, sliced on spinach and mushrooms, with a light English mustard sauce over); and Somerset Trout, split open, filled with grated cheddar and chopped onion, baked slowly in the oven and served with a cordon of hot cream. I could go on and on, but I must curb my enthusiasm and get on with the story.

We 'borrowed' (for a small fee) an old market stall from one of the vegetable suppliers, Hotel Purveyors (how's that for a plug?) We set the stall up in the restaurant foyer and loaded it each day with all sorts of fresh English goodies: fruit, vegetables and cheeses that were displayed with artistic flair (well, we thought so!) It really went down well, with customers spending time looking it over and being amazed at the selection of English food. I must admit that after I had got into the research, I too was surprised at the amount of products we took for granted, being English. (Rule Britannia and all that!).

Anyway, we did so well that we won the competition! The directors of the group went around each of the hotels and marked them for originality, presentation, quality, etc. We were really pleased with the result, so two fingers (one finger in some cases) to the other grand hotels, the Selfridge and the Tower, to name but two. The directors had arranged for the winning team – the chef, catering manager and restaurant manager, together with their partners or friends – to have a long weekend, all expenses paid, in the Bordeaux and Cognac areas of France, with a tour round a vineyard, the cellars and lunch with the owner in the Chateau (Clos Fourtet) – *bloody marvellous*! Then we went up to the Cognac region where we were guests of the brandy producer, Baron Ottard. This is a really lovely brandy, it's the only one we drink now (and you can get it in Tesco's, plug plug.) We had dinner at the famous Chateau Cognac, where Francis I of France was born, before which we were given a tour of the cellars of the Chateau with some tasting involved, lovely! Dinner was served in the hall, we had a young brandy to start with at the reception, and the brandies gradually improved in age as the meal progressed, bloody marvellous!

Next day we went out to the main distillery outside the town and had a very enjoyable tour. If you ever get the chance to do it, I recommend it! Then it was lunch at a local restaurant, a lovely place on the banks of the river. One whole wall of the restaurant was covered with racks containing bottles of brandy from all the producers, and when one of the companies was in for lunch, a bottle of theirs was placed on a small side table by the main table, so that all the other diners could see which companies were entertaining, subtle advertising or what! It was during this meal that my wife was shown the correct way to eat mussels.

We were taken to another cellar for a tour, it was a sparkling wine producer. At the end of the tour we arrived at a table that had been set up for tasting, (more like a drinking table because we weren't going to spit this out!) The wine tasted like a first class Champagne, it was really good. It looked like Champagne, tasted like it, was bottled like it, but as it was not in the Champagne area it had to be called sparkling wine. We thought it tasted better than some Champagnes that we get back home (now there's a controversial statement for you!) We hoped to find it when we got back home, but we could not remember the name! Anybody out there know? What about the directors of Thistle?

A while before all this we had a change of manager (shock)! Miss Fitzgerald had got a transfer to the Royal Horseguards Hotel in White-hall, and she asked me if I would be interested in joining her if the head chef's job became available. While I was flattered and thanked her, I elected to stay where I was (as it turned out, it would not have made any difference to the future, but more of that later.)

The new manager was called Mr Charman, or 'Prince', as he was soon nicknamed (Get it? Oh well , please yourself!) He was Charman by name but certainly not by nature, as I soon found out. From 'day one' of him taking over, I had problems. He just did not seem to like me, I don't know why.

This period at the Royal Westminster was one of frustration and dis-belief, especially on the stock-takes. For example, how could about 300 pounds of caviar appear on stock when we did not have, never used, never ordered caviar. When I pointed this out, amongst other mistakes, I was told, 'Oh, it's too late to change, the figures have already been sent off to head office!' 'Well phone up or fax them and tell them of the mis-takes, and give them the proper figures,' I said. Stonewall silence! Funny how you get the feeling trouble is brewing, eh!

This was only one example. I could go on, but I think the reader will have got the gist of my problems by now. Also, 'Prince' was inventing a lot of complaints about the food and service (he would make a very good fiction writer!) The fact was, business was going well, John 'I' and John 'D' always checked that the customers were happy with everything, and the answer was always yes. We had lots of regular customers so we must have been doing something right.

Near the end of my time at the Royal Westminster, my office was taken away to be used as a wine store for the restaurant, 'Fair enough,' I said, 'but where will my new office be?' Again, stonewall silence, bloody frustrating eh! I got fed up trying to get an answer so I turned part of the stores into my office. You know who didn't like it, but by then it was tough! (I must change the subject because I am getting very bitchy. I could write another four pages on the problems that were foisted on me by 'Prince' and his cohorts, but I won't ... sod it, yes I will! Oh, OK then, I won't, the reader can draw his or her own conclusions on the matter!)

I will always remember a company seminar held to improve the standing, quality and overall performance of the group. This was held at the Tower Hotel and lasted two days (yes, we were allowed to go home each evening). All the general managers, catering managers, head chefs and restaurant managers were required to attend. It wasn't too bad, the lunches were OK and we had about an hour's lecture from Bob Paynton (of Chicago Pizza fame), telling us how good he was and how he succeeded in life (and to think that they paid him as well!) Then in the evening we were sent in our groups to various restaurants in town for a meal to see if we could learn anything from them for our own places. We were sent off to a small, well-known restaurant in Pimlico/Victoria but we weren't too impressed. It had a musty smell, the food was served luke warm – not a very good evening. The next day we had to produce a paper of our thoughts about the evening and whether we could use any of the ideas from there. Our main answer was *no*! and that we thought we were doing it better now!

Then the fateful day came. I was asked to go Mr Charman's office and when I arrived I found the personnel director and the general manager there. The upshot of this was that I was given my marching orders! I won't bore you with the details, but the letter of dismissal was about 20 lines long, and I could disprove about 15 of them. But they were determined, so after packing up my belongings and answering the usual questions from the lads (why? wherefore? etc), I left and went home.

A few days later I arranged a meeting with the main director and the personnel director in one of the other hotels and pointed out the numerous lies in the letter of dismissal they had given me. After refusing to let me tape the conversations between us, they wrote me out a nice reference and settled a fee. I was told that any queries from other prospective employers should be sent to the personnel director, not to Mr Charmer, so put that in your pipe and smoke it, as they say!

And so it was that life moved on ...

Thatchers

Christmas 1980

A glass of mulled Claret
£1.05

Pâté en Croute
A smooth pâté with tomatoes
and baked in puff pastry
£1.90

Smoked Salmon
£4.25

Avocado Troika
Blended with egg, dill cucumber and
anchovies in vinaigrette dressing
£2.25

Thatchers' Cocktail
A mixture of prawns, lobster and other seafood in a tomato and
brandy mayonnaise, served on a bed of melon
£2.95

Mousse Bowes-Lyon
A light mousse of smoked salmon, brandy,
cream and pimentos
£2.25

Sardines Pisane
Poached in white wine, served on a bed of
spinach and mashed with a tomato and
cheese sauce
£1.55

Crème Fleur de Lys
Turtle soup with port and diced mushrooms
and a topping of whipped cream
£1.40

Tortue Claire Réforme
£2.50

French Onion Soup
£1.15

Game soup with sherry and cream and garnished
with celery and carrots

* * * *

Scampi Phillipa
cooked in butter, served with toasted flaked
almonds and sherry, on a bed of rice
£5.60

Rouget en Papillotte Westminster
Red mullet, cooked in butter with white wine,
mushrooms, artichoke hearts and rosemary.
Finally, baked in the oven in a
thin paper case
£4.25

River Trout
Grilled or
shallow fried
£3.95

Dover Sole
A whole Dover Sole
served on or off
the bone
£6.95

Sirloin
One steaks are cut from Scotch Beef and are garnished with
tomato, straw potatoes, béarnaise sauce and watercress
£4.95

Lamb Cutlets
£4.50

Fillet
Cooked in butter with mushrooms,
chipolata sausages, bacon and watercress
£6.25

Roast Turkey
Traditional Christmas Fayre served with savoury chestnut stuffing,
chipolata sausages, bacon and cranberry sauce
£4.50

Entrecôte Mary-Ann
Cooked in butter with white wine, chopped tomato
and garnished with pâté and spring onions
£5.25

Escalope of Venison Saffrin
Cooked in butter with a saffron, cream, brandy
and mushroom sauce
£7.50

Supreme of Chicken Archiduc
Breast of chicken cooked in a Madeira sauce
with paprika and sour cream, garnished
with a spinach tartlette
£4.50

Noisettes of Lamb Noel
Cooked in butter with apple, cream and
kirsch sauce
£5.35

Potatoes
Croquette
Vapeur
Roast
£0.65

Vegetables
A selection of fresh
seasonal vegetables
£0.80

Salads
Tomato
French
Green
£0.80

* * * *

Christmas Pudding
served hot from the trolley
with Brandy sauce
£1.25

The Cheese Board
£1.25

Coffee and Mince Pies
£0.75

Sweets
from the trolley
£1.25

Appetisers

SMOKED SALMON £3.50

PARMA HAM AND MELON £2.70

PRAWN COCKTAIL £1.90

POACHED EGGS WINDSOR £2.90
Placed on mushrooms, crabmeat and smoked salmon, masked with a lobster sauce and glazed

AVOCADO TETBURY £2.00
The flesh mixed with radish, celery and fresh cream

PRINCE OF WALES PATE £1.85
A country pate with port, herbs and leeks

ROYAL COCKTAIL £2.50
A mixture of prawns, smoked salmon and fresh trout, mixed in a brandy mayonnaise

CREAM OF ALTHORP £1.25
Chicken, watercress and mushroom soup with cream and white wine

CONSOMME BONNINGTON £1.25
A strong beef consomme garnished with egg royale

GORDONSTOUN CREAM SOUP £1.25
Carrot soup garnished with leeks mushrooms and cream

ROYAL CAERNARVON £2.50
A broth of fresh fish with white wine and herbs

Thatchers
Restaurant

THE ROYAL WEDDING OF
H.R.H. THE PRINCE OF WALES & LADY DIANA SPENCER.

Fish

RIVER TROUT HIGHGROVE £5.10
Cooked in butter, filled with a prawn, crab and chive hollandaise and glazed

SCAMPI BELVIERE £6.40
Cooked in a sauce of port mushrooms, cream and smoked salmon, served on a bed of rice

DOVER SOLE CLARENCE HOUSE £7.50
A whole sole cooked in white wine with a tarragon and cream sauce

CORNWALL LOBSTER £12.50
Diced lobster with a crab, celery, brandy and cream sauce, served in a nest of rice, prawns and crabmeat.

Grills

FILLET £6.50

LAMB CUTLETS £5.25

RUMP £5.30

SIRLOIN £5.80
All our steaks are cut from Scotch Beef and are garnished with straw potatoes and watercress

A choice of cold meats and a selection of salads £5.25

A Gardners Pride of Vegetables from: 80p

A choice of:—
New — Sautee — Fried — Macaire
Fried Potatoes 65p

Cover Charge 40p

All prices are inclusive of V.A.T. at current rates.
Service is not included and is left to the discretion of
our patrons.

The Royal Westminster Hotel   Buckingham Palace Road   London, SW1.   Telephone 834-821

Main Dishes

FILLET STEAK SPENCER £6.10
Sliced and cooked in butter, garnished with pate and tomatoes, masked with champagne, herb and cream sauce and glazed

BREAST OF CHICKEN STORNOWAY £4.90
Cooked in butter with cream, thin strips of vegetables and covered with a cherry brandy sauce

SIRLOIN PRINCE OF WALES £6.15
Cooked in butter and masked with port, mushrooms and, caerphilly cheese and glazed

ESCALOPE OF VEAL ST. PAULS £5.30
A veal escalope stuffed with spinach and pate, served with a risotto and brandy butter

LAMB NOISETTES LADY DIANA £6.10
Cooked in butter and fresh mint, masked with a cream, sherry, mushroom and chicken liver sauce.

Desserts

A selection from our sweet trolley £1.25
or

LOVES DUET £1.60
Fresh peach and grapes soaked in pernod, topped with whipped cream

SORBET DIANA £1.50
Lemon sorbet laced with madiera and topped with chocolate cream

ROYAL HAPPINESS £1.35
Lemon and strawberry sorbet laced with cherry brandy

A SELECTION OF BRITISH CHEESES £1.40

COFFEE AND SWEETMEATS 75p

199

A Taste of London
£7.95 Inclusive of V.A.T.

St. James's Pâté
(A Rough Country Pâté with Port, wit.
served with a Port Jelly
or
Potted Shrimps Whitehall
(Placed on a mound of Russian Salad
and masked with a Sweet Mayonnaise

*****

Goujons of Sole Parliament Square
(Strips of Sole cooked in Butter with
Fresh Pimentoes and Mushrooms
or
Sirloin Duke of Wellington
(Steak cooked in Butter and Masked with a Mushroom
and Madeira Sauce Garnished with a Savoury Stuffed Tomato

*****

Covent Garden Basket
(Selection of Fresh Vegetables and Potatoes)

*****

Speakers Corner
(The 'Last Word' in Sweet Trolleys or a
selection of English Cheeses from Leadenhall Market)

*****

The Knightsbridge Event
(Choice of Coffee or Speciality Teas
served with Petits Fours)

NATIONAL EATING OUT WEEK
THATCHERS RESTAURANT
Royal Westminster Thistle Hotel, Buckingham Palace Road, London SW1W 0QT
Telephone: 01-834 1821   Telex: 916821

200

HAPPY NEW YEAR

Start the year as you mean to go on with our special New Years day breakfast.

The Great Thatchers Refresher
Pineapple juice served cold and creamy, topped with a spoonful
of lemon sorbet, to cut through the smog of last night
(Tomato, Orange and Grapefruit juices available on request)

To progress despite all!
A choice of tea, lemon tea or coffee
Choose your favourite beverage and don't worry you won't
feel this bad for another year.

Onward ever onward!
Please select from our range of fresh croissants
rolls, toast and traditional preserves.

Depending on your condition!
Cornflakes or Rice Krispies — if you can face the noise.
Weetabix — an oblong cereal to match your eyes.
Alpen — for our guests who wish they were somewhere
else.
Allbran — for our regular customers.
(Don't worry, the chef feels much worse than you)

If by now you have sufficiently recovered!

Haddock Monte Carlo
Poached haddock, poached egg, masked with a cream
sauce and topped with tomato.

Kippers in a Kilt
Scottish kippers, rolled in oatmeal and grilled.
(Bottles of Whisky and Bagpipes available on request)

Piggies Sympathy
Three chipolata sausages, wrapped up in bacon and grilled, served
on fried bread and garnished with tomato,
mushroom and slices of spiced apple.

Amnesia Relief
Try to remember ! ! !

Any permutation of boiled,
fried, poached or scrambled eggs, bacon, sausages, cold ham,
tomatoes and mushrooms.

£3.50 including Value Added Tax

Y NOW YOU SHOULD BE READY TO FACE THE COMING YEAR WITH
SMILE, SO HAVE A GOOD DAY AND A HAPPY AND PROSPERGUS YEAR.

The Crystal Room
Queens Hotel, Crystal Palace
Head chef, June-December 1985

I saw an advert in one of our local papers for the position of head chef in the newly refurbished top-floor restaurant in the Queens Hotel. I wrote in with my CV, had an interview and got the job. It was quite a challenge: no menu, no staff, not much equipment and they wanted to open in a month! (Bloody hell, get your skates on, Frankie boy!)

The main problem with the Crystal Room was getting the deliveries up to it. The service lift stopped a floor below so everything had to be carried up a narrow flight of stairs to the kitchen.

I sat in one of their small party rooms for about a week, planning an à la carte menu, drawing up a list of supplies that were needed, sorting out the suppliers. Unfortunately, we had to use a local butcher who, although his overall quality was good, charged well-over-the-top prices. I was told that the previous owners had left a large amount of unpaid bills, hence the rather limited choice of butchers. The vegetable supplier was also a local man. He tried his best but the trouble was that he could not get (or sometimes didn't know) the special fruit and vegetables that I would normally have been able to order, so my hands were tied a bit which didn't help.

The head chef in the banqueting kitchen was not very helpful, we used to start about 2 pm (we were supposed to only do dinners, more of this later) and all of our deliveries were just left where they were delivered and not checked. If anything was missing, tough! So we had to spend about the first hour lugging all the stuff from the basement kitchen to the roof before we could start any work.

When the menu was passed by the general manager, I started to take stock of the equipment we would need. The main things we needed were fridges, an ordinary one and a freezer, so the manager gave me a letter of authority to take to a local firm and off I went. Imagine my surprise when it turned out to be a second-hand shop selling household goods! Anyway, I made the best of it and got the biggest fridge and freezer they had. They had to bring them through the front of the hotel and up the customers' lift to the restaurant, as I pointed out that they would not be able to get them up the back stairs. By now I had a hunch that things were going to be an uphill battle, but I felt that once we had overcome the initial problems, everything would settle down into a routine (what a fool!)

I managed to get Carl Evans as my sous (remember him? Royal Court Hotel, Carlton Club), and also another lad called Steve Allen who started at the Selfridge Hotel as chef de partie. Old Bill (from the Westminster Hotel) came as our porter, so we had a small but hard-working team. We spent a week gradually getting the mise en place sorted out, the pâtés etc made, the stocks ordered and packed away and generally getting the feel of the place, deciding the best way to serve the various dishes. Most of the main courses were plated and the vegetables silver served.

We had been employed on a five-day week basis, evening only service and closed all Bank Holidays and every Sunday. Those was the terms of employment (the Bank Holiday section is worth remembering as it comes up again a bit later). I was quite pleased with the menu and its layout, as apart from standard grills and some classic dishes, we had a good sprinkling of special house dishes. One of my tongue-in-cheek, play-on-words creations was 'egg of the menthe', poached eggs on a riz pilaf base, masked with a creamy mushroom and creme de menthe sauce. It tasted quite nice, even if I do say it myself. Another was Ceylonese cocktail, tuna mixed with a curried mayonnaise on a shredded lettuce base and topped with flaked almonds. Then there was Dover sole venture, filleted and poached in white wine with a cream and chopped mango chutney and chopped anchovies sauce, then glazed.

As we settled in and business gradually got better as word spread that we were open again, we received quite a few compliments on the food – and the view was not bad either! The general manager told us that he would like to hold a round table lunch in the restaurant, and we agreed that it might help to promote the Crystal Room if we had a number of local businessmen in for lunch to see what we could do. The only trouble was that it turned out to be on a regular basis, yet the manager didn't want to pay us extra. So we devised a system whereby whoever came in to do the round table lunch – usually for 20 people – would have the night off. Since it might give the business a boost and establish the restaurant a bit more securely, we were willing enough to do it. So all round it was a good team effort.

Tom Ott, the manager, was an Austrian with a droopy moustache. When he was dressed up in his uniform I could imagine him as Wild Bill Hickock. The waitresses, like Tom, lived in the staff annexe behind the hotel, so in a way they were captive staff! All the staff seemed to get on well with one another; a couple of waitresses were a bit 'scatty', but they all worked well that was the main thing.

My 'office' looked like (and probably was) an old wardrobe stuck in a corner of the kitchen. This lack of space made it a bit difficult to keep the bookwork up-to-date etc, not that anyone seemed to be very bothered about it – a bit 'shonky', I thought.

The directors were nice. One was Mr Patel, who owned a local cash and carry warehouse and used to drive around in a nice 'Roller'. The other was a pleasant Jewish guy of about 50. Both men put a lot of effort and money into the hotel and restaurant, trying to make it work. The trouble was, I think, that they were too trusting of the management, which is probably why the standards eventually collapsed and the directors ended by getting rid of the management. But by then it was too late, and they had to sell the hotel. Shame, because I think that if all efforts had been pooled for the common good instead of individual aggrandisement, things might have worked out better.

Christmas was approaching and I had prepared a small selection of seasonal menus for December so that parties could have a choice. We got quite a lot bookings, from twos and fours right up to 30-plus, so although it was hard work, it was satisfying to see all these customers coming in.

At the beginning of November the head chef in banqueting began to drop hints about wanting us to help him over the Christmas period (Christmas Day and Boxing Day), but I pointed out that we were supposed to be off on the Bank Holidays and in any case, we would be too busy with our own family Christmases. Anyway, we said no thanks to his offer of £50 a day to work. Then, shortly before Christmas, we had just finished a busy week and were preparing to serve the sweets for a full restaurant of happy customers when the general manager and the head chef of banqueting came up and asked me to come down to the office with them. When we arrived the manager told me that they were having trouble getting staff to do the Christmas and Boxing Day lunches and that we would have to work! I pointed out that 1) I was not interested because we always have a family Christmas and 2) according to our contract of employment, we were supposed to be off on all Bank Holidays.

'Well, if you don't you're fired!' was the general manger's response. I was quite upset (people who know me will appreciate the understatement) at this blatant threat,. 'Stuff you!' I said, or words similar, and I went back upstairs. Both Carl and Steve had a feeling that something was cooking and had been 'holding off' serving the various sweets that had been ordered until they had found out why I was 'taken away' during service. When I told them that I had just been fired and the reason why, they both went down to see the general manager, only to be given the same ultimatum. Both, to their credit, also said 'stuff you' or words to that effect. Steve later told me that he had to restrain Carl from getting over the desk and 'making contact' with the general manager.

Anyway, we were all back in the kitchen gathering up our knives etc., Tom and his staff were going mental, wanting the sweets for this party and the sweets for that party. We had about six different sweets on offer so you can imagine the confusion that was building up. It was of some bittersweet satisfaction to say, 'Sorry, we've been sacked, we don't work here any more!' So we went home and left them to it, not a very happy Christmas that year!

At this point I would like to apologise to any of the customers that night who may have had their evening spoilt by our actions, but I think that when they read this, they will understand.

The footnotes to this tale are:

1. We arranged after Christmas to see Mr Patel at his warehouse to try and sort out the problems, but to no avail. He had to side with the general manager's authority, fair enough. During the discussion we pointed out how he was being well overcharged by the suppliers. I offered to give him the names of some other suppliers, so that he could compare prices and see for himself how much more he was paying, so in that, we managed to 'put the boot in', though gently, of course! It's not a thing that I normally do, but in special cases …

2. This concerned my son's 21st birthday party. A few months before I had booked and paid for one of the banqueting suites at Queens Hotel for the Saturday after Christmas. I had also booked the disco and the bar staff etc. When the general manager fired me he casually said, 'Oh, by the way, I expect you will be cancelling your booking for the room?' 'Oh no, I won't', I said, 'and if you do, I'll sue. Don't worry, you'll have no trouble from us.' 'Oh!' was all he said.

The party went ahead, fancy dress – it was hilarious! Nearly everyone turned up decked out in some costume or other. We had done our own food (part of the agreement) and we had a free bar. The bar staff were great, and I told all the staff involved that if they wanted a drink or some food, or even to join in the dances, then they were welcome (as long as they didn't abuse the drink offer!) Despite the problems I'd had before Christmas, we all had a very good evening.

And as far as work was concerned, it was 'Hey Ho, ever onwards!'

THE CRYSTAL ROOM ROOF-TOP RESTAURANT: Our Chef de Cuisine would be delighted to prepare any particular dish, not on this menu, (given advance notice) or to discuss the extra-special occasion with you. Please ask the Restaurant Manager for further information.

SOUPS: Chef's selection of tasty "home-made" soups. Prepared using only traditional stocks and the pick of the finest, fresh ingredients.

Minestrone: (our own famous recipe), made with an abundance of rough cut vegetables, diced ham pieces and pasta.

Cream of Watercress and Chicken (Creme Althorp): Cooked in white wine and chicken stock, garnished with tender pieces of diced chicken and fresh watercress leaves.

Cream of Chicken and Mushroom (Creme de Cendres): Chicken and mushroom, cream soup, delicately flavoured with sherry, garnished with thin strips of chicken and truffle.

Lobster Bisque: Freshly made, with lobster, brandy and cream, using the classic recipe; garnished with finely diced lobster tail.

Vichysoisse: Traditional cream soup, finely sieved potato, with a hint of leek, finished with cream and chopped chives. (served hot or ice-cold).

Gazpacho: (a reminder of spanish nights!); a thin, garlic, pimento and cucumber-based soup — served with croutons and finely diced onions, on crushed ice.

Consomme Varoch: A fish-based clear soup, delicately flavoured with tender seaweed and served with a garnish of prawns, chopped seaweed and puff pastry fleurons.

APPETISERS: A selection of hot and cold Hors D'oeuvre dishes, designed to whet the appetite.

Smoked Salmon "Blini": A generous portion of thinly cut smoked salmon garnished with half-lemon and served with freshly prepared "russian style" batter pancakes.

Gourmet's Platter: Freshly carved slices of smoked salmon, complimented with three large "head-on" King Prawns, lots of lemon and cocktail sauce.

As a main course with five King Prawns and additional salmon.

Prawn Cocktail: Served on a bed of lettuce, using best quality peeled prawns, with a piquant cocktail sauce, garnished with lemon and king prawn.

Avocado Prawn: A healthy portion of prawns, bound in our own-recipe cocktail sauce; served with half, sliced, avocado pear.

Avocado "Royalty": Scooped out flesh of half avocado pear, chopped and mixed with grated carrot and celery, black pepper and fresh basil — "perfectly delicious".

Melon and Parma Ham: Choice slices cut from the best melons available, draped with thinly sliced parma ham (cut to order); ground black pepper to taste.

Melon (chilled): Ogen, Honeydew, Charanti, etc., as available. Only the best, will be served.

Egg of the "Menthe": A fabulously unusual dish of poached egg, served on pilaff rice and masked with a creme de menthe flavoured mushroom sauce.

Pate "Maison": Guaranteed "Home Made" using venison, pork, brandy and cream, with a "roughly smooth" consistency!

Deep Fried Mushrooms: A favourite on any menu. Selected button mushrooms, breadcrumbed, deep fried, and served with hollandaise sauce.

Cocktail "Ceylonese": Flaked tuna served on a bed of finely shredded lettuce, masked with a light curried mayonnaise, sprinkled with toasted flaked almonds.

Mousse "Crystal" — "CHEF'S SPECIAL": A dish created especially for "The Crystal Room"; a creamy, cold, lobster mousse partnered by a similar portion of smoked trout mousse; served plated, with a cool and creamy watercress sauce.

FISH DISHES:

Grilled Dover Sole: A large, whole dover sole, grilled, served with parsley butter and half lemon.

Dover Sole (Venture): A whole sole, filleted and poached with white wine — finished with a creamy, finely chopped, fruity, chutney and anchovy sauce.

Quenelles of Sole (St. Nazaire): Shaped forcemeat of sole, poached with a sauce of red wine, shallots, prawns, mushrooms and cream, 'something unusual for fish lovers'.

Scampis (Frit): Breadcrumbed, deep fried, served with tartare sauce.

Scampis (En Papillotte): Scampis cooked in an individual envelope, with butter, finely sliced onions, green pimento, seasoning and flavoured with pernod — served with wild rice.

Fillets of Red Mullet (Catherine): One of the world's fish delicacies; cooked slowly in butter, served on a bed of leaf spinach and masked with a bearnaise sauce, finished with a cordon of hot cream.

Grilled Halibut Steak: Chargrilled for maximum flavour retention, served with parsley butter and small shaped, boiled potatoes.

ENTREES:

Fillet Steak Tartar: Prime Fillet Steak, chopped to order and mixed with finely chopped onion, egg yolk and seasoning to taste — prepared at the table — served with fingers of hot toast.

Coq-au-Vin: A 'no-nonsense' chicken casserole, based on the traditional recipe, using pork, mushrooms, onions and red wine.

Breast of Chicken (Ann-Marie): Tender breast of chicken, simmered slowly in a sauce of white wine, flavoured with stem ginger, apple and cream.

Pepper Steak: A trimmed sirloin steak, covered with crushed black peppers, pan-fried and finished with fresh cream and brandy sauce.

Noisettes of Lamb (Ashdown): Three delicate fillets of loin of lamb, cooked in butter, coated with a sauce of white wine, mushrooms and fresh mint; glazed with thin slices of 'Belle-Paesse' Cheese.

Veal Escalope Marsala: Thinly sliced, tenderised veal escalope, cooked slowly in marsala flavoured cream sauce.

Tournedos Rossini: Fillet steak, topped with pate, served on a croute, and masked with a rich madeira sauce.

GRILLS:

It is our policy to use only prime cuts for all our grills. Also as a special feature of our "Crystal Room Restaurant", we have installed one of the latest American, 'Lava-rock', Chargrills, which ensures that all our steaks retain their natural juices and succulent flavours during the cooking process.

'T' Bone Steak garni	(16 oz)	Fillet Steak garni	(7 oz)
Entrecote Steak garni	(8 oz)	Rump Steak garni	(10oz)
Lamb Cutlets garni	(3 pieces)	Veal Chop garni	(8 oz)

Crystal Room Chop Steak: A full ½-lb of Prime, Chopped, Pure Beef Hamburger, (chargrilled to retain the juices) and served on a toasted English muffin, with lettuce, sliced tomato and smooth mayo-relish, served with a side order of deep-fried onion rings.

Chateaubriand (For two — 30 mins): A double fillet, cut from the centre, grilled to order and carved at the table. Served with a full selection of seasonal vegetables (or salad) and potatoes. Bearnaise Sauce served separately.

COLD BUFFET-PLATTER: A plated selection of cold meats. Choose from sirloin of beef, home cooked Ham, Roast Chicken. (price includes a side salad to choice).

THE CRYSTAL ROOM — ROOFTOP RESTAURANT

207

Fisherman's Wharf
George Street, Croydon
Head chef, June-September 1986

Again, I saw this position advertised in the local paper. The manager interviewed me and I had a look round the nearly empty shells of the restaurant and kitchen. (The restaurant had not opened yet.) The kitchen was split by hard walls so you couldn't do much with it, but it wasn't bad for service.

I inherited two staff. One was a sous chef, an alcoholic Arab (!) and the other was a small black porter who talked more than he worked: brilliant! But as they both buttered up the manager, they were great guys!

One day we went to a restaurant in Wimbledon that was closing down, to see if there was any equipment we could use. We found a few items, loaded them onto a lorry and returned to the restaurant where we unloaded them and started to give the kitchen a deep clean, ready for opening. The manager had organised the delivery of the dry stores and the cleaning materials and once we had received and packed them away, he ordered the fresh food. We were getting organised for the big opening day!

The restaurant was in a fairly good position in George Street, Croydon, just off the main shopping street. It was mainly a fish restaurant with a few meat and vegetarian dishes. The menu had already been planned and printed by the manager – fair enough, as it was only a few weeks until we opened, and I was told that after the restaurant was up and running, I would be able to make up my own menu and change it every few months. The restaurant was open for lunch and dinner Monday to Friday, dinner only on Saturday, and closed Sundays and Bank Holidays, so not too bad.

We managed to get another two staff through local advertising. The chef de partie was Brian Sewell (I think) and a black girl, Cynthia Lynsdale, was commis. Brian hadn't done much in the way of cooking but he was eager and a quick learner; Cynthia had done a bit and had also been to college. She was quite good and I thought she would go far (New Zealand, Australia? Sorry, I know it's a corny joke but I couldn't resist it!) So, we had our team! Myself and the drunk on sauce, Brian on the vegetables and doubling up on the salads, and Cynthia on the starters and salads.

The restaurant was set out quite nicely, some banqueting seating around the edge with tables along the middle. Part of the restaurant was raised up, the decor was nice, clean and bright. The waiters/waitresses came in mainly on a casual basis, doing two, three or four shifts a week. Not quite the way to get a good consistent service, but who am I to say! The manager always knew best (that's probably why the other place closed down, you are wiser afterwards aren't you?)

Business was good at first, Fisherman's Wharf being a new place and all that. But then we had to start to fight the other restaurants in the area for customers. On the whole, I think we did quite well despite the fact that we had to sober up our sous a few times before service and I had to send him home once as he was too far gone!

I found out that the reason he kept his job was that he used to invite the manager to the numerous parties and semi-orgies that he went to a lot. The manager was obviously a very frustrated person! The rest of us got on well and started to form a fairly good team.

However, after a couple of months I was getting peeved off because the manager insisted on placing the orders and after I had given him a list of our requirements, he would, in his infinite wisdom, trim the orders down, so consequently we started to run out of things halfway through the evening. This didn't help to please the customers and was very frustrating for us, especially as the manager had the cheek to come into the kitchen and ask me why! I just used to say, 'If you had ordered what I had written down, we would have had enough to cope.' Very restrained of me, don't you think?

The manager was one of those pushy, I-know-best types, the sort of person who is loved universally! He used to come and interfere in the kitchen, he wanted to serve his friends first – never mind the paying customers, feed the freeloaders first! In short, a complete pain in the arse (excuse my French!)

By the time three months had passed (quite quickly, I must say), I had come to the conclusion that things would never get any better. The manager kept putting off a new menu that I was keen to introduce. I had a few specialities in mind as well as creating a few dishes with connections to a Fisherman's Wharf, for example 'the Dockyard Platter', a mixture of seafood, deep fried and served with three different dips, 'Fisherman's Delight', a large piece of cod steak poached with prawns and seaweed, and so on. I thought that by now any of our regular customers would have been through our classical menu and would be looking for something different to try. Besides, it would also give us a chance to readvertise the restaurant, boasting of our new menu. But the manager, a real ostrich, just wanted to poodle along as we were, so I got the message. What had started out as a great adventure with lots of potential turned out to be a nightmare, frustrating and causing me to lose interest. Once that starts to happen, you are best out of it! So out of it is where I went – sad, but there you go!

The footnote to this chapter is that the manager and his drunk chef managed to close the place in a few months. Poetic justice, perhaps?

APPETISERS

Prawn Cocktail	£2.50	Salad Nicoise	£2.50
Crab Cocktail	£3.75	Mediterranean Prawns	£5.75
Brandade of Smoked Trout	£2.25	Melon as available	
Smoked Scotch Salmon	£5.75	Avocado with Prawns	£3.75
Pate Maison	£2.25	Avocado with Vinaigrette	£1.95
Whitebait	£2.50	Asparagus as available	
Grilled Sardines	£2.50	Speciality Fish Soup	£1.95

ENTREES

DOVER SOLE

Grilled	Served with lemon and tartare sauce	£8.70
Meuniere	Pan fried in butter with lemon juice and parsley	£8.70
En Goujons	Cut into strips, breadcrumbed, deep fried, served with tartare sauce	£8.70
Bonne Femme	Filleted and served in a white wine, mushroom and parsley sauce	£9.30
Lydia	Filleted and served in a white wine sauce with prawns and asparagus	£9.30
Mornay	Filleted and served in a rich cheese sauce	£9.30
Murat	Cut into small strips, pan fried in butter with artichoke and potato	£9.30
Castiglione	Filleted and served in a white wine sauce with lobster, mushrooms and tomato	£9.60
Walewska	Filleted and served in a rich cheese sauce, garnished with lobster	£9.60

LOBSTER

Thermidor	Prepared in a white wine sauce with shallots, mustard and cream, returned to the shell and glazed with parmesan cheese	£16.50
Mornay	Prepared in a rich cheese sauce and served in the shell	£16.50

CRAB

Freshly Poached	Dressed and served cold with salad and fresh mayonnaise	£11.50

SALMON

Poached	Served with new potatoes and Hollandaise sauce	£8.75
Cold	Served with seasonal mixed salad	£8.75

PINK TROUT

Whole Fish	Grilled or poached served with Hollandaise sauce	£6.95
Filleted	Served with a ginger and lime sauce	£6.95

COVER CHARGE - 55p   PRICES INCLUDE V.A.T. AT 15%

SCAMPI

Deep Fried	Coated in breadcrumbs, served with tartare sauce	£6.95
Provencale	Cooked with tomatoes, parsley, shallots and crushed garlic, served in a bed of rice	£7.25

SCALLOPS

Mornay	Poached and served with rich cheese sauce	£7.75
Brochette	Grilled on a skewer with bacon, mushrooms, peppers and onions, served with rice	£7.75
Pan Fried	Served wrapped in bacon	£7.75

HALIBUT

Mirabeau	Grilled with anchovies, garnished with stuffed olives	£8.25
Poached	Served with new potatoes and Hollandaise sauce	£8.25

TURBOT

Grilled or Poached	Served with new potatoes and Hollandaise sauce	£8.95

SKATE

Deep Fried or Beurre Noir	Served with noisette butter, capers and lemon juice	£5.50

PLAICE

Grilled	Whole fish on the bone served with tartare sauce	£5.50

HELIGOLAND FISH PIE

	A selection of seafood in a rich wine sauce crusted with potatoes	£5.50

MEAT

	Prime fillet steak, grilled	£7.95
	Sirloin steak, grilled, with mushrooms and tomatoes	£7.25

VEGETABLES

Seasonal vegetables (per portion) £1.00	Potatoes, fried, new, creamed or saute	.75p

SALADS	Prepared to choice	£1.50
SWEETS	Choice from our sweet trolley, served with fresh cream	£2.25
CHEESEBOARD	Cheddar, blue Stilton or brie served with celery	£2.00
COFFEE	Freshly brewed and served to your requirements	.95p

A 12½% Service Charge will be added to the total bill

We are happy to accept cheques up to £50 with a bankers card

212

The Waverley Court Hotel
Bedford Corner Hotel
Aquarius Hotels, Holborn
Head chef, September-November 1986

This position was one of my shortest ever! I was engaged as the executive chef overseeing both hotels. My brief was to reorganise and upgrade the conditions and service and increase the business in both.

The Waverley Court was already doing good business in its brasserie, but its restaurant clientele was dismal, practically non-existent! The boss had started up an outside pastry delivery service to the other local restaurants – not a bad idea to help business, but the trouble was that the poor chef at the Bedford Corner spent most of his time trying to keep up with the orders and didn't have enough time left to concentrate on the service at the hotel and on trying to build a reputation for good service. A Catch 22 situation really.

The other problem was the delivery driver, he was the boss's chauffeur who turned up when he thought about it and delivered when he had the time! Consequently, deliveries were very haphazard, especially if the driver had to run the boss around or do any errands for him. We used to get grief from the customers looking for their orders, so one of my first decisions was to cancel the delivery service until we could set up a proper service. The boss wasn't too happy until I explained that it was only creating bad feeling from the other restaurants and that if he was going to do this type of delivery service, we had to make sure that we had the staff and the equipment to do it properly – in other words, spend some money!

The Bedford Corner Hotel was going to be the hardest to get up and running as it only had one chef! The kitchen and the equipment badly needed updating, not necessarily with new equipment – good second hand would do to kick off with. Then there was the problem of staff. I suggested that we get a good pastry chef so that we could be sure of quality products being turned out, also it would free the chef there and enable him to concentrate on the customers and get the service and quality more upmarket.

On the face of it, it was a real challenge to get both places running smoothly and hopefully building a reputation for both as well.

At the Waverley, we had Carl Evans as one of the sous chefs, which was lucky. The other sous was a young guy who was not very co-operative, so that made it a bit harder to put changes into action. The lads in general were hard-working, they did long hours without complaint and generally did a good job, but they had no sense of rhythm, everyone doing all sorts, instead of being slotted into sections so that they could concentrate on just a few things instead of trying to do it all.

After a few weeks of sussing out the problems in both places, talking to the chefs, finding out what sort of problems they had found and incorporating them into my assessment of the situation, I devised a plan of action and a working agenda that would hopefully bring the two hotels up to scratch (especially the Bedford Corner). But this would involve investment! The idea was to supply both hotels with a good class sweet trolley or selection as well as supplying outside trade, and also to employ a proper delivery driver so that we could confidently deliver on time and get the right orders to the right places.

I had a meeting with the general manager and the boss and outlined all my ideas. To boost the restaurant trade at the Waverley I suggested that maybe we could sort out a separate entrance for the restaurant. At that time you had to walk into and through the hotel to get to the restaurant. We should also, I suggested, promote the restaurant more, and in due course make it bigger, as it could only seat about 20. Also, we could reorganise the menu and style of service at the brasserie. The Bedford Corner needed to be knocked out and started from scratch, quite literally (but again this was looking into the future; a little investment in equipment would do for now). In short, everything depended on cash investment! It depended on how committed the boss was in bringing the hotels up a grade or two, maybe three! If you want to play with the big boys then you have to invest for now and also the future!

I was told that they would look at my suggestions, then come back to me and let me know what they had decided.

After about a week I was called into the boss' office and ... sacked! All I can assume was that the boss was too tight to part with his money or that he didn't really want to increase business. I don't know.

So, I was out on my bum again. But, as the song says, 'Pick yourself up, dust yourself down and start all over again!'

So I did just that ...

The Sloane Club
Lower Sloane Street, London SW1
Head chef, December 1986-April 1990

I heard that the Sloane Club chef was about to leave via the 'grapevine', so I wrote in, got an interview with the managing director, Mr Hussey and was asked if I would be willing to come and prepare a lunch for the rest of the directors. 'Fine with me,' I said, so a day was arranged and I got in touch with the chef, gave him a list of what I would need, then duly turned up and did a 'Ready, steady, cook' session. I can't remember exactly what I offered them, but it was choice of a couple of starters and a couple of meat dishes. One was a classic, the other was one of my own creations and I seem to remember a fish dish as well as a traditional fruit salad and another type of sweet. After the lunch I got washed and changed and waited to be called up to the office to find out what they thought. Mr Hussey said that they were very pleased and offered me the job there and then. Great! Brilliant! Super! (OK, that's the end of the Jim Bowen impersonation!) Anyway, I was very happy.

The Sloane Club was run along the lines of a gentlemen's club (shades of the Carlton), a members-only establishment, but operated like a hotel. It had about 120 rooms, a large restaurant with a small kitchen behind it, a nice-sized lounge (where afternoon tea was served), and three or four rooms that could be used for private parties, all set in a lovely old building. The members came from all over the world, so it would be a good challenge to get traditional *and* international-style menus up and running. I was due to work with the existing chef for his last two weeks so that he could give me the 'run through' and allow me to settle in. He was leaving to start up a business in antique miliary artifacts (uniforms, weapons etc), quite a change of direction. The last I heard was that he was looking for a small warehouse, so business must have been doing well.

The staff I inherited were: the chef's wife who doubled up as a breakfast chef and pastry chef; a Scottish sous; a couple of commis; and a couple of casual chefs.

Business was not that great. The lunch service was a carvery operation and the evening was a sort of table d'hôte-cum-à-la-carte. The menu changed daily, so lots of room to improve!

Most of the staff 'lived in'. The company had a large house just opposite in Sloane Gardens which it used to house the staff. All the laundry was done at the club in the basement, even the chefs' whites. After a short time we changed to a proper laundry for our uniforms, which the company supplied. They were taken away, washed and returned sparkling white – the usual arrangement with any catering establishment, while they carried on the 'in-house' laundry.

I remember some of the live-in staff. Margaret was Scottish, about mid-20s, a real happy-go-lucky type. Sometimes she would get her knickers in a twist but on the whole she was easy to get on with. Margaret was one of the chambermaids and she also used to do the laundry.

Maureen was what they call 'formidable'. She was 40ish with years and years and years (sorry, I didn't mean that many years, I got carried away) of service to the club. I was told that she kept a parrot in her room. (How useless can I get with such information?) She was the breakfast head waitress but used to do lunch service and occasionally dinners as extra. She started out by being a bit awkward, but we soon became friends. Maureen was not frightened to speak out if she thought something was wrong – a real straight talker! She had a hard outer shell, but inside she was a softie. I was very sad when I heard a few years later that she had died. She'd had a lump but left it too late before seeing a doctor. A real shame, a sad loss!

Then we had Liam, an Irishman (what a surprise!) who was one of the head waiters and also did most of the dinner and cocktail parties. Liam knew most of the members by name, he too had been there years and years (no, I won't go on!) He had a rather warped sense of humour so we got on well. Another head waiter was Patrick, who always seemed to be in a daze and far away (I know the answer to that, the further the better!) But once you could 'tap into' him he was not a bad sort.

A few of the reception staff, mainly the girls, also lived in. There must have been about 15 of the payroll staff living in, quite handy in emergencies, no need for panic phone calls, just nip across the road and knock on the door.

Amongst the other staff who were there at the time was Dave Jennings, the maintenance guy, a brilliant bloke who could turn his hand to anything. Dave had quite a happy disposition with a sarcastic twist. We used to get on well (I like to think so, anyway). If we had any problems in the kitchen, plugs, wiring etc, we only had to mention it and it was 'sorted'.

Then we had Mark. Everybody knew Mark, he was our day kitchen porter, about six foot (no, he only had two feet, smart alec!), a very happy chap but a bit slow on the uptake. He was always laughing and singing (well, that's what he called it; a bloody racket, we called it!) He worked like a Trojan, a really good kitchen porter, and he was never late – more often than not he was early, which for a kitchen porter is really something! Show Mark how to do something a certain way and he would religiously do it that way forever. He was always willing to help others, he used to help out with the veg prep, show him once and away he'd go like the clappers!

The overall feeling among the staff was that we, like the Sloane, were a club. Many of them would go 'en masse' to the local pub just across the road for social evenings (most evenings!)

My general brief was to bring the club 'up a bit' and try to increase the restaurant and party business. I was given a fairly free hand (what a difference from the Waverley!) It was a good feeling to know I was trusted.

After the first week the existing chef decided that he would go early. That was OK by me as I was eager to get going and try out some ideas. The only trouble was, the sous decided to leave as well (he came back about a year later looking for a job and wondered why I said no), so it was a case of 'put ideas on hold, head down and full steam ahead!' Sort out the immediate problems and pick up the ideas later.

The only ones left in the kitchen besides myself were the ex-chef's wife, a black girl about 20ish, 6 ft and largish with huge 'melons'. She was quite a good worker with a 'sunny' disposition, who could take a joke and give it back. I do like a happy kitchen! There were also a couple of guys from the agency (Chef's Centre – Mike Moore was the boss, still is, always sent good blokes! How's that for plug for a friend?) So I had to start recruiting quickly or else I would start to 'drown'. After quite a while of chefs coming and going, we eventually settled down with a good crew. It took a while but I think it was worth it.

The other directors used to pop down to the kitchen every now and again to have a little chat and see how things were going; it made one feel quiet 'at home'. They always 'ate in' when they were in the area, which in itself was good as it showed that 1) they had faith in the food and service and 2) it kept the staff alert. The three main directors were quite friendly with all the staff and often passed on their thanks or any other comments after they had eaten.

We used to roast the main joints downstairs and the chateau potatoes upstairs. We used the upper kitchen to prepare and serve the various starters and vegetables on the menu. One of the sous, and a chef de partie or commis, would go up to control the service in the evening and make sure that any orders were sent down by the chute system that we had, using 'bullets'. Everything had to go up by lift and you can imagine what a bitch it was when the lift broke down and the whole caboodle had to be taken up and brought down by hand (after a few days of this we would have muscles growing everywhere!) You really needed that after a busy night – not!

By now I had set up two brigades, one early, one late (it was run along the lines of the Royal Westminster, so I won't bother you with the details again. If you have forgotten, then turn back the pages!)

Some of the guys stayed a while. Les Moorehead was one. He was a sous and was with us for two years or more. He was quite a capable bloke but inclined to worry about the job and let it get to him. He was reliable and could always be counted on to help out with extra time and days when we had staffing problems or holidays (as is usual in kitchens). I always made it up to them, either in extra time off later or pay. Les was about in his late 20s or early 40s (just kidding, Les!) with a ginger beard, though he was much better looking than Robin Cook, the Labour MP.

A sous that was only with us for a short time was an English guy, about 40, with good references, who had worked in some prestigious places. He was OK when I was there but went to pieces when left on his own. He seemed to disintegrate from a confident chef to one that couldn't control a kitchen. It's weird how a person can seem to be good and then spoil the illusion. I always put all staff on a fortnight's trial – 'make or break,' I used to tell them.

Another sous was a chap called Gary Chappel. He was good, very confident, a good leader, not frightened to tell the waiters off (this is sometimes called the national sport of chefs – telling waiters off). Gary worried for the job without letting it get to him (conscientious, they call it). He had had a few good sous positions before he came to us so he was used to command and he also helped the lads build up their confidence in themselves. Very good all round. He always had a surprised look about him, peering through his glasses. Gary later emigrated to Australia but came back. He got the position as executive chef at the Westbury Hotel, and was there for about two years. (OK, who's going to correct me?) But he got a bit too involved in the job and nearly had a breakdown. Luckily he recognised the symptoms in time and emigrated (he's a boy, ain't he?) to New Zealand and that was the last I heard from him. So if you know Gary, give me my regards and if you read this, Gary, how are you? How's the family, any chance of a free holiday? (Don't hurt to ask does it?)

Another long-serving chef was Lionel Williams, a Welshman who was our pastry chef. He was with us for about two years or so and was excellent with pastry, it literally melted in your mouth. He had previously worked in a large bakery back home in Wales, so he was not too used to doing mousses etc, but he was a quick learner and after we had shown him the basic ways for mousses, caramels etc, he gained confidence and started to experiment and use my books that I kept in my office for ideas on sweets. We used to make all the sweets on site, even our own Christmas puddings, cakes and mince pies. Lionel would start on the puddings and cakes about August then nearer the time, he would make a couple of hundred mince pies up and we would freeze them ready for the first rush.

Lionel was very easy to work with, always laughing and joking, with a loud infectious laugh – a real happy bunny. He could take being ribbed and give it back without getting upset. He was gay and quite camp, and used to dress outrageously in suits made out of lurex etc. It really saddened me when one of the chambermaids, who I met a couple of years later, told me that poor old Lionel had caught Aids and had died at home in Wales – only young and a great loss. It was even sadder because when I knew him he was very careful, so I don't really know how he came to catch the disease.

On breakfast and staff lunch we had ... Peter! (Yes Peter from the Royal Westminster), good old dependable Peter, always on time, always turning out good work. We used to forget about breakfast because Peter was so thorough with his service and mise en place. How are you, Peter? Where are you now? Let us know!

One of the other chefs was Christophe, a young French lad. He was of the same persuasion as Lionel. Christophe started as a chef de partie and later we promoted him to sous chef. He was quick to learn, reliable and had a good sense of humour, so we had some laughs as I tried out my meagre French on him and he helped me with some of the pronunciations.

Lionel, Christophe and one of the chaps upstairs in reception all shared a flat together. The chap upstairs was a Brazilian and used to arrive to work wearing tight pedal bike outfits, showing off his 'manhood'. Maureen used to say that she bet he'd left a lot of girls disappointed. 'Wish I was bit younger,' she used to say, 'I'd make him change his leaning!' The last I heard (and saw) of this guy was on a TV programme. They were going around different nationalities' restaurants during the World Cup and they went to this newly opened Brazilian restaurant/club in, I think, Notting Hill and spoke to the owner. Well, bugger me (wrong expression, I know), it was the bloke from the Sloane Club! He'd obviously saved his money and opened his own place. Best of luck, to you, I hope it's going well – let me know!

The last I heard of Christophe was that he'd gone back to France. Anyone with information?

We were quite lucky with our porters as they were all hard-working and not frightened to do any deep cleaning, scrub and disinfect the fridges which we did once a week, fetch and carry, help with bringing in the deliveries etc. All in all, I think we helped each other without hassles, quite a good bunch of guys and occasionally girls.

Upstairs behind the kitchen, behind the restaurant (with me so far?) there was the wash up for the restaurant crockery etc, and who did we have in to do the 'honours'? Yes old reliable Bill (Phipps). It's nice when you don't have to keep chasing staff to do their work. Although Bill came under the restaurant manager's control, if he had any problems he always came to us to sort it out for him, quite nice I thought.

While I was there we had a few restaurant managers come and go. One I particularly remember was an Armenian, very smooth and smart. Unfortunately he could talk up a storm but he could only work up a faint breeze! He and the then house manager used to eat dinner together in the restaurant, with wine. They started to get carried away with their positions and ran up a drinks bill, so that was soon stopped! Didn't go down too well upstairs.

Another time, we were sent on a two-day course to Cliveden, the same company that was running the Sloane Club. These two managers opted to stay the night there (I went home) and they ran up a drinks bill while playing snooker all evening, thinking it was 'on the house'. They were very surprised to have the bill presented to them (I never found out if they did pay it or not).

Another time, Mr Hussey sent us out for lunch at the Connaught Hotel to see if we could learn anything from them. I went in a suit, the two managers wore black coats and pinstripes – talk about subtle! We had a very good lunch, I remember that I had rabe de lièvre, absolutely first class! But we decided we were probably on a par with the Connaught anyway. I believe in letting the competition worry about what we are doing, not us worrying about them!

The restaurant manager who stayed longest was a Mr Hughes, who came to us by way of one of the officers' messes in the RAF. He was always spick and span, friendly enough in a creepy sort of way. I tried to have a good working relationship with him, but it was hard going, as he never seemed to stick up for us, whereas we always tried to help him out of his problems.

I will always remember the saga of the scones that we used to serve with the afternoon teas. Lionel used to make a big batch up and then freeze them, then we used to cook about 20 at a time. Bloody good they were! Anyway, Mr Hughes used to insist that the Filipino tea waiter kept them in the hot plate to keep them hot, so they used to dry out and go 'biscuity'. Do you think I could get through to him that scones should not be kept hot as it spoilt them? Not a bloody chance! So, every now and again it would be brought up at the weekly Heads of Department meetings that Mr So and Mrs So and So had complained about the scones. I got so fed up trying to explain to the management why we were getting complaints, that I considered making a tape and just pressing play when the subject was brought up. (I never did!)

Often during the evening service when we had the à la carte menu as well as the carvery, Mr Hughes would wander about the restaurant with orders still on his pad, not in the kitchen. Then he would bring in about four or five checks at once, then complain that check number whatever was waiting for a long time for their starters. Not surprising, was it! The system we devised to try and contain this 'late check' problem was that as soon as the check was received, it would be time dated and then any part of the check that was to be prepared downstairs was sent down by 'bullet', the dish or dishes prepared and dressed up, then sent up to be served. So it was very important to receive the order as soon as possible to keep the waiting time to a minimum. The other problem was actually getting the waiting staff to take the orders in: they always had something else to do or it was not their table. It was as if they were frightened of the customers. In reality they were just unorganised. When it was brought up at the HoD meeting, the questions went 'straight out the window'. The waiters thought we were making trouble for them, instead of realising that we were trying to help them get organised.

At the club we had a membership secretary, quite a nice, 'awfully, awfully' type, who was not very organised, always going to do this or that, but never quite succeeding. She seemed more into personal image building than club membership building.

During my time at the club Mr Hussey had a few personal secretaries. The one that I remember was called Annie, a typical 'Sloane Ranger' (said in the nicest way, Annie). She was actually very nice, friendly with no 'class' problem. I remember once, she and her family had gone to a charity party somewhere in the West End and she asked if we could do a later dinner for them. I said I didn't mind, so we laid on a special meal. I seem to remember that it was on a Sunday evening, so I came into work later that day and stayed on to do the dinner for them. When Annie got married, she had a society wedding and after she came back from honeymoon, she was playing the wedding tape for Mr Hussey and the rest of the directors. Somehow or other it was played through all the televisions in the club so everybody enjoyed seeing Annie get married (ahhh!)

My time at the club was, all in all, a very satisfying time, as I was allowed a relatively free hand with the menus. We used to have a carvery operation for lunch with a small cold buffet and salad display and an à la carte menu changed monthly, with another carvery operation for dinner. I used to love creating and experimenting with dishes, most of which were well received. We used to have a fresh sweet trolley (at least four of the dishes changed daily), and a good English cheeseboard.

One of the most manic times of the year was two weeks of the Chelsea Flower Show. The club would then be 'heaving' with a waiting list (if only we could have had this all year round!) We used to run a large cold, decorated buffet with six or seven different salads to choose from, plus the sweet trolley laden with strawberries and cream, amongst other sweets. We had two sittings for both lunch and dinner, and did just carvery and cold buffet for dinner, as we didn't have enough time to offer à la carte service. We used to do quite a lot of private parties during the year, all without complaint, not bad eh!

One couple I will never forget. They always had a birthday party for the wife with all the family and friends attending – about 20 people, I recall. The reason I will always remember them is that the wife had the same birthday as mine! When we used to meet about a week or so before the party to plan the menu etc., we would wish each other a happy birthday. I always made sure everything was OK for this party, as I used to have the day off myself, and my wife and I would go out for a country lunch. (There are some nice places just by Edenbridge way!)

Each year just before Christmas, we had the staff Christmas dinner. We took over the restaurant for the evening and brought in casual chefs and waitresses so that all the staff could relax and enjoy the evening. We got all the food organised and ready for cooking and serving, then we left it up to the casuals, usually friends of mine. (Hello, Barry!) It was all very nice and civilised, the staff were mixed on the tables so that you would be talking to people from other departments, which stopped people talking 'shop' all night. During the staff bash we used to have a secret ballot for the most popular staff member. The year that Lionel won he caused a great laugh because in his excitement, he nearly kissed Mr Hussey as he was presented with his prize. A good laugh was had by all.

I had to do the weekly and monthly costing sheets as well as the percentages sheet. I quite enjoyed this, as it kept me informed on my spending levels. Unfortunately the returns from the breakfast, restaurant and parties were not always ready in time, so that the percentages were often moving up and down – a bit frustrating but never mind. The accounts office manager always said that it was OK, so I didn't worry too much as the official figures were satisfactory.

It was quite hard work at the Sloane Club and as we were never fully staffed it meant a lot of hours put in to keep up the standards we had set. In the evenings I used to do the starters and main à la carte in the downstairs kitchen. I should have had a commis or chef de partie with me, but more often that not I was by myself. We used to do most of our own butchery, pâtés, pies, cold buffet, decorating, salads and all the sweets. The satisfaction in doing all these things from scratch and having them well received made all the effort worthwhile.

I like to think that I managed to bring up the quality and also the amount of business during my time there. Most nights we were hitting 50 customers, sometimes we went over 60, which was very good. Lunches, though, were still up and down as most members who were staying were on business, so they were out most of the day. As we couldn't take from off the street, we had our hands slightly tied.

During the summer, Cliveden hosted a fortnight of military band music in the open air. People used to book and arrive with their packed supper and have it on the lawns as the bands played (the food, I mean). For two years the staff set up an outing. We laid on a good cold buffet with sweets and cheese, tablecloths, cutlery, glasses, even candelabras. We had wines, beers, soft drinks, and used to purloin a couple of tables from our friends in the restaurant and lay everything out 'fit for a king'. Once we all had our photos taken by the local paper and our spread was voted 'best supper of the night'. We all had a good time, and a coach was laid on there and back, so we didn't have to worry about drinking and driving (not that I think it would have worried many of the staff anyway!)

The directors bought a large house in just behind the large Peter Jones store on the corner of Sloane Square, and proceeded to turn it into an exclusive, small (about ten bedrooms, I think) hotel, designed to attract the more affluent and upwardly mobile Americans. I was asked to go there and help with the planning of the kitchen. This I did, drawing up a diagram and making a list of the equipment that would be needed. My plans were approved and the kitchen was born! The tall black girl took over as chef there and, as far as I know, did a good job. On the opening night we prepared canapes and the pickings at the club and transported them over. Whoever is there now, I hope it's OK for you – let us know!

About this time the directors had a chance to buy (I think) the Chemists Club in New York and the idea was to make it into the American Sloane Club. But they were having trouble with the American red tape, so they had the idea of getting one of their friends, a Mr Desavory, onto the board of the Sloane Club in the hope that he would be able to cut through the red tape, as he had many influential friends in the US. I don't know the ins and outs, but they did not get the club and Mr Desavory ended up buying out the Sloane Club from them – bit of a shock to all concerned, especially the staff. Mr Desavoury didn't make any significant changes and life continued as before. Then the club was sold again, this time to Norfolk Capital Hotel Group, but as before not many changes were made. The club was unique and it was hard to change its format.

We carried on as before, then after a year or so, Mr Hussey started to hassle me over the staffing, food costs, percentage figures etc. In the end we agreed to differ. He paid me off (fairly well) and I agreed to say that I was leaving for family reasons (to keep his immediate bosses sweet and stop the staff from asking awkward questions). I must admit that it hurt a lot, as I had put a lot of sweat, time and energy into the club and I believe we did a very good job against all the odds.

When I found out that Mr Hussey was going to give the job to his stepson, it hurt even more. I then understood why he was being such a pain in the arse and hassling me so much over the past months. I was mad to think that this pumped-up guy was going to come in and screw up everything I had built up and in time I was proved right. (I heard later from some of the suppliers that this guy thought he was God! Apparently he used to complain if river trout were not all the same size and weight – a bloody miracle is needed for that to happen! If the apples, oranges, bananas and pears were not the same size he would send them back, also they had to be the same colour and so on. Apparently a couple of the suppliers told him to find someone else to bother, which is unusual for them; they usually bend over backwards to supply.)

Most of the kitchen staff left because they got fed up with the new chef staying in the office most of the time and not doing any actual work. They also got fed up with his constant arguments with his stepfather (served you right, Mr Hussey). Towards the end he had to run the place on casual chefs. It was bittersweet satisfaction when I learnt that the club was to close for refurbishing and both Mr Hussey and his stepson had to go. (It has now reopened under new owners and I would like to wish them lots of luck for the future.)

At this time I came up against that weird word ... ageism! I found out that I was considered too old to run a hotel or restaurant kitchen. They now recruit whizz kids to run them. Funny but a few years ago you would not be considered for an executive chef/head chef position unless you were 40 and had the experience in good-class establishments. Now, with some, if you have managed to read a cookery book, are about 20 and have an idea what cooking is all about, then you're in!

CLUB CARVERY

STARTER FROM THE CLUB MENU

SEPTEMBER

TUESDAY 1ST SEPTEMBER, 1987

Cold Buffet Selection

Roast Loin of Pork

Lamb Kidneys Turbigo

ROAST OF THE DAY
Roast Foreribs of Beef
with Yorkshire Pudding

SELECTION OF PUDDINGS

£13.50

COFFEE AND MINTS   75p

CLUB MENU

BORTSCH

POACHED EGG IN A POTATO NEST
GARNISHED WITH ONIONS, BACON AND MUSHROOMS

VENISON AND PORK PATE EN CROUTE

GRAPEFRUIT MARINATED IN WHITE WINE
WITH THINLY SLICED PIMENTOES

SMOKED EEL FILLETS IN GARLIC AND BASIL BUTTER

BRAISED RIVER TROUT WITH ROSEMARY AND ALMONDS

BEEF STROGANOFF

NOISETTES OF PORK WITH A KIRSCH AND APPLE GARNISH

SUPREME OF CHICKEN WITH TOMATO EN CROUTE
WITH MADEIRA SAUCE

ESCALOPE OF VEAL CORDON BLEU

ICE CREAM OR SORBET OF THE DAY

SELECTION OF PUDDINGS FROM THE TROLLEY

CHEESE AND BISCUITS

£14.50

COFFEE AND MINTS 75p

My swan song to this book is a poem that I wrote a little while ago. I think that it's a fitting end to my story!

Ageism

Ageism as a word is a funny thing
The youngsters say it with such 'zing'
'It'll never affect me!' we hear them cry
'Oh yes it will,' the oldies sigh
'It will catch you, never fear
It looks far, but it will soon be near!'
When you're young, and in your prime
Do you really have the time
To talk or listen to their advice?
Or sometimes even to be nice!
'They're gone, they're past it!' you all shout
Until the day your turn comes about
Then ageism isn't such a funny thing!

T H E   E N D   (but my life goes on!)